BALL

Itard, Segu—

D0893361

DATE DUE			

LB
1067
.B187

711809

Missouri Western College Library
St. Joseph, Missouri

ITARD, SEGUIN AND KEPHART

THOMAS S. BALL, Ph.D.

Pacific State Hospital

ITARD, SEGUIN AND KEPHART

SENSORY EDUCATION — A LEARNING INTERPRETATION

711809

CHARLES E. MERRILL PUBLISHING COMPANY
Columbus, Ohio   *A Bell & Howell Company*

MISSOURI WESTERN COLLEGE
4525 Downs Drive
ST. JOSEPH, MISSOURI 64507

This book is respectfully dedicated to

WARREN L. JONES

THE SLOW LEARNER SERIES
edited by Newell C. Kephart, Ph.D.

Copyright © 1971 by Charles E. Merrill Publishing Company, Columbus, Ohio. All rights reserved. No part of this book may be reproduced in any form, electronic or mechanical, including photocopy, recording, or any information storage and retrieval system, without permission in writing from the publisher.

International Standard Book Number: 0-675-09191-8

Library of Congress Catalog Card Number: 70-154658

1 2 3 4 5 6 7 8 9 10 — 75 74 73 72 71

Printed in the United States of America

Foreword

The slow learner is a very complex organism, displaying a large number of problems in a wide variety of different learning situations and behavioral conditions. Not only is there a wide range of deviant or deficient responses but also they interact with each other so that his problems are intertwined into a complex mesh frequently difficult to untangle. Often the most puzzling aspects of the treatment may be the questions of what problem to attack first, which problems can be attacked simultaneously and what problems must wait upon the solution of prior problems.

With such a complex of problems, it is to be expected that there would be differing points of view among professionals in the field. For reasons of their own, investigators will be interested in different types of problems. One worker will become intrigued with one aspect of the child's behavior while another worker will find this aspect unengaging but will be attracted by another aspect of the behavior. These many different approaches will naturally lead to many schools of thought, some of which can be graced with the appellation "theory" and some of which remain merely points of view.

For the most part, these various approaches are neither contradictory nor mutually exclusive. They result from different angles of view upon the problem and, therefore, are more supplementary than irreconcilable. The teacher or practitioner, who must deal with the entire range of problems needs an array of these approaches which he can use in combination or in succession as he deals with different types of problems, or different aspects of behavior.

In education, however, we too often tend to pick and choose. We like to think that somewhere there is one true, all-inclusive theory and that all others are inadequate or incorrect. We, therefore, pit one point of view against another and, on the basis of the resulting arguments, choose one position over the other. We then tend to apply the chosen position and its resulting methods and techniques to all problems of all children in all situations. With such a complexity of problems as that presented by the slow learner, this limited approach is doomed to failure.

When such a choice has been made, too frequently, it seems to follow that this position must be espoused to the exclusion of all others. Differences in terminology and dissimilarities in descriptive constructs lead to the feeling that an "either-or" decision is required. It is quite possible, however, that two apparently conflicting theories might both be correct. Physics, for example, lives happily with both the corpuscular and the wave theory of light, using one to solve certain problems and the other to solve different problems. In an organ as complex as the central nervous system, it is quite possible that more than one mechanism for learning may be operative at the same time. It would follow that more than one teaching principle may be needed either simultaneously or in succession. It is not desirable, therefore, to settle on one approach and reject all others as inaccurate. Rather various positions should be integrated together and each used as the problem seems amenable to that approach.

In the present volume, the author has performed a great service by bringing together several points of view current in the literature today. He has addressed himself particularly to the relationship between the operant conditioning position and that of the so-called cognitive theorist. These positions are complimentary rather than opposing. The cognitive theorist is primarily concerned with what behaviors should be taught, in what order and for what purpose. When he has made this determination, he turns to operant conditioning as at least one method of accomplishing his aims. In like manner, the behavior modifier does not modify behavior haphazardly. He must turn to other poins of view to augment his knowledge. Thomas Ball has properly pointed out that, beneath the political jockeying and interprofessional maneuvering, there lies a vast substratum of interdependence. This realization and the subsequent enrichment of both conceptualization and practice can demonstrably increase the efficiency of teaching. The teacher will bring more ideas and greater ingenuity to the classroom, resulting in greater flexibility in learning presentations with consequent increased opportunity for the child who finds learning difficult or confusing.

Not only is it desirable to achieve an integration between current positions but it is also essential that these be integrated with what has gone before. Scientific knowledge grows by accretion. New discoveries are added to previous knowledge. Such new discoveries refine and augment what has been learned before but seldom do they refute it. In like manner, new data are suspect if they appear to disprove past knowledge. The stress on scholarship in universities and graduate schools emphasizes this philosophy.

The two great pioneers in the field of the slow learning child were Itard and Seguin. Dr. Ball has performed a further service by identifying the roots of our present thinking in the works of these earlier investigators. With this historical perspective the field is seen, not as a series of opportunistic whims, but rather as a steadily growing, compact body of scientific information.

It is hoped that this volume will aid the student to see this field in perspective, both historical and contemporary, and also that it will aid the teacher in evaluating the long-term value of the many techniques, methods and materials with which he is bombarded daily. The education of the slow learning child is a vital concern to the entire educational profession in this country. It is hoped that this concern will induce its leaders to resist the temptation of temporizing; rather, they will foster complete and well-grounded long-range educational programs. The present volumn should help point the way toward such a goal.

Newell C. Kephart
Glen Haven Achievement Center
Fort Collins, Colorado

Preface

In writing this book I have striven to develop an interpretive framework for the field of sensory education. In so doing I have approached the literature selectively rather than comprehensively. Regarding Kephart, I have dealt with key concepts and fundamental assumptions in some detail. Other contemporary systems are essentially ignored and there is no attempt to provide an exhaustive review of the literature. This strategy is consistent with the need to scrutinize carefully the foundation of at least one contemporary system rather than to get lost in an appraisal of an excessively complex superstructure. If the strategy is deemed successful, it should be applicable to other systems. Itard and Seguin are included because these men were the true pioneers and innovators of sensory education. It is felt that the assumptions upon which the entire field was based might best be understood by returning to their original sources.

The initial section of this book is devoted to an analysis and evaluation of Itard and Seguin within a modern frame of reference. For explanatory concepts I have drawn heavily upon operant conditioning and Russian research on the orienting reflex. The second segment contains chapters dealing with escape-avoidance conditioning and generalized imitation. In both chapters the goal is synthesis. Thus, despite the acknowledged differences and contradictions between Kephart's cognitive system and Lovaas' operant orientation, and between contemporary and historic developments, it does appear possible to view important aspects of Kephart, Lovaas, Itard and Seguin within the common frame of reference of escape-avoidance conditioning. This does not mean that the work of any of these men is totally reducible to this model. It does, however, suggest a previously unrecognized interrelationship which might form the basis for discussion and mutual reinforcement regarding overlapping areas of interest and activity. In the chapter on generalized imitation it is demonstrated that both the underlying theoretical assumptions and the technical specifics of recent developments in imitation training were anticipated in the nineteenth-century work of Itard and Seguin.

The final section is devoted to a review and evaluation of Kephart's theory and correlated treatment program. It is shown that some of Kephart's most powerful support comes from the Russians. Not only does Kephart's system coincide with and complement their work on the orienting-exploratory response; his program for the development of gross motor generalizations also appears to provide a prior developmental step missing in the Russian work. The section ends with a synopsis in which Kephart's approach is integrated with others discussed throughout the volume.

The writer gratefully acknowledges the financial support received through the Bureau of Research of the California Department of Mental Hygiene and the support and encouragement of Dr. Herbert Dörken, Chief of Research. I wish also to thank Valerie Ackerland for carefully reading the manuscript and providing many highly valued constructive criticisms of the material. I am indebted to Hayden Mees who first opened my eyes to the clinical implications of the operant approach, and to Ivar Lovaas and Cecil Colwell who showed me how it could be creatively applied in a hospital setting. In the sensory-motor training area I owe much to my long-standing collaboration with Clara Lee Edgar and to my more recent association with Michael Maloney. Lastly, I wish to thank Newell Kephart, my former major professor and now my editor, for the inspiration, support and encouragement he has given me over the years.

Thomas S. Ball

Contents

part 2

Threads of Continuity

part 3

Kephart — A Contemporary Approach

ITARD, SEGUIN AND KEPHART

Courtesy of Kennedy Galleries, Inc.

For those who ask, "How can you work with children such as these?", the truth is simply this — we fly on the same wings.

part 1

Pioneers in Sensory Education

chapter 1

Itard and the Wild Boy
of Aveyron

A classic has been defined as *a work that is frequently cited but seldom read*. This definition applies especially well to Itard's *The Wild Boy of Aveyron*, a description of his work with a feral child found in a wooded area near Paris approximately 170 years ago.

It was not until several years after completing my doctorate that I finally read this work. It was a beautiful, deeply moving experience, timed at precisely the right moment in my life and career. Partly by accident, and partly by sheer good fortune, I had had the opportunity to work with people whose perception of and dealings with children of atypical development held a personal element of greatness. Although their theoretical differences were marked, there was a common denominator that ran through their personalities and techniques, identifiable when one looked beyond their formal writings. My preparation for Itard also entailed exposure to certain critical experiences including intensive work with institutionalized idiots. It is not in jest when I say I have learned more from idiots than I have from many learned professors—it is a fact of my experience. And I have discovered something else—the sublime pleasure of finding nascent humanity where I expected only a negation of human qualities.

As I have read and reread Itard, the hiatus of years that separates our lives has slowly disappeared. Each time, he becomes more of the teacher-physician-scientist-humanitarian and sensitively responsive human being. Although I do not view this in a mystical sense, my mind has become

the scene of a dialogue involving three parties: great men of my contemporary experience, Itard, and myself. As I know these contemporaries
better, I know Itard better. With enhanced understanding of Itard, I
understand more deeply my own reactions to what I have personally
experienced. Out of the chemistry of these interactions I begin to come
in contact with what I would like to call *wisdom*. It is with whatever
wisdom I can bring to bear upon this topic that is so close to my heart
that I proceed with the dialogue.

The nature of my quest in this broad area of therapeutic and research
endeavor coincides especially well with a recent statement by Wheeler
(1968):

> Wisdom is the realm of knowledge that concerns human choice and
> action, rather than simply knowing facts about things. Its acquisition
> comes only if there is a deep personal experience, a participational
> element as well as an intellectual element. Only rarely can one
> acquire practical wisdom just through books, for the reader's per-
> sonal creative participation is not a necessary precondition to the
> kind of knowledge available from books. What is needed in acquir-
> ing wisdom is a form of revelation that allows the experience, as
> well as the perception, of the fruits of wisdom. (p. 32)

I believe, with Hoffer (1955), that compassion is the one true anti-
toxin of the soul. This is the point at which our dialogue begins and,
when we have gone full circle, at which it must end. As Hoffer knows,
all other human qualities, for instance, loyalty, patriotism (and I would
include intelligence and its machine-extensions) can potentially subserve
destructive ends. But I am optimistic for a society that can approach
its least defensible members, its children who are unable to cope and
adapt, with compassion. There is hope for such a society—this compassion is a measure of its capacity constructively to love others and, ultimately, itself. For we cannot confront and deal with these children, however pervasive their impairment, without dealing with ourselves. It is in
the elemental nature of this confrontation, with its potential for creative
human involvement and self-discovery, that we encounter both the profound challenge and the enduring inspiration of Itard's work.

Itard organized his case report around the five principal aims govern-
ing his educational strategy (see page 9). There is a seeming directness
and simplicity in this presentation, but the order and directness is more
apparent than real. In the end, it obscures the continuity of his efforts.
For this reason, I decided to abandon his outline and develop my own

approach to analysis, an approach that cuts across Itard's system of classification.

The process of analyzing Itard's work can be compared with a unique mining expedition. It is a terrain with many colorful gems lying right on the surface. Here I include Itard's work on imitation—the pleasant and exciting surprise of finding he had largely anticipated the modern concept of imitation training and worked out practical techniques almost identical to those employed 160 years later. But there are also gems lying beneath the surface that are, for me, of a more subtle and brilliant value, gems that must be extracted from his material. They relate to some of the far-reaching implications of specific training efforts. They are linked with what Kephart calls *training in generalization rather than specificity.*

In many respects I understand Kephart better through Itard than I do through Kephart himself. This is because I see in Itard's work with Victor a brilliant and penetrating, yet exhaustive, clinical documentation of sensory education carried from its most rudimentary level on to the development of abstract functioning. In part, the limitations of this material lie in the fact that it is based on a single case. But what it lacks in this respect is more than compensated by the breadth and scope of what can be truly described as a monumental effort—a work of genius. And it turns out that Itard's presentation does, in fact, have great generality. I can find in many of his experiences and observations exact counterparts to my own and those of others. Since Itard is the point of departure, the fountainhead of the field of sensory education, it is obviously important to understand his original work as clearly as possible within a modern framework. The same point has been made forcefully and eloquently by Eugene Doll (1967):

> Probably no field of education has ignored its past so cavalierly as have educators of the mentally retarded in the last 15 years. Teachers of the normal still glean inspiration from Rousseau, Pestalozzi, Herbart, Froebel, Parker, and Dewey, but who among us knows Seguin, Howe, Wilbur, W. E. Fernald, Farrell or Anderson? Even the recent revival of Montessori came to us largely from general education—and characteristically it is the disciple, Montessori, rather than the master, Seguin, who is revived. What is the virtue of preserving and attending to older materials, and what problems offer themselves for investigation and research? It is probably true that the bulk of this heritage has been handed down to us, second- or third-hand. One finds today papers and systems advocating many of the techniques used by W. E. Fernald or E. R. Johnstone fifty years ago. The newest methods, perhaps unawares, revamp the

devices of Seguin and Goddard in terms of modern statistics. But we are missing the inspiration of some of the clearest expositions of basic principles by the great minds of the past — who evolved them from first-hand experience rather than gleaning them from books. We are depriving ourselves of balanced points of view from the days when the whole of the field could still be grasped by one person—before we were led down tangential alleyways by the current plethora of publication. Individual pages, moreover, bristle with suggestive techniques or incisive comments. (pp. 181-82)

I have only gradually become aware of the true dimensions of Itard's contribution and discovered an amazing serendipity in this work. This serendipity arises from the fact that, from the conclusion of his initial efforts at stimulating the senses to the beginning of reading instruction, Itard pursued a program of sensory training which, according to Kephart's theory, represented a seriously inappropriate teaching strategy. Judged from Kephart's standpoint it was severely inappropriate for two basic reasons: (1) it ignored the sensory-motor component as a foundation for the learning process, and (2) it focused on a type of discrimination training that emphasized a narrow specificity and seemingly impaired the development of perceptual organization and conceptual generalization. But it is precisely because of these *misdirected* perceptual training efforts that we are able to see those subtle and far-reaching implications of perceptual training seldom recognized by today's educational experts.

SYNOPSIS OF VICTOR'S HISTORY PRIOR TO TRAINING

A feral child, of approximately 11 or 12 years of age, was found in a wooded area near Paris in September of 1799. From the outset, this boy aroused a great deal of curiosity and much speculation regarding his educability. What the curious actually saw when he was brought to Paris is described by Itard (1932)[1] as follows:

A disgustingly dirty child affected with spasmodic movements and often convulsions who swayed back and forth ceaselessly like certain animals in the menagerie, who bit and scratched those who opposed him, who showed no sort of affection for those who attended him; and who was in short, indifferent to everything and attentive to nothing. (p. 4)

Responsibility for the boy's welfare was assumed by the National Institute for the Deaf and Dumb. It was through this organization that he was confined to the care of Jean-Marc-Gaspard Itard, a young otologist who eventually undertook his education. He assumed this monumental task despite a most discouraging evaluation by Pinel, founder of modern psychiatry, who even in Itard's day was a man of undisputed preeminence. Itard summarized Pinel's report as follows:

> Proceeding first with an account of the sensory functions of the young savage, citizen Pinel showed that his senses were reduced to such a state of inertia that the unfortunate creature was, according to his report, quite inferior to some of our domestic animals. His eyes were unsteady, expressionless, wandering vaguely from one object to another without resting on anybody; they were so little experienced in other ways and so little trained by the sense of touch, that they never distinguished an object in relief from one in a picture. His organ of hearing was equally insensible to the loudest noises and to the most touching music. His voice was reduced to a state of complete muteness and only a uniform gutteral sound escaped him. His sense of smell was so uncultivated that he was equally indifferent to the odor of perfumes and to the fetid exhalation of the dirt with which his bed was filled. Finally, the organ of touch was restricted to the mechanical function of the grasping of objects. Proceeding then to the state of the intellectual functions of this child, the author of the report presented him to us as being quite incapable of attention (except for the objects of his needs) and consequently of all those operations of the mind which attention involves. He was destitute of memory, of judgment, of aptitude for imitation, and was so limited in his ideas, even those relative to his immediate needs, that he had never yet succeeded in opening a door or climbing upon a chair to get the food that had been raised out of reach of his hand. In short, he was destitute of all means of communication and attached neither expression nor intention to his gestures or to the movements of his body. He passed rapidly and without any apparent motive from apathetic melancholy to the most immoderate peals of laughter. He was insensible to every kind of moral influence. His perception was nothing but a computation prompted by gluttony, his pleasure an agreeable sensation of the organ of taste and his intelligence the ability to produce a few incoherent ideas relative to his wants. In a word, his whole life was a completely animal existence. (pp. 5-6)

Pinel rejected the notion that the boy was a feral child. Instead, he believed him to be a helpless idiot only recently abandoned by his parents. He considered him incurable—certainly *not* the subject of an intensive educational effort.

Itard saw the parallels with a classical picture of idiocy but rejected Pinel's conclusions. His own position was based on his belief in the fact that Victor had actually survived for years in a primitive condition apart from society. His interests were aroused regarding the nature of the intellectual development of such an individual. This boy, whom Itard named Victor, presented, as it were, a natural experiment on the effects of environmental deprivation on intelligence. For Itard, Victor's intellectual functioning was but the natural outcome of such deprivation. In his primitive condition there were few needs to be satisfied and none of the intellectual stimulation provided through language and formal education. In short, Victor's intellectual functioning was appropriate to these circumstances. Itard held out the hope that by providing the necessary stimulation he might overcome the psychologically crippling effects of prolonged deprivation. He realized, however, that to justify his position he had first to prove that Victor was, in fact, a feral child. This he did by documenting Victor's aversion to all of the so-called pleasures and comforts of society; for instance, his repugnance to sleeping in a bed. He further verified the background by evidences of unique adaptations to a primitive environment and a concomitant lack of even rudimentary human training and example. These evidences included Victor's tendency to trot or gallop, mastication with the incisors in rodent-like fashion, numerous body scars suggesting bites of animals and repeated, deep scratches. Yet perhaps the best evidence of all is derived from his specific and selective responsiveness to stimuli related to survival in the wild.

On the basis of such inferential data plus the reports of inhabitants of the area in which he had been found, Itard concluded:

> We shall find above all that he had been seen more than five years before entirely naked and fleeing at the approach of men, which presupposes that he was already, at the time of his first appearance, habituated to this manner of life, which could only be the result of at least two years' sojourn in uninhabited places. Thus this child had lived in absolute solitude from his seventh almost to his twelfth year, which is the age he may have been when he was taken in the Caune woods. It is then probable, and almost proved, that he had been abandoned at the age of four or five years, and that if, at this time, he already owed some ideas and some words to the beginning of an education, this would all have been effaced from his memory in consequence of his isolation. (pp. 9-10)

He assessed Victor's state as:

> . . . much less an adolescent imbecile than a child of ten or twelve months, and a child who would have the disadvantage of anti-social habits, a stubborn inattention, organs lacking in flexibility and a sensibility accidentally dulled. From this last point of view his situa-

tion beame a purely medical case, and one the treatment of which belonged to mental science. (p. 10)

Interpreting Victor's condition within a medical and educational framework, Itard mapped out a strategy of educational therapy based upon five principal aims:

> 1st Aim. To interest him in social life by rendering it more pleasant to him than the one he was then leading, and above all more like the life which he had just left.
> 2nd Aim. To awaken his nervous sensibility by the most energetic stimulation, and occasionally by intense emotion.
> 3rd Aim. To extend the range of his ideas by giving him new needs and by increasing his social contacts.
> 4th Aim. To lead him to the use of speech by inducing the exercise of imitation through the imperious law of necessity.
> 5th Aim. To make him exercise the simplest mental operations upon the objects of his physical needs over a period of time afterwards inducing the application of these mental processes to the objects of instruction. (pp. 10-11)

He was put to bed at the close of the day, allowed to eat an abundance of preferred foods, provided with frequent opportunities to go outside, and subjected to few demands and restraints upon his freedom. As Victor slowly adapted to his new environment, Itard planned gradually to reduce the time he devoted to such satisfactions and introduce instructional experience. Toward this end his meals became fewer and less plentiful, his hours of sleep shortened and his excursions grew less frequent. Yet Itard recognized in Victor a rare love of nature. He hoped that this source of satisfaction could be retained and even used positively to reinforce the boy's new life experience.

SENSORY EDUCATION

Itard's therapeutic work with Victor begins with an example of sensory education at the most basic and fundamental level. My interpretive approach to this work and its present-day implications draws upon the theoretical framework of operant conditioning and upon the concepts and methodology stemming from Pavlov's original formulation of the orientation reaction. A brief review of the most salient concepts from both of these fields and their complementary interrelationships may set the stage.

OPERANT CONDITIONING

The term *instrumental learning* encompasses both operant conditioning and escape-avoidance conditioning. Instrumental learning is voluntary and adaptive, in contrast to classical conditioning which is reflexive and involuntary (Pavlov's dog, conditioned to salivate reflexively in response to a tone, is an example). To demonstrate operant conditioning, one must first find an appropriate reinforcer. Something known to reward the individual may serve the purpose. This step is crucial because,

> . . . reinforcement gives you a means of control over the behavior of the animal. It rests on the simple principle that whenever something reinforces a particular activity of an organism, it increases the chances that the organism will repeat that behavior. (Skinner, 1951, p. 26)

Skinner substituted "reinforcement" for "reward" to distinguish operant conditioning from reward training. Reward training usually entails the use of an incentive. When the individual "delivers" the requested behavior, he gets his reward. From the start he knows what is wanted. However, in operant conditioning, the subject need not be aware of what is wanted. The trainer has a predetermined notion of the behavior that he plans to develop or "shape." And the behavior is *ongoing* when the reinforcement is delivered.

Unlike the administration of rewards for a completed task, the administration of reinforcement during the process of shaping requires exact timing. Split-second timing is possible by associating a signal, such as the sound made by a Halloween "cricket," with food. If the subject is invariably fed after hearing the cricket, the sound itself will come to function as a *conditioned* reinforcer. Equipped with a "cricket," the trainer can pay close attention to the subject's ongoing behavior and administer this reinforcement at just the right moment.

Skinner provides an excellent example of shaping behavior by *successive approximations* as he explains how "to teach the dog to lift its head in the air and turn around to the right."

> As a guide to the height to which the dog's head is to be raised, sight some horizontal line on the wall across the room. Whenever the dog, in its random movements, lifts its head above this line, reinforce immediately. You will soon see the head rising above the line more and more frequently. Now raise your sights slightly and reinforce only when the dog's head rises above the new level. By a series of gradual steps you can get the dog to hold its head much

higher than usual. After this you can begin to emphasize any turning movement in a clockwise direction while the head is high. Eventually the dog should execute a kind of dance step. (Skinner, 1951, p. 27)

If, after the dance step is learned, the dog is never again reinforced, the behavior will gradually disappear or "extinguish." One way to make the behavior resistant to extinction is to reinforce it unpredictably or "intermittently" after it is first learned. The pattern with which such reinforcements are delivered is called a *schedule of reinforcement*.

Complex behaviors can be shaped by applying the same principles employed in teaching the dog its dance step. Skinner describes the training of a pigeon taught to peck a card inscribed with PECK while avoiding one with the words DON'T PECK. This procedure, powerful enough to make a pigeon appear to "read," is of great significance in child rearing. A parent may inadvertently be caught in the trap of selectively reinforcing a child's disruptive behavior. Just as "the squeaky wheel gets the most grease," so also does maladaptive behavior often get the most attention and, hence, reinforcement. It is often difficult to convince parents that such behavior can be extinguished, but it *can* be done.

Relative to the example of reinforcing annoying behavior, it is possible that, while the mother reinforces such behavior, the child's father ignores it. Therefore, in the father's presence that behavior is extinguished and a discrimination is developed. The appearance of the mother becomes, then, a *discriminative stimulus* (S^D); that is, it signals the occasion when he can obtain a reward for annoying behavior. Many other examples are possible. A red traffic light is a discriminative stimulus marking an occasion when crossing the street may be punished, either through physical injury or negative social consequences, such as citation by a policeman. Conversely, a green light marks an occasion when crossing the street will avoid negative consequences and lead us on our way toward such positive reinforcers as lunch in the restaurant across the street. Still simpler examples are possible: a rat may learn that when, and only when, a green light is on, pressing a lever in a Skinner box leads to the presentation of a food pellet.

Discriminative stimuli do not elicit responses in the sense that a blow below the knee cap elicits the patellar reflex. Rather, they serve as cues that mark a time or place of reinforcement, positive or negative, being presented or removed. The importance of discriminative stimuli is underscored by Bijou and Baer (1961) who state:

A great part of psychological development, therefore, is simply the process of learning the discriminative stimuli which signal important reinforcers. (p. 50)

Consider the "reading" performance of Skinner's pigeon. How did he do it? This leads us again into the classical problem of assessing what cues are effective in a discrimination learning situation. It is quite conceivable, for example, that the pigeon responded simply to the difference in *lengths* of the lines of print in PECK and DON'T PECK. He need not have used any other cue. Kephart (1960) believes that many children with learning difficulties read in much this fashion with the "look and say" method of reading instruction.

THE ORIENTATION REACTION

In his excellent and extremely readable review of the literature on the orientation reaction, hereinafter referred to as the OR, Lynn (1966) describes it as follows:

> When an animal is presented with a new stimulus it pricks up its ears, looks in the direction of the stimulus and alerts itself to deal with possible eventualities which the stimulus may herald. It is this response which Russian physiologists and psychologists call the 'orientation reaction.' . . . Apart from the simple turning towards the source of the novel stimulus, it has become evident that the orientation reaction involves a large number of physiological changes. The purpose of these changes, in general terms, is to make the animal more sensitive to incoming stimuli so that it is better equipped to discern what is happening, and to mobilize the body for whatever action may be necessary; for 'fight or flight' as Cannon expressed it. (pp. 1-2)

In addition to the obvious physical components of the OR (the organism's turning its head in the direction of the stimulus, general muscle tonus rises, and the EEG changes toward increased arousal, i.e., faster and lower amplitude activity), there are also the following vegetative changes: (1) vasoconstriction in the limbs and vasodilation in the head, (2) appearance of galvanic skin reaction, (3) increased amplitude and decreased frequency of respiration, and (4) reduced heart rate.

Of special relevance to the present topic is the fact that, with the occurrence of the OR, *sense organs become more sensitive*. This occurs in a non-specific fashion, i.e., the organism is sensitized to all incoming stimuli, regardless of modality. The non-specific nature of the OR is further underscored by the fact of intersensory facilitation. For example, Sokolov reports many studies in which the arousal of an OR to a tone resulted in an increase in sensitivity to visual stimuli (Maltzman & Raskin, 1965).

In one experiment it was first established that a subject did not respond to a given light intensity either behaviorally or physiologically. A loud sound was then introduced which evoked an OR. In the presence of the OR the weak light was detected behaviorally and physiologically. With repeated presentations, however, the OR to the sound extinguished and the visual stimulus was no longer detected.

Just the *opposite* effect can also be produced experimentally, in that it is possible to *raise* an animal's threshold for stimulation through long-term environmental deprivation (Melzack & Scott, 1957). This notion is certainly consistent with the findings of researchers who have assessed the effects of stimulus deprivation on the arousal reaction, a concept closely related to the Russian orientation reaction. Thus, according to Bexton, Heron & Scott (1954):

> There is much evidence from recent neurophysiological studies to indicate that the normal functioning of the waking brain depends on its being constantly exposed to sensory bombardment, which produces a continuing "arousal reaction." . . . when stimulation does not change it rapidly loses its power to cause the arousal reaction. Thus, although the one function of the stimulus is to evoke or guide a specific bit of behaviour, it also has a non-specific function, that of maintaining "arousal" . . . . (p. 70)

Drawing upon Berlyne's (1960) system of categorization, Lynn (1966) described the characteristics of stimuli eliciting the orientation reaction as follows:

1. Intensity
2. Color
3. Conditioned Stimuli (signal stimuli)
4. Surprise
5. Complexity, Uncertainty, Incongruity
6. Conflict
7. Novelty

Stimuli of moderate to high *intensity* elicit an OR. If, however, the stimulus becomes excessively intense, other reactions may set in; for example, the startle-defensive reaction. *Color* stimuli are more likely to elicit ORs than are achromatic ones.

A number of stimuli, such as one's name or the warning "look out," elicit ORs through learning, and these are grouped under the heading of *conditioned* or *signal stimuli*.

Unanticipated changes in experimental conditions, such as sudden deviations from the habitual order of presenting stimuli, can produce an orientation reaction. Lynn characterizes such changes as *surprises.*

Complexity, incongruity and *uncertainty* are seen to elicit ORs when one considers that infants orient more readily to complex geometric designs than to simpler ones. Orientation reactions in adults are readily evoked by incongruous pictures.

Orientation reaction in an animal during a discrimination learning experiment results from exposure to positive and negative stimuli, those in the category of *conflict*. The animal continues making ORs to the stimuli until the discrimination becomes perfect; then the ORs disappear.

Novelty is the most prepotent factor and, in its absence, *habituation* occurs. Thus, once the new stimulus is presented and repeated a number of times, the organism no longer pays attention and the OR, in both its physical and physiological aspects, disappears.

While the factor of intensity is easily understood, it should be realized that novelty can be evoked under extremely simple conditions, such as a light touch to the skin. This characteristic served as the point of departure for a recent research study (Ball, Midgley, Ackerland, Nies & Hord, 1969).

A subject, blindfolded, can be touched lightly on the back of the hand. This simple touch constitutes a novel stimulation, and is sufficient to produce a well-defined OR which includes a clear-cut galvanic skin response. The galvanic skin response, or GSR, consists of a minute, though readily measurable, rise in electrical conductivity of the skin related to palmar sweating. If the touch is repeated several times at the same intensity, in the same location, and at a constant rate, the OR gradually disappears (habituates). One way to elicit a new OR would be simply to touch the subject in a new location; for instance, on the other hand.

SENSORY TRAINING AND THE ORIENTING RESPONSE

By relating the facts of operant conditioning with those of the OR[2], Ball & Porter (1967) trained profoundly retarded, sensorily deprived, institutionalized blind children to directional orientation to an auditory signal. This writer then decided to replicate the study and assess learning in terms of the GSR component of OR acquisition.[3] In the second study, prior to training, subjects showed no more response to their own names than they did to "nonsense" stimuli. This was true for *both* behavioral and GSR indicators. The training procedure entailed "shaping" these subjects to pull back on a lever, an act which terminated a continuous buzzing sound activated by the experimenter prior to each training trial. Initially the experimenter placed his hand over the subject's and moved his hand for him.

At the completion of the manipulation, the experimenter turned off the buzzer, rewarded the subject and allowed him to release his grip. Over several trials it was possible for the experimenter gradually to withdraw from participation so that the subject, unassisted, reached out for the handle and then pulled back on it. Eventually, the subject learned to respond to the buzzing sound as the discriminative stimulus or signal for the start of a new trial.[4] Once this occurred, duration of the buzzing sound was gradually reduced. Eventually, a brief sound could elicit orientation to the task and the motor response. The next step was to add the child's name to the sound and then fade out the tone until he was responding solely to his name.

Since the child's name was followed by both a motor response and a food reward, it became a conditioned stimulus of *signal significance*. Evidence of this newly acquired signal significance was found when, following training, GSR orienting responses to the child's name were significantly greater than those to the nonsense stimuli. As a result of training, for the first time, the child's name could have functioned as an S^D for completely new learning experiences.[5]

Another element, such as intersensory facilitation, could have been added to the above experiment. As noted previously, Sokolov found that the arousal of an OR to a tone caused a previously subliminal light to be detected. For the sake of discussion, assume that the blind retardates would have responded with an OR to a touch to the skin and that this OR could have momentarily facilitated reception of auditory stimulation. Had this occurred, it would have *enhanced* the acquisition of the children's names as conditioned stimuli of signal significance. It could have speeded up the conditioning process.

Assume further that following training the children's names were no longer used and because of this kind of environmental deprivation they began to lose their signal significance. In this case, the operant would have been extinguished as the result of a loss of signal significance of the S^D as an auditory stimulus. Had touch facilitated its initial acquisition, it could function to restore the signal significance of the name, to make it available again as an S^D. Now if a conditioned operant had been related to that S^D (for instance, had the child faced the adult in response to hearing his name), it is conceivable that the end result of a touch to the skin could be the reappearance of the conditioned operant.[6]

It could be argued that the above-mentioned blind retardates failed to orient to their names either behaviorally or physiologically due to long-term environmental deprivation. The specific training overcame the results of such deprivation. This model for the facilitation of learning through sensory stimulation seems to apply quite well to some of the initial procedures Itard utilized with Victor. Thus, Itard reasoned that training in attention would not succeed if the sense organ involved were pervasively lacking in sensitivity. For Victor, such was the case for touch, taste and smell. His lack of response to extremes of temperature was particularly striking.

> Several times during the course of the winter I have seen him crossing the garden of the Deaf and Dumb, squatting half naked upon the wet ground, remaining thus exposed for hours on end to a cold and wet wind. It was not only to cold but also to intense heat that the organ of the skin and touch showed no sensitivity. When he was near the fire and the glowing embers came rolling out of the hearth it was a daily occurrence for him to seize them with his fingers and replace them without any particular haste upon the flaming fire. He has been discovered more than once in the kitchen picking out in the same way potatoes which were cooking in boiling water, and I can guarantee that he had, even at that time, a fine and velvety skin. (pp. 14-15)[7]

He also proved insensitive to certain powerful olfactory stimuli; for example, quantities of snuff failed to produce sneezing or the secretion of tears.

Itard concentrated initially on developing tactual sensitivity to temperature changes by applying heat to the skin in a variety of ways: Victor was clothed, put to bed, housed warmly and given frequent and prolonged baths. Marked changes in his responses to temperature variation did occur. He carefully tested his bath water with his finger before entering the tub. If it was lukewarm, he refused to bathe.

We cannot discount the possible roles of modeling and imitation in the development of such behaviors. It is quite possible that Victor observed Itard and others testing their bath water before entering the tub and thereby learned to do likewise. The problem of interpreting the various changes in Victor's responses to heat variations was further complicated by the fact that, concurrently with the baths, Itard conducted a variety of additional programs of stimulation, such as dry rubs and avoidance conditioning with static electricity. In addition, Victor was exposed to various sources of social stimulation. Yet there is evidence supporting Itard's belief that he had really accomplished a heightening of tactual sensitivity to thermal stimulation. This derives from the fact that he was eventually able to utilize cold as a negative reinforcer in an application of escape-avoidance conditioning to establish the wearing of clothing, a practice that Victor initially rejected. A much more tenuous, yet intriguing, line of evidence arises in a seeming generalization from tactual training to the olfactory sense.

The sense of smell had also gained by this improvement. The least irritation of this organ provoked sneezing, and I judged by the fright that seized him the first time this happened, that this was a new experience to him. He immediately ran away and threw himself on his bed. (p. 19)

The use of snuff was prevalent in that day and Victor probably observed the practice. Yet in emphasizing the apparently unexpected, reflex-like nature of Victor's response, Itard seemed clearly to imply that it was anything but a simple act of imitation. Within three months Itard achieved what he termed "a general excitement of all the senses." Victor's touch "showed itself sensitive to the impression of hot or cold substances, smooth or rough, yielding or resistant" (p. 18).

Itard also suggested that a generalized improvement of taste and smell resulted from the specific program of stimulation applied to the skin.

The simultaneous improvement of the three senses, touch, taste and smell, resulting from the stimulants applied to the skin whilst these last two remained unaffected is a valuable fact, worthy of being drawn to the attention of physiologists. It seems to prove, what from other sources appears probable, that the senses of touch, smell and taste are only a modification of the organ of the skin; whereas those of hearing and sight, more subjective, enclosed in a most complicated physical apparatus, are subject to other laws and ought in some measure to form a separate class. (p. 20)

Despite the admitted difficulties in interpreting the degree to which the results are attributable to intersensory facilitation rather than other influences, the idea is exceedingly interesting. Itard's claim is consistent with Sokolov's findings regarding intersensory facilitation of the OR[8] (see page 13).

Although the interpretation of the effects of Victor's therapeutic baths and thermal treatments must remain tentative, it nonetheless provides a model of the lowest common denominator for sensory education, a simple stimulation of the more primitive senses. The possible applicability of this model is suggested by the results of research involving relatively simple sensory stimulation.

In one such study (Schaffer & Emerson, 1968) the short-term effects of changes in arousal level, brought about by brief sessions of environmental stimulation, were related to developmental status in normal infants. The "stimulator" smiled and talked to the infant, stroked his face and hands, picked him up and held him. A period of twelve minutes of stimulation prior to testing resulted in a ten-point increase in *Developmental Quotient* for the stimulated infants, with essentially no change for a control group.

It was concluded that experiential deprivation can produce a temporary loss of arousal level in normal infants with a consequent decrement in developmental test performance. They also concluded that under extreme and chronic conditions of environmental restriction a real, rather than apparent, deterioration may occur. This is consistent with the position taken by Hunt (1961) and also that of Bexton, et al. (1954). (Also see Sayegh & Dennis, 1965).

The selective importance of certain kinds of tactual stimulation to development was convincingly revealed in a fascinating series of studies by Harry F. Harlow (1958). Dr. Harlow removed infant monkeys from their mothers and gave them substitutes which he called "surrogate mothers." One type of surrogate, covered with a wire mesh, provided the monkey with milk for nursing. The other surrogate, covered with sponge rubber and an outer layer of terrycloth, did not provide for a great deal of tactual and contact comfort. The infant monkey showed a marked preference for the terrycloth mother and would cling to her while nursing from the wire mother. The infant also used the terrycloth mother as a "home base" to which he clung as he tentatively explored unfamiliar objects placed nearby.

If an exceedingly simple stimulation of the senses can have a marked influence on developmental status, this fact has far-reaching implications for the entire field of sensory education. Thus, for all programs of sensory education, however diverse and even contradictory their theoretical positions, a good deal of stimulation is provided at this primitive level. In the course of interpreting the results of such programs, it is necessary to consider first the explanatory value of this highly parsimonious factor in accounting for the results. For example, Kephart's (1960) and Delacato's (1959) treatment approaches for brain-damaged children, although they superficially appear similar, actually stem from divergent theoretical frameworks. Yet both approaches have this in common — they involve a great deal of tactual stimulation. It is conceivable that whatever positive results are obtained from both systems are due to this common factor. The possible contribution of this factor must be more carefully assessed. For example, in a recent study by Edgar, Ball, McIntyre and Shotwell (1969), institutionalized pre-school age, organically impaired, severely retarded children were given a program of sensory-motor training based on Kephart's approach. In several of the procedures intensive tactual, visual and auditory stimulations were involved. Although a control group received a modified nursery school program containing individualized attention and a great deal of stimulation, the input on the tactual level was necessarily less. Over an eight-month period the experimental group gained significantly more in Gesell developmental age than the control group (6.0 months v. 2.2 months). However encouraging these results, further training and stimulation studies of this type will need more precisely to control for the possible effects of tactile stimulation and, additionally, experimenter effects including the phenomenon of "self-fulfilling prophecy" (Rosenthal, 1966).

ATTENTION TRAINING (PART I)

Although it may be true that Itard's work was guided by a restricted, sensationistic theoretical orientation (Talbot, 1964, p. 27), at times, he expressed a broad conception of the significance of training that transcended a narrow sensationism. In the following quote from Itard we see evidence of a remarkably contemporary-sounding orientation:

> . . . such . . . is the intimate relation which unites physical with intellectual man that, although their respective provinces appear and are in fact very distinct; yet the borderline between the two different sorts of function is very confused. Their development is simultaneous and their influence reciprocal. Thus while I was limiting my efforts to the exercise of the senses of our savage, the mind took its share of the attention given exclusively to the education of these organs and followed the same order of development. In fact it seemed that in instructing the senses to perceive and to distinguish new objects, I forced the attention to fix itself on them, the judgment to compare them, and the memory to retain them. Thus nothing was immaterial in these exercises. Everything penetrated to the mind. Everything put the faculties of the intelligence into play and prepared them for the great work of the communication of ideas. (p. 67)

A similar degree of sophistication is clearly evident in his interpretation of Victor's lack of attention. Pinel took Victor's lack of attention at face value and considered it an indication of hopeless idiocy. Itard never accepted this point of view. His own view was influenced by his observations of Victor's responses to a variety of sounds, some significantly related to his previous existence, others to his new environment.

> It is easily conceived that in the midst of the forest and far from the society of all thinking beings, the sense of hearing of our savage did not experience any other impressions than those which a small number of noises made upon him, and particularly those which were connected with his physical needs. Under these circumstances his ear was not an organ for the appreciation of sounds, their articulations and their combinations; it was nothing but a simple means of self-

preservation which warned of the approach of a dangerous animal or the fall of wild fruit. These are without doubt the functions to which his hearing was limited, judging by the slight response obtained from the organ given a year ago to all sounds and noises except those bearing upon his individual needs; and judging on the other hand, by the exquisite sensibility which this sense showed for such sounds as had some such connection with his interests. When a chestnut or a walnut was cracked without his knowledge and as gently as possible; if the key of the door which held him captive was merely touched, he never failed to turn quickly and run towards the place whence the sound came. If the organ of hearing did not show the same susceptibility for the sounds of the voice, even for the explosion of firearms, it was because he was necessarily little sensitive and little attentive to all other impressions than those to which he had been long and exclusively accustomed. (pp. 26-27)

Itard's own position regarding the function of attention is as follows:

If then, after the early days of childhood, attention is given naturally only to such things which have recognized or suspected connection with our tastes, it is understood why our young savage, having only a small number of requirements, would exert them upon a small number of objects. Unless I am deceived, that is the cause of this absolute inattention which struck everybody at the time of his arrival at Paris, and which at the present moment has almost completely disappeared because he has been made to feel the connection which all the new things about him have with him. (p. 27)

Interpreted within the framework of operant conditioning, the above statement expressed the idea that Victor's gross lack of attention was due to the almost total absense of discriminative stimuli related to survival in the wild. With the presentation of relevant discriminative stimuli, such as the cracking of walnuts, attention proved exceptionally keen. Such sounds both evoked an OR (as a signal stimulus) and served as a discriminative stimulus for an instrumental response eventuating in reinforcement; in this case, eating the nut. Unlike the case of tactual sensitivity, insofar as audition was concerned, Itard had clear-cut evidence of *intact sensibility*. Yet it appeared that many of the discriminative stimuli of civilized life (e.g., the gunshot) failed to function as such and, more basically, failed to elicit an OR.[9] Itard thus tackled the problem of teaching Victor to make appropriate instrumental responses to the myriad discriminative stimuli controlling the everyday behavior of civilized man.

Itard's initial attempt at training entailed a hopeless strategy repeated thousands of times since: attempting to train profoundly impaired children through the use of standard children's toys.

> I have successively shown him toys of all kinds; more than once I
> have tried for whole hours to teach him how to use them and I have
> seen with sorrow that, far from attracting his attention, these various
> objects always ended by making him so impatient that he came to the
> point of hiding them or destroying them when the occasion offered
> itself. Thus, one day when he was alone in his room he took upon
> himself to throw into the fire a game of ninepins with which we had
> pestered him and which had been shut up for a long time in a night
> commode, and he was found gaily warming himself before his
> bonfire. (p. 20)

Itard, however, was far from discouraged by this temporary setback.
He simply devised a new strategy which, it appears, stemmed from his
awareness of how attention was learned in the wilderness.

> I succeeded sometimes in interesting him in amusements which had
> connection with his appetite for food. Here is one, for example,
> which I often arranged for him at the end of the meal when I took
> him to dine with me in town. I placed before him without any sym-
> metrical order, and upside down, several little silver cups, under one
> of which was placed a chestnut. Quite sure of having attracted his
> attention, I raised them one after the other excepting that which
> covered the nut. After having thus shown him that they contained
> nothing, and having replaced them in the same order, I invited him
> by signs to seek in his turn. The first cup under which he searched
> was precisely the one under which I had hidden the little reward due
> to him. Thus far, there was only a feeble effort of memory. But I
> made the game insensibly more complicated. Thus after having by
> the same procedure hidden another chestnut, I changed the order of
> all the cups, slowly, however, so that in this general inversion he was
> able, although with difficulty, to follow with his eyes and with his
> attention the one which hid the precious object. I did more; I placed
> nuts under two or three of the cups and his attention, although
> divided between these three objects, still followed them none the
> less in their respective changes, and directed his first searches towards
> them. Moreover, I had a further aim in mind. This judgment was
> after all only a calculation of greediness. To render his attention in
> some measure less like an animal's, I took away from his amusement
> everything which had connection with his appetite, and put under
> the cups only such objects as could not be eaten. The result was
> almost as satisfactory and this exercise became no more than a simple
> game of cups, not without advantage in provoking attention, judg-
> ment, and steadiness in his gaze. (pp. 20-21)

Thus, by the utilization of extrinsic reinforcers (food and trinkets) in the
context of the "shell game" of carnival fame, Itard developed a rudi-

mentary kind of attention. The technique parallels, in certain respects, Harlow's (1949) later development of *learning set* training which was subsequently applied to retardates by Zeaman & House (1963).[10]

In conclusion, it appears that Itard's shell game attention training procedure was successful in "provoking attention, judgment, and steadiness in his [Victor's] gaze." It is also suggested that he was dealing with the problem of distractibility and developing task-oriented behaviors at a level that may be prerequisite to more complex levels of discrimination learning.

ATTENTION TRAINING (PART II)

The next significant step in visual discrimination training took, as its point of departure, Sicard's method of instruction for deaf mutes.

> I began then with the procedure ordinarily used first in that celebrated school [Sicard's] and drew on a blackboard the outline of some objects that could best be represented by a simple drawing, such as a key, scissors, and a hammer. Repeatedly, and at such times as I saw that I was being noticed, I placed each of these objects upon its respective drawing and when I was sure that in this way he had been made to feel the connection, I endeavored to make him bring them successively to me by pointing to the drawing of the one I wanted. Nothing came of this. I repeated the experiment several times and always with as little success; he either refused stubbornly to bring the one of the three things which I indicated, or else brought the two others with it and gave them all to me at the same time. I am convinced that this was merely calculated laziness which did not let him do in detail what he found quite simple to do all at once. (Itard, pp. 38-39)

Seeing that he could not induce this simple matching procedure through a standard approach that worked well with deaf mutes, Itard made one of his many intuitive and extremely creative revisions of strategy. On a somewhat different level, this strategy was to be repeated over 150 years later by Haeussermann (1958). Capitalizing on the need for preservation of sameness (compulsivity) of autistic children, Haeussermann devised a technique for tricking them into performing a formboard test.

> The examiner can skillfully "spill" a nest of cubes or a formboard or other item to be assembled, and, leaving it there, pretend to be busy in another part of the room. The child, believing himself unobserved, may be found to assemble the toy, often with an aggrieved

expression. It may appear that he is annoyed to find order disturbed and is almost compulsively forced to restore it before he once more can return to his withdrawn state. By increasing the difficulty of the demand, such as reversing the formboard, on a subsequent attempt, one may then find a clue to the child's level by observing whether he is able to adapt to the higher demand. (Haeussermann, p. 32)

In terms of his tendency to be excessively orderly and his extreme resistance to change in his immediate environment, Victor corresponds well to Haeussermann's autistics. It should be noted, however, that Victor's behavior did not otherwise conform to the classical picture of autism. Itard fully exploited the possibilities of manipulating this compulsive trait in the service of performance as indicated in the following quote:

I bethought myself then of a means which would force him to give particular attention to each of these objects. I had noticed for some months past that he had a most decided taste for order; so much so that sometimes he would get up from his bed to put a piece of furniture or a utensil which had accidentally got moved, back again into its usual place. He was even more particular about the things hanging upon the wall: each had a nail and a particular hook, and when any of these had been changed he was not quiet until he had himself corrected them. All I had to do then was to arrange in the same way the things upon which I wished him to exercise his attention. By means of a nail I suspended each of the objects below its drawing and left them there for some time. When afterwards I came to give them to Victor they were immediately replaced in their proper order. I repeated this several times and always with the same result. (p. 39)

By all appearances it would seem that Itard had achieved the goal of teaching Victor the matching procedure. Yet he did not equate appearance with reality. In Kephart's terms, he felt it necessary to explore the *process* whereby Victor solved this task. In somewhat different terms, it could be said that he undertook to evaluate the cues that were effectively utilized by Victor to perform this discrimination task.[11] The important point is that Itard was *never* content to accept Victor's performances at face value. This essential procedure of evaluating the process involved is repeated again and again. It is at the very core of Itard's greatness and depth as a teacher and a scientist. In this instance, Itard suspected that the seemingly "correct" matching procedure may have been based on a process that did not really entail matching at all.

Nevertheless, I was far from attributing this to his discrimination, and this classification could well be only an act of memory. To reas-

sure myself I changed the respective positions of the drawings and
this time I saw him follow the original order in the arrangement of
the objects without any allowance for the transposition. As a matter
of fact, nothing was easier than for him to learn the new classification necessitated by this change, but nothing more difficult than to
make him reason it out. His memory alone bore the burden of each
arrangement. I devoted myself then to the task of neutralizing in
some way the assistance which he drew from it. I succeeded in fa-
tiguing his memory by increasing the number of drawings and the
frequency of their transpositions.

His memory now became an insufficient guide for the methodical
arrangement of the numerous articles, so that one would expect his
mind to find assistance by comparing the drawing with the things.
What a difficult step I had overcome! I was convinced of this when
I saw our young Victor fasten his gaze and successively, upon each
object, choose one, and next look for the drawing to which he wished
to bring it, and I soon had material proof by experimenting with the
transposition of the drawings, which was followed on his part by the
methodical transposition of the objects. (pp. 39-40)

So Itard succeeded in forcing Victor to give up memory for order as his
sole cue by evolving a situation in which memory was insufficient. Victor
was thus pushed into utilizing a more mature process or cue system. It will
be seen that progress with Victor was largely a matter of passing through
a whole sequence of such systems or strategies, each one a bit more mature
than the last. It is a measure of Itard's clinical brilliance and inventiveness
that he could identify each system and find a means of pushing Victor onto
the next higher level. The entire sequence is strikingly similar to Kephart's
(1968) discussion of the necessity of working through the atypical child's
resistance to learning generalized solutions to problems.[12]

Having induced Victor to carry out the matching procedure in a fashion
that actually did involve matching, Itard was encouraged to believe that
he had taken a temporary detour that would permit him to follow the
remaining steps of Sicard's program. But such was not the case.

This result inspired in me the most brilliant hopes. I had believed
there were no more difficulties to conquer, when there arose a most
insuperable one which obstinately held me back and forced me to
renounce my method. It is well known that in the education of the
deaf and dumb this first procedure is followed by a second and much
more difficult one. After having been made to feel by repeated comparisons the connection of the thing with its drawing, the letters
which form the name of the object are placed on the drawing. That
done, the drawing is effaced and only the alphabetical signs remain.
The deaf mute sees in this second procedure only a change of draw-

ing which continues to be for him the sign of the object. It was not so with Victor who, in spite of the most frequent repetitions, in spite of a prolonged presentation of the thing below its word, could never solve the problem. I was easily able to account for this difficulty and it was easy for me to understand why it was insurmountable. From the picture of an object to its alphabetical representation, the distance is immense and it is so much the greater for the pupil because he is faced with it during the first stages of his instruction. If deaf mutes are not held back at this point the reason is that, of all children, they are the most attentive and the most observing. Accustomed from their earliest childhood to hear and speak with their eyes, they have more practice than anyone else in the recognition of relations between visible objects. It was necessary then to look for a method more in keeping with the still torpid faculties of our young savage, a method by which the surmounting of each difficulty prepared him for a still more difficult task. (pp. 40-41)

So once again, for the purpose of establishing a process that was to fill a gap in what would be an orderly learning sequence for the typical deaf student, Itard invented a discrimination training program.

Upon a board, two feet square, I pasted three pieces of paper of very distinct shapes and decided colors. One was circular and red, another was triangular and blue, the third was square and black. By means of holes pierced in their centers and nails driven into the board, three pieces of cardboard of the same shapes and colors were placed there and left for some days upon their respective models pasted on the board. Then I lifted them and gave them to Victor and they were replaced without any difficulty. I assured myself by reversing the board and then changing the order of the figures, that this first result was not a matter of routine but was due to comparison. After some days I substituted another board for the first. I had pasted the same figures on it, but this time they were all of a uniform color. In the first case the pupil had the double indication of shapes and colors to aid him in recognition, in the second case he had only one guide, comparison of the shapes. At almost the same time I showed him a third where all the figures were the same but the colors different. The same tests always gave the same results, excepting that I do not count mistakes due to lack of attention. The facility with which he executed these easy comparisons obliged me to present some new ones to him. I made additions and modifications in the last two presentations. I added to the one with the different shaped figures some new shapes much less distinct and to the one with the colors some new colors which differed only in shade. There was, for example, in the first a rather long parallelogram besides a square, and in the second a pattern in sky blue beside one of grayish blue.

He made some mistakes and showed some uncertainty about these, which disappeared after some days' practice.

These results emboldened me to new changes always more diffi- cult. Each day I added, curtailed, and modified, provoking new comparisons and new judgments. (pp. 41-42)

In the first problem Itard provided Victor with a great deal of what has been called *cue redundancy* (Trabasso & Bower, 1968) by providing him with relevant cues from two different stimulus dimensions, in this case, form and color. He then induced him to match on the basis of a single dimension. Finally, he had him make progressively finer discrimina- tions along a single dimension, sky blue v. grayish blue.

In effect, Itard, through his discrimination training procedure, achieved what Zeaman and House (1963) might consider a "break through" in the training of retardates: he had taught Victor to attend to relevant dimen- sions. This accomplishment was immediately followed by an apparently rapid learning of increasingly complex cues along these dimensions.

Following a temporary interruption,[13] Itard proceeded to a more com- plex level of training, described as follows:

This favorable change allowed us to take up again our course of exercises where we had broken it off. These I submitted to new mod- ifications which were designed to stabilize his judgment still further. For the figures pasted on the board, which I have said were com- pletely colored shapes representing geometrical figures, I substituted linear outlines of these same shapes. I also contented myself with indicating the colors by little irregular samples quite unlike the col- ored cards. I may say that these new difficulties were only a game to the child; a result which was sufficient for the end I had in mind when adopting this system of direct comparisons. The moment had come to replace this by another which was much more instructive and which would have presented insurmountable difficulties if the way had not been smoothed in advance by the success of the meth- ods just used. (p. 45)

Thus, when given the blue cardboard triangle, Victor had to match it to an outline of a triangle with a swatch of blue on it. Matching a solid figure with an outline form is one of the transfer problems subsequently used by Lashley (1938) in one of his famous experiments on the evalua- tion of cues in figure discrimination.

Lashley clearly demonstrated the need to evaluate various cues. For example, just because a rat learns to choose a door marked with a white triangle, as against one marked with a white circle, it does not necessarily mean that the triangular shape is a positive cue. The wide white base would be sufficient and the remainder of the figure might be disregarded.

Itard subsequently dispensed with colored cardboard forms and proceeded to apply the matching technique to teaching the letters of the alphabet. Once again, although Victor seemingly performed the task on the basis of matching, such was not the case. Yet Itard detected the strategy and skillfully dealt with it. In this instance Itard sensed that something was wrong because Victor mastered the task too rapidly! When he discovered Victor's strategy for evading the full demands of the task, he devised still another successful counter-strategy:

> I ordered to be printed as a big character upon a piece of cardboard two inches square each of the twenty-four letters of the alphabet. I had an equal number of spaces cut in a plank a foot and a half square. Into these the pieces of cardboard could be inserted, without the use of paste, so that their places could be changed as required. I had an equal number of characters of the same dimensions made in metal. These were meant to be compared by the pupil with the printed letters, and were to be arranged in their corresponding places.
>
> The first trial of this method was made, in my absence, by Madame Guérin. I was very much surprised on my return to learn from her that Victor distinguished all the characters and arranged them properly. He was immediately put to the test and performed his task without any mistake. Though delighted with such an immediate success I was still far from able to explain its cause, and it was only some days after that I discovered this by noting the way in which our pupil proceeded to make this arrangement. In order to make the work easier he devised of his own accord a little expedient which in this task allowed him to dispense with memory, comparison and judgment. As soon as the board was put between his hands, he did not wait until the metal letters were taken out of their places but he himself took them and piled them upon his hand, following the order of their arrangement so that the last letter, after all were taken from the board, was the first on the pile. He began with this and finished with the last of the pile, thus beginning the board at the end and proceeding always from right to left. Moreover, he was able to improve upon this procedure; for very often the pile collapsed, the characters fell out and he had to straighten everything up and put it in order by the unaided efforts of attention. So the twenty-four letters were arranged in four rows of six each, making it easier to lift them up by rows only, and even to replace them in the same way by taking letters from the second row only when the first was replaced.
>
> I do not know whether he reasoned as I suppose, but at least it is certain that he executed the performance in the manner described.

It was then a true routine, but a routine of his own invention, and one which was perhaps as much to the credit of his intelligence as was a method of arrangement hit upon shortly afterwards to the credit of his discernment. It was not difficult to set him off by giving him the characters pellmell whenever he was given the board. At last, in spite of the frequent transpositions to which I submitted the printed characters by changing their places, in spite of insidious arrangements, such as the O beside the C, and E beside the F, etc., his discrimination became infallible. (pp. 45-47)

Perceptual training based on matching procedures like those developed by Itard have their modern counterparts in reading readiness programs for normal children, and special training materials for children with learning problems. Throughout the United States alone, millions of class hours are devoted to such activities and millions of dollars are spent for teachers' salaries and a massive output of teaching materials. But what are the implications of all this effort? Parents, and also the "education experts," view these programs enthusiastically. Indeed, the eager first-grader viewed at his desk matching forms and letters in his reading readiness workbook seems to be "making progress." It all seems to lead to an inescapable conclusion that, since letters and words are complex shapes, in learning to match the shapes he is being prepared for reading. But let's evaluate this facile, "common sense" assumption. It may hold for most normal children who respond well to all kinds of teaching approaches, even some that are seemingly contradictory in nature. But what of the *atypical* child? What are we doing to him? A further consideration of Itard's work yields some highly relevant clues to this problem.

In looking at what Itard emphasized in his perceptual training program we see that he placed great stress on evoking even finer cue discriminations, as with increasingly similar shapes and colors differing only in shade. In terms of Kephart's (1960) system of perceptual training, it could be said that he failed to train for perceptual generalization. Thus, according to Kephart, perceptual learning follows the course of a very early differentiation of perceptual elements, lines and angles, out of an initial globular mass. Form perception develops through an integration of these elements into an *organized whole* in the Gestalt sense of the term. He believes that this organized whole, or integrated form, is absolutely essential to more advanced, abstract learning. However, many children break down at the level at which details, having been differentiated, must be integrated into constructive form (Kephart, 1960). If this is correct, for these children, Itard's program, with its emphasis on differentiation of detail, would serve to fixate this problem rather than remedy it. So also would many of the currently accepted readiness techniques.

It is interesting to note that Trabasso (1968), working in a frame of reference remote from Kephart's, clearly implies a similar concern regarding the implications of discrimination training.

> A final word or two about attention and the learning environment. A series of experiments . . . have shown that you can pare down the initial or attentional phase and hence speed up the overall learning rate by increasing 1, the *number*, and 2, the *vividness* or saliency of relevant stimulus cues. These same experiments have shown however that such quicker learning can be inefficient or eccentric. If more stimulus patterns or cues are provided than are needed to solve, they will not all be used or learned. Furthermore, what *is* learned may be learned in odd, sometimes undesirable ways. A child who distinguishes t's from f's because "t's are purple," has really only learned an unfortunate association which sooner or later will impede his reading progress. (p. 36)

Pursuing the implications of Trabasso's statement we could devise a readiness program that may actually accelerate learning for most children, but handicap a minority. If this program were utilized as blindly and uncritically as those in current vogue, the child who distinguishes t's from f's because "t's are purple" might end up with the diagnosis of "primary reading disability" and be placed in a special class for children with presumptive brain dysfunction. Because most children thrived academically, the program would receive support from parents and "experts." The embarrassment of the failure of a significant minority could be circumvented with the most convenient of rationalizations: "There is something wrong with his brain." With such a neatly reinforcing system of self-deception, the readiness program might prevail indefinitely!

It is possible that we could be overwhelmingly successful in programming perceptual training materials without foreseeing their long-range implications for later learning. Sidman & Stoddard's (1966) remarkable errorless learning program is reminiscent of Itard's emphasis on discriminating small differences of a dimension. Yet it seems probable that had Victor received Sidman's program, Itard would have faced the same problems he later encountered. There are subtle, far-reaching problems of this kind that deserve much more attention than they are receiving among the more staunch adherents of operant conditioning.

Though rarely recognized, there exists a highly critical problem that transcends the mechanics of reading. It is this — what are the implications of perceptual training for the eventual development of conceptual thinking and creativity? Happily, due to the tremendous scope of his educational experiment, Itard provided some fascinating glimpses into this issue, also.

READING INSTRUCTION

Itard's matching exercises with letters of the alphabet marked the end of readiness training.[14] He then proceeded to instruct Victor in reading itself.

> In exercising it upon all these letters, the end I had in view was to prepare Victor for a primitive but correct use of the letters, namely the expression of needs which can only be made known by means of speech. Far from believing that I was already so near this great step in his education, I was led by the spirit of curiosity rather than the hope of success to try the experiment which follows.
>
> One morning when he was waiting impatiently for the milk which he always had for breakfast, I carried to him his board which I had specially arranged the evening before with the four letters *L.A.I.T.* Madame Guérin, whom I had warned, approached, looked at the letters and immediately gave me a cup of milk which I pretended to drink myself. A moment after I approached Victor, gave him the four letters that I had lifted from the board, and pointed to it with one hand while in the other I held the jug full of milk. The letters were immediately replaced but in inverted order, so that they showed *T.I.A.L.* instead of *L.A.I.T.* I indicated the corrections to be made by designating with my finger the letters to transpose and the proper place of each. When these changes had reproduced the sign, he was allowed to have his milk.
>
> It is difficult to believe that five or six similar attempts were sufficient, not only to make him arrange methodically the four letters of the word *Lait* but to give him the idea of the connection between the word and the thing. At least this is the justifiable inference from what happened a week later. One evening when he was ready to set out for the Observatory, he was seen to provide himself on his own initiative with the four letters in question, and to put them in his pocket; he had scarcely arrived at Citizen Lemeri's house, where as I previously said he goes every day for some milk, when he produced them and placed them on a table in such a way as to form the word *LAIT*. (pp. 47-48)

But once again, Itard was unwilling to accept a performance at face value. He was to discover that the process underlying Victor's performance was more specific and constricted than he had supposed. Thus, at a later time he observed:

> I have given an account of the first step made in recognizing written signs, and I am not afraid to signalize it as an important epoch in his education, as the sweetest and most brilliant success that has ever been obtained upon a creature fallen as was this one, into the lowest extremity of brutishness. But subsequent observations, by throwing light upon the nature of this result, soon came to weaken the hopes that I had conceived from it. I noticed that Victor did not use words which I had taught him for the purpose of asking for the objects, or of making known a wish or a need, but employed them at certain moments only, and always at the sight of the desired things. Thus for example, much as he wanted his milk it was only at the moment when he was accustomed to take it and at the actual instant when he saw that it was going to be given him that the word for this favorite food was expressed or rather formed in the proper way. In order to clear up the suspicion that this restricted employment of the words awoke in me I tried delaying the hour of his breakfast but waited in vain for the written expression of my pupil's needs although they had become very urgent. It was not until the cup appeared that the word *lait* (milk) was formed. I resorted to another test. In the middle of his lunch and without letting it appear in any way to be a punishment, I took away his cup of milk and shut it up in a cupboard. If the word *lait* had been for Victor the distinct sign of the thing and the expression of his want of it, there is no doubt that after this sudden privation, the need continuing to make itself felt, the word would have been immediately produced. It was not, and I concluded that the formation of this sign, instead of being for the pupil the expression of his desire, was merely a sort of preliminary exercise with which he mechanically preceded the satisfaction of his appetite. It was necessary then to retrace our steps and begin again. I resigned myself courageously to do this, believing that if I had not been understood by my pupil it was my fault rather than his. Indeed, in reflecting upon the causes which might give rise to this defective reception of the written signs, I recognized that in these first examples of the expression of ideas I had not employed the extreme simplicity which I had introduced at the beginning of my other methods of instruction and which had insured their success. Thus although the word *lait* is for us only a simple sign, for Victor it might be a confused expression for the drink, the vessel which contained it, and the desire of which it was the object. (pp. 67-69)

The operant approach provides a convenient framework for conceptualizing much of what occurred in these two initial training incidents. But

in order to do this we must add the concept of *chaining* to what we have
already learned about operant conditioning. A beautiful example of chaining can be found in Keller's (1954) amusing description of a complicated
sequence of acts carried out by a rat (Pliny) trained by operant conditioning methods.

> Pliny's accomplishment amounted to this. He would first pull a
> string that hung from the top of his cage. This pull would cause a
> marble to be released from an overhead rack. When the marble fell
> to the floor, he would pick it up in his forepaws and carry it across
> the cage to a small tube that projected vertically two inches above the
> floor. He would then lift the marble to the top of the tube and drop
> it inside, whereupon a pellet of food was automatically discharged
> into a nearby tray. Pliny would then approach the tray, sieze the
> pellet, eat it, and turn again to repeat the sequence of acts. In this
> way, he earned his living, day after day.
>   Here, then, is a chain of operants, each induced by its own
> specific cue. . . . Visual or tactual stimulation from the string and
> its surroundings probably set off the string-pulling response. String-
> pulling brought into action a new set of stimuli, provided by the
> marble as it arrived. These made up the cue for the grasping and
> carrying responses that put the animal in the presence of another
> visual compound, the tube. The lifting and letting-go responses that
> permitted the marble to drop into the tube produced, in turn, the
> sound of the food-magazine which led to tray-approach and, finally
> stimulation from the food itself. With completion of the eating
> behavior, the entire sequence began again. (p. 24)

Now we return to Victor. Prior to training, the appearance of pitcher
and cup served as discriminative stimuli (S^Ds) for the presentation of
milk, a primary reinforcer (S^R). Into the breakfast context, Itard injected
the previously mastered task of inserting letters in recesses on a board.
Victor copied the letter arrangement presented and then removed by Itard.
This was no more than a variation on the previously learned matching
task. When Victor correctly repeated the letter sequence, he was reinforced with milk. The whole procedure can be summarized as follows: the
appearance of pitcher and cup served as S^Ds for Victor's laying out the
letters, an act that was an S^D for Itard to provide Victor with reinforcement. We thus have a chain involving both Victor and Itard.

That this was a simple chain of S-R connections is suggested by the
second episode in which Itard discovered the limitations of Victor's performance. For Itard's term, "sign," we can substitute the expression, "ini-

tial discriminative stimulus in the chain;" in this case, pitcher and cup. Thus, the chain was not activated until the initial visual cue (pitcher), the occasion for the response of laying out the letters, was presented. Conceptualizing the sequence as a simple chain enables us to avoid more complicated explanations, such as Itard's final remark that the word *Lait* might be confused with the expression for the drink, the vessel, and the desire for milk. We need only say that the appearance of the initial S^D was required for the "running off" of the chain.

The fit of the operant chain explanation is not nearly as satisfactory when applied to Victor's picking up the letters on his own initiative and taking them to Citizen Lemeri's house. Prior to conditioning with the letters, chains involving a milk-drinking ritual had been established both at Victor's home and at the Lemeri residence. When the *Lait* spelling procedure was established we could expect some generalization to the second chain. Discriminative stimuli for a departure to the observatory, for example, donning of overcoats, could serve as the initial S^Ds in a chain extending to the act of milk-drinking occurring on arrival. It is noteworthy that the initial S^D in the longer chain, that is, donning overcoats, took place in a location in which the letters were available (Victor's home). Yet if we are to stick to our notion of the mechanistic specificity of the chain, as suggested by Victor's failure to "request" milk at home when the pitcher and cup were hidden, it is difficult to reconcile his "anticipating" the need for the letters while still at home.

To return to Itard's adjustment of Victor's programming, it should be noted that he identified the difficulty and, much as he had done earlier in connection with training Victor to match objects with their outline representations, he backed up and evolved intermediate steps in programming.

> Several other signs with which I had familiarized him showed the same lack of precision in application. An even more considerable defect was inherent in the method of expression we had adopted. As I have already said, this consisted in placing metal letters on a line and in the proper order, in such a way as to form the name of each object. But the connection which existed between the thing and the word was not immediate enough for his complete apprehension. In order to do away with this difficulty, it was necessary to establish between each object and its sign a more direct connection and a sort of identity which fixed them simultaneously in his memory. The objects first submitted to a trial of this new method of expression had therefore to be reduced to the greatest simplicity, so that their signs could not in any way bear upon their *accessories*.*[15] Conse-

---

*Here, and throughout the book, an asterisk following italicized words in an extract indicates *author's italics*.

quently I arranged on the shelves of a library several simple objects such as a pen, a key, a knife, a box, etc., each one on a card upon which its name was written. These names were not new to the pupil. He already knew them and had learned to distinguish them from each other, according to the method of reading which I have already indicated.

The problem then was merely to familiarize his eyes with the respective display of each of these names under the object which it represented. This arrangement was soon grasped as I had proof when, displacing all the things and instantly replacing all the labels in another order, I saw the pupil carefully replace each object upon its name. I varied my tests, and the variation gave me the opportunity to make several observations relative to the degree of the impression which these written signs made upon the sensory apparatus of our savage. Thus, leaving all the things in one corner of the room and taking all the labels to another, I wished by showing them successively to Victor to make him fetch each thing for which I showed him the written word. On these occasions, in order for him to bring the thing it was necessary that he should not lose from sight for a single instant the characters which indicated it. If he was too far away to be able to read the label, or if after showing it to him thoroughly I covered it with my hand, from the moment the sight of the word escaped him he assumed an air of uneasiness and anxiety and seized at random the first object which chanced to his hand.

The result of this experiment was not very reassuring and would in fact have discouraged me completely if I had not noticed that after frequent repetitions the duration of the impression upon the brain of my pupil became by imperceptible degrees much longer. Soon he merely needed to glance quickly at the word I showed him, in order to go without haste or mistake to fetch the thing I asked for. After some time I was able to extend the experiment by sending him from my apartment into his own room to look in the same way for anything the name of which I showed him. At first the duration of the perception did not last nearly so long as that of the journey, but by an act of intelligence worthy of record, Victor sought and found in the agility of his legs a sure means of making the impressions persist longer than the time required for the journey. As soon as he had thoroughly read the word he set out like an arrow, coming back an instant later with the thing in his hand. More than once, nevertheless, the name escaped him on the way. Then I heard him stop in his tracks and come again towards my apartment, where he arrived with a timid and confused air. Sometimes it was enough for him to glance at the complete collection of names in order to recognize and retain the one which had escaped him. At other times the image of the word was so effaced from his memory that I was obliged to show it to him afresh. This necessity he indicated by taking my hand and making me pass my index finger over the whole series of names until I had shown him the forgotten one.

This exercise was followed by another which by offering his memory more work contributed more powerfully to develop it. Until then I had limited myself to asking for only one thing at a time. Then I asked for two, then three, and then four by showing a similar number of the labels to the pupil. He, feeling the difficulty of retaining them all, did not stop running over them with eager attention until I had entirely screened them from his eyes. Then there was no more delay or uncertainty. He set off hurriedly on the way to his room whence he brought the things requested. On his return his first care before giving them to me was to look hastily over the list, comparing it with the things of which he was the bearer. These he gave me only after he had reassured himself in this way that he had neither forgotten anything nor made a mistake. This last experiment gave at first very variable results but finally the difficulties which it offered were in their turn surmounted. The pupil, now sure of his memory, disdained the advantage which the agility of his legs gave him and applied himself quietly to this exercise. He often stopped in the corridor, put his face to the window which is at one end of it, greeted with sharp cries the sight of the country which unfolds magnificently in the distance, and then set off again for his room, got his little cargo, renewed his homage to the ever-regretted beauties of nature, and returned to me quite sure of the correctness of his errand.

In this way memory, reëstablished in all its functions, succeeded in retaining the symbols of thought while at the same time the intelligence fully grasped their importance. Such, at least, was the conclusion that I thought I could draw when I constantly saw Victor, wishing to ask for various things, either in our exercises or spontaneously, making use of the different words of which I had taught him the meaning by the device of showing or giving him the thing when we made him read the word, or by indicating the word when he was given the thing. Who could believe that this double proof was not more than sufficient to assure me that at last I had reached the point to gain which I had been obliged to retrace my steps and make so great a detour? But something happened at this juncture which made me believe for a moment that I was further from it than ever. (pp. 69-72)

Referring to the final paragraph in the preceding quote, it can be seen that reading the word was paired with receiving the objects symbolized by the word. The printed word thus became an S^D for *receiving* the object. When the object received was desired, the act of word presentation was reinforced and became a conditioned operant. Like a rat pushing a lever which leads to the presentation of a food pellet, for Victor, presenting the word cards led to the presentation of a reinforcing object. Therefore, Victor had learned to request things through reading. The visual cue of seeing the pitcher and cup, previously necessary to set the stage for laying out the letters for the word *Lait,* was no longer necessary. It thus became possible for Victor to respond solely in terms of his desire for an object.

As can be seen, Itard succeeded in teaching Victor to match the word to the object. In the course of doing this he encountered, but was not deterred by, the problem of limited memory. Itard was, as before, not content to accept Victor's performance at face value. He was to identify a serious limitation of generalization.

> One day when I had taken Victor with me and sent him as usual to fetch from his room several objects which I had indicated upon his list of words, it came into my head to double-lock the door and unseen by him to take out the key. That done I returned to my study, where he was, and, unrolling his list, I asked him for some of the things on it, taking care to indicate none which were not also to be found in my room. He set out immediately, but finding the door locked and having searched on all sides for the key, he came beside me, took my hand and led me to the outer door as if to make me see that it would not open. I feigned surprise and sought for the key everywhere and even pretended to open the door by force. At last, giving up the vain attempt, I took Victor back into my study and showing him the same words again, invited him by signs to look about and see if there were not similar objects to be found there. The words designated were stick, bellows, brush, glass, knife.[16] All these things were to be found scattered about my study in places where they could easily be seen. Victor looked at them but touched none of them. I had no better success in making him recognize them when they were brought together on a table and it was quite useless to ask for them one after the other by showing him successively their names. I tried another method. With scissors I cut out the names of the objects, thus converting them into single labels which were put into Victor's hands. By thus bringing him back to our original procedure, I hoped that he would put upon each thing the name which represented it. In vain. I had the inexpressible grief of seeing my pupil unable to recognize any of these objects or rather the connection which joined them to their signs. With a stupefied air which cannot be described he let his heedless glance wander over all these characters which had again become unintelligible. (pp. 72-73)

Itard's insight was penetrating, but I take exception to his statement that the words became "unintelligible." The word for book (see preceding note), for example, was no less intelligible than before. What was unintelligible was the second discriminative stimulus, that is, the specific book in Itard's room. Keller's description of chaining once again provides a convenient explanatory model. Thus, returning to Pliny — what if, for the marble, a hard rubber ball of identical weight had been substituted? It would have worked in the tube, but in terms of color, texture, and transparency, it would constitute a new set of stimuli in place of the well-established discriminative stimulus, the marble. As such, it may have been ineffective as the occasion for the response of lifting the ball and dropping it into the tube.

That the problem was not a function of irrelevant cues related to the setting of Victor's room is revealed by the following:

> I placed the same objects again under his eyes, and induced him to indicate them one after the other as soon as I successively showed him the names. I began by asking him for the book. He first looked at it for rather a long time, made a movement towards it with his hand while trying to detect in my eyes some signs of approval or disapproval which would settle his uncertainty. I held myself on guard and my expression was blank. Reduced then to his own judgment he concluded that it was not the thing asked for, and his eyes wandered, looking on all sides of the room, pausing, however, only at the books which were scattered upon the table and mantelpiece.
>
> This examination was like a flash of light to me. I immediately opened a cupboard which was full of books and took out a dozen among which I was careful to include one exactly like the one Victor had left in his room. To see it, quickly carry his hand to it and give it to me with a radiant air was for Victor only the affair of a moment. (pp. 74-75)

Itard, with another insight, eventually formulated the problem as follows:

> It was evident that my pupil, far from having conceived a wrong idea of the meaning of the symbols, had only made too rigorous an application of them. He had taken my lessons too literally and as I had limited myself to giving him the nomenclature of certain things in his room he was convinced that these were the only things to which it was applicable. Thus every book which was not the one he had in his room was not a book for Victor, and before he could decide to give it the same name it was necessary that an exact resemblance should establish a visible identity between the one and the other. This is a very different procedure in nomenclature from that of children, who, when beginning to speak, give to particular terms the value of general ones but keep the restricted meaning of the particular term. (p. 75)

For Victor, discriminating the word and fetching the specific book may be likened to Pliny's seeing the string and subsequently pulling it. Picking up the book and carrying it to Itard can be compared with picking up the marble and inserting it in the tube. For Pliny, the reward at the end of the chain was food; for Victor, social approval. Changing the marble to a rubber ball would be, for Victor, the counterpart of switching books. We thus see that Victor's problem was not in the mechanics of reading. It resided in the lack of generalization in the second discriminative stimulus to the chain.

Itard traced the failure of generalization to the training program.

> What could account for this strange difference? If I am not mistaken it grew out of an unusual acuteness of visual observation which was the inevitable result of the special education given to his sense of sight. By the method of analytical comparison I had trained this sense organ so thoroughly in the recognition of the visible qualities of objects and the differences of dimension, color and conformation, that he could always detect between two identical things such points of dissimilarity as would make him believe there was an essential difference between them. (pp. 75-76)

Itard said, almost precisely as would Kephart, that an overemphasis on differentiating small differences (details) impeded the development of concepts. In effect, he suggested that lack of generalization was a function of Victor's earlier course of perceptual training! So here we can see a significant sequence: (a) a seemingly successful course of perceptual training as a basis for reading readiness, (b) a seemingly successful attainment of rudimentary reading skills, (c) a failure to attain adequate conceptualization presumably based on (a).

The above training problem can be related to a modern discrimination learning framework (Zeaman & House, 1963). Thus, it appears that Victor was responding to the correct dimensions and the correct cues in those dimensions, for example, rectangularity in the shape dimension. But there was inadequate generalization among these cues: slight variations in shape, color, and the like, resulted in a breakdown in the concept of *book*.

Incorrectly assuming that the problem lay exclusively in the realm of visual discrimination training, Itard sought to remedy the problem by shifting his emphasis to generalization.[17]

> With the source of the error thus located, the remedy became easy. It was to establish the identity of the objects by demonstrating to the pupil the identity of their uses or their properties. It was to make

him see common qualities which earned the same name for things apparently different. In a word, it was a question of teaching him to consider things no longer with reference to their differences but according to their similarities.

This new study was a kind of introduction to the act of comparison. At first the pupil gave himself up to it so completely that he was inclined to go astray again by attaching the same idea and giving the same name to things which had no other connection than the conformity of their shapes or uses. Thus under the name of book he indicated indiscriminately a handful of paper, a note book, a newspaper, a register, a pamphlet. All straight and long pieces of wood were called sticks. At one time he gave the name of brush to the broom, and at another that of broom to the brush, and soon, if I had not repressed this abuse of comparison, I should have seen Victor restricted to the use of a small number of signs which he would have applied indiscriminately to a large number of entirely different things which had only certain general qualities or properties in common. (p. 76)

Training generalization on the level of visual discrimination apparently eventuated in the very opposite of his previous problem; that is, from excessive discrimination Victor had passed to overgeneralization.

In the next clinical episode, Itard effected a major departure in his procedure of teaching generalization: he suddenly switched to providing Victor the experience of *practical manipulation* of the objects to be discriminated (see page 128). For this writer, it represents the critical turning point in the entire teaching program.

In the midst of these mistakes, or rather fluctuations, of an intelligence tending ceaselessly to inaction but continually provoked by artificial means, there apparently developed one of those characteristic faculties of man, and especially thinking man, the faculty of invention. When considering things from the point of view of their similarity or of their common qualities, Victor concluded that since there was a resemblance of shape between certain objects, there ought in certain circumstances to be an identity of uses and functions. Without doubt this conclusion was somewhat risky. But it gave rise to judgments which, even though obviously found to be defective, became so many new means to instruction. I remember that one day when I asked him in writing for a knife, he looked for one for some time and contented himself with offering me a razor, which he fetched from a neighboring room. I pretended it would do and when his lesson was finished gave him something to eat as usual. I wanted him to cut his bread instead of dividing it with his fingers as was his custom. And to this end I held out to him the razor which he had given me under the name of knife. His behavior was consistent, he tried to use it as such, but the lack of stability of the blade prevented this. I did not consider the lesson complete. I took the razor and, in the actual presence of Victor, made it serve its proper use. From then on the instrument was no longer and could not be any longer in his eyes a knife. I longed to make certain. I again took his book and showed him the word *couteau* (knife) and the pupil immediately showed me the object he held in his hand and which I had given him a moment ago when he could not use the razor.[18] To make the result convincing it was necessary to reverse the test. If the book were put in Victor's hands while I touched the razor, it was necessary that he should fail to pick out any word, as he did not yet know the name of this instrument. He passed this test also. (pp. 76-77)

The above passage records what, to this writer, was the first indication of Victor's forming a high-level *concept* in the context of reading instruction. It is extremely significant that Victor equated a resemblance of shape with an identity of functions. Itard provided him with precisely what was needed, a practical experience, a purposive manipulation of the object in a meaningful context. Here we have what Kephart would describe as a *veridical experience;* that is, the experience of things as they work in the real world.

Itard revealed the fact that the real road to conceptual differentiation is through functional manipulation. Practical manipulation of the object yields S^Ds that are simply not available through a purely visual presentation. In Victor's case, visual similarities led to an overgeneralization. Practical manipulation and the discovery of veridical (Kephart, 1968) differences (i.e., you can't readily cut bread with a razor but you can with a knife), yielded new S^Ds. These new and relevant S^Ds were inherent in the *behavior* of the implement in a *practical, purposeful* action-context. This is the basic assumption underlying all of Kephart's writing from *The Slow Learner in the Classroom* (1960) to the present time. It is the foundation of his entire sensory-motor training program. A major difference between Kephart and Itard is in timing: Kephart would emphasize such training *before* the advent of reading instruction. He would underscore the dangers of developing a reading proficiency based upon a faulty, or even distorted, experimental background. Itard had to learn this important lesson after the fact.

In the next anecdote we see Victor take a highly significant step in problem solving.

But very often his expedients were happier, more successful and better deserving the name of invention. Quite worthy of such a name was the way by which he provided himself one day with a pencil case. Only once in my study had I made him use one to hold a small piece of chalk too short to take up with the end of his fingers. A few days afterwards the same difficulty occurred again but Victor was in his room and had no pencil-holder at hand to hold his chalk. I put it to the most industrious or the most inventive man to say, or rather do, what he did in order to procure one. He took an implement used in roasting, found in well-equipped kitchens but quite superfluous in one belonging to a poor creature such as he was, and which for that reason had remained forgotten and corroded with rust at the bottom of a little cupboard — namely a skewer. Such was the instrument which he took to replace the one he lacked and which by a further inspiration of really creative imagination he was clever enough to convert into a real pencil-holder by replacing the slide with a few turns of thread. . . . What also added to the importance of this result when considered as a proof of actual progress and as a guarantee of future improvement is that, instead of occurring as an isolated incident which might have made it appear accidental, it was one among many incidents, doubtless less striking, but which, coming at the same period and evidently emanating from the same source, appeared in the eyes of an attentive observer to be diverse results of a general impulse. It is, indeed, worthy of notice that from this moment many routine habits which the pupil had contracted when applying himself to the little occupations prescribed for him, spontaneously disappeared. While rigidly refraining from making forced comparisons or drawing remote conclusions, one may, I think, at least suspect that this new way of looking at familiar things which gave birth to the idea of making new applications of them, might be expected to have precisely the result of forcing the pupil out of the unvarying round of, so to speak, automatic habits.[19] (pp. 78-79)

In Kephart's (1968) terms, Itard had, at this point, significantly overcome Victor's rigidity (the above-mentioned "routine habits") in his effort to teach generalization.

Itard encountered new difficulties when faced with the problem of teaching part-whole relationships. Once again, he proved himself more than equal to the task. He first dealt with the problem of part-whole relationships in a concrete action-context. Once established, he reduced this idea to a subtle gestural indication.

Thoroughly convinced at last that I had completely established in Victor's mind the connection of the objects with their signs, it only remained for me to increase the number gradually. If the procedure by which I established the meaning of the first signs has been thoroughly grasped it will be seen that it could be applied only to a limited number of objects and to things small in size, and that a bed, a room, a tree, or a person, as well as the constituent and inseparable parts of a whole, could not be labeled in the same way. I did not find any difficulty in making the sense of these new words understood, although I could not, as in the preceding experiments bind them visibly to the things they represented. In order to be understood it was sufficient for me to point to the new word with a finger and with the other hand to show the object to which the word belonged. I had little more trouble in making him understand the names of the parts which enter into the composition of the whole object. Thus for a long time the words fingers, hands, forearms could not offer any distinct meaning to the pupil. This confusion in attaching the signs was evidently due to the fact that he had not yet understood that the parts of a body considered separately formed in their turn distinct objects which had their particular names. In order to give him the idea I took a bound book, tore off its covers, and detached several of its leaves. As I gave Victor each of these separate parts I wrote its name upon the blackboard. Then taking from his hands the various pieces, I made him in turn indicate their names to me. When they were thoroughly engraved on his memory, I replaced the separated parts and when I again asked their names he indicated them as before; then showing him the whole book without indicating any part in particular, I asked him the name. He pointed to the word book.

This is all that was necessary to render him familiar with the names of the various parts of compound bodies; and to avoid confusion between the names of the separate parts of the general name of the object, I was careful in my demonstrations to touch each part directly and, when applying the general name, to content myself with indicating the thing vaguely without touching it. (pp. 79-80)

What follows is the crowning achievement of Itard's efforts — positive evidence of the attainment of genuine abstraction in the reading context. Note how Itard continued to emphasize the practical manipulation of objects. His experiment to test for generalization of the concepts of *big* and *little* is as simple and direct as it is ingenious.

From this lesson I passed on to the qualities of the bodies. Here I entered into the field of abstractions and I entered it with the fear of not being able to penetrate or finding myself soon halted by insurmountable difficulties. None showed themselves, and my first lesson was grasped instantly although it bore upon one of the most abstract qualities, that of extension. I took two books of similar bindings but of different sizes, the one an octodecimo, the other an octavo. I touched the first. Victor opened his book and pointed to the word *book*. I touched the second. The pupil indicated the same word. I began several times and always with the same result. Next I took the little book, and giving it to Victor, made him put his hand flat upon the cover which it hid almost entirely. I then made him do the same thing with the octavo volume; his hand covered scarcely half of it. So that he could not mistake my intention I showed him the part which remained uncovered, and induced him to stretch out his fingers towards this part which he could not do without uncovering a part equal to that which he covered. After this experiment which demonstrated in such a tangible manner to my pupil the difference in size of these two objects, I again asked him the name. Victor hesitated. He felt that the same name could no longer be applied indiscriminately to two things which he had just found so unequal. This was what I was waiting for. I wrote the word *book* upon two cards and placed one upon each book. I next wrote upon a third the word *big,* and the word *little* upon a fourth. I placed them beside the others, the one on the octavo and the other upon the small volume. Having made Victor notice this arrangement I took the labels again, mixed them several times, and then gave them to him to be replaced. This was done correctly.

Had I been understood? Had the respective sense of the words *big* and *little* been grasped? In order to be certain and to have complete proof, this is what I did. I got two nails of unequal length. I compared them in almost the same way as I have done with the books. Then having written upon two cards the word *nail* I gave them to him without adding the two adjectives big and little, hoping that if my preceding lesson had been thoroughly grasped he would apply to the nails the same signs of relative size as he had served to mark the difference of dimension of the two books. He did this with a promptness that rendered the proof still more conclusive. Such was the procedure by which I gave him the idea of size. I used it with the same success to render intelligible the signs which represent the other sensible qualities of bodies such as color, weight, resistance, etc. (pp. 80-81)

Itard's test of the adjectives *big* and *little* demonstrated Victor's ability to apply these terms correctly to new objects in the absence of additional specific training. But generalization may occur at still higher levels.[20]

Higher-level generalization is revealed in the following anecdote pertaining to training of verb forms in reading. As on previous occasions, Victor's conceptual grasp was made manifest in a situation involving an incongruity.[21]

After the explanation of the adjective, came the verb. To make this understood by the pupil I had only to submit to several kinds of action an object of which he knew the name. These actions I designated as soon as executed, by the infinitive of the verb in question. For example I took a key and wrote its name upon the blackboard. Then *touching* it, *throwing* it, *picking* it up, *kissing* it, *putting* it back in its place, and so on, I simultaneously wrote in a column at the side of the word *key*, the verbs *to touch, to throw, to pick up, to kiss, to replace,* etc. For the word *key* I then substituted the name of another object which I submitted to the same functions, pointing at the same time to the verbs already written. It often happened that in thus replacing at random one object by another in order to have it governed by the same verbs, there was such an inconsistency between them and the nature of the object that the action asked for became odd or impossible. The embarrassment in which the pupil found himself generally turned out to his advantage as much as to my own satisfaction; for it gave him the chance to exercise his discernment and me the opportunity of gathering proofs of his intelligence. For example, when I found myself one day, after successive changes of the objects of the verbs, with such strange association of words as *to tear stone, to cut cup, to eat broom,* he evaded the difficulty very well by changing the two actions indicated by the first two verbs into others less incompatible with the nature of their objects. Thus he took a hammer to break the stone and dropped the cup to break it. Coming to the third verb (eat) and not being able to find any word to replace it, he looked for something else to serve as the object of the verb. He took a piece of bread and ate it. (p. 82)

Itard indicated that, given the appropriate object (for example, a key), Victor would execute the appropriate action (touch it, throw it, etc.). It was only when the verb and object combination dictated an unfeasible course of action, such as eating the broom, that he substituted a more appropriate object. Victor thus adapted the action and evolved a novel solution to maximally approximate the action required by the verb. What seems implied is that Victor related both *tear* and *cut* to the more general concept of *subdivide.* Victor's flexibility and resourcefulness in this context reflected the same qualities revealed in the solution to the previously discussed pencil-holder problem.

To the writer, these demanding tests provided a high-level challenge to Victor's intellectual resources. Itard provided evidence of a considerable conceptual attainment in the language sphere, an attainment that, historically, seems scarcely appreciated. This lack of appreciation may be largely the result of Itard's somewhat derogatory appraisal of his own work. Instead of emphasizing the failure to achieve speech (see Itard, p. 86), he should have stressed Victor's impressive language attainments as manifested through reading.

NOTES

[1] This and all subsequent references to and quotations from Itard's work are taken from the following single source: J.M.G. Itard, *The Wild Boy of Aveyron,* trans. G. & M. Humphrey (New York: Appleton-Century-Crofts, 1932,

1962). All quotations from this book are used by the permission of the publisher. Authorship of other extracts throughout is indicated in the text.

[2] In their first volume, Bijou & Baer opened the door for the incorporation of a psycho-physiological approach into the operant framework:

> Note that an internal response is not necessarily an unobservable response. As research in the area of physiological psychology proceeds, it is to be expected that present techniques for observing internal behavior and stimulation will be greatly improved, and new techniques developed. Hence, present limitations to a study of internal "mediating" events may be temporary. In general, a natural science approach to psychological development is not restricted to stimulus and response events *outside* the organism; it is restricted to *observable* stimulus and response events in any locale (1961, pp. 80-81).

[3] The project eventually developed into a dissertation (Porter, 1968).

[4] In the initial study, two subjects learned, by successive approximations, to walk across the room and to pull the handle when called by name.

[5] For a closely related example from the field of classical conditioning, see K.N. Irzhanskaia & R.A. Felberbaum, Effects of stimulus sensitization on ease of conditioning, in Yvonne Brackbill & George G. Thompson (eds.), *Behavior in Infancy and Early Childhood: A Book of Readings* (New York: The Free Press, 1967), pp. 246-49.

[6] Note that the touch is *not* used as a reinforcer for the operant, since it occurs before the operant appears. It makes the S^D *available* to the subject. The circumstances may be compared with what happens when a driver, preoccupied with other matters, runs a stoplight. Though the light falls on his retina, it fails to register in his conscious awareness. The same light would function as intended on other occasions. But, from a practical standpoint, it is no more available to him as an S^D on this occasion than if the signal light had been replaced by an infra-red bulb. He failed to stop, not because he lacked appropriate training, but because he lacked the necessary OR.

[7] Melzack & Scott's sensorially deprived dogs also showed an unusual deficiency of response to intense heat (1957).

[8] I have belatedly discovered that the work of Ayres (1964) has inspired two studies which more closely approximate Itard's program of primitive sensory stimulation than anything I have encountered in the literature. They are studies by Julia Van Deusen Fox: Cutaneous Stimulation: Effects on Selected Tests of Perception. *The American Journal of Occupational Therapy*, 1964, **18**, 53-55, and Improving Tactile Discrimination of the Blind: A Neurophysiological Approach, *The American Journal of Occupational Therapy*, 1965, **19**, 5-7.

[9] It is difficult to see why the gunshot did not produce a startle pattern, which occurs reflexively under such circumstances.

[10] What if the subject of a learning set procedure fails to give up the place cue? Several years ago, this author encountered just such a problem during the course of an informal learning set experiment with a severely retarded child. The equipment consisted of a cardboard screen, two sets of styrofoam cups

(black and white; orange and green), and candy rewards. The procedure followed Harlow's except that, instead of sliding a tray back and forth, the experimenter held a finger on each of the cups and released the one the subject grasped. If no food was found under the one selected, the screen was immediately replaced and the subject was not allowed to pick up the remaining cup.

The subject perseverated with the place cue; he always picked up the cup in the position in which he last received a reward, ignoring the correct color cue. The writer then stumbled on the idea of trying out what he later identified as simply a variation of Itard's "shell game." Setting aside the screen, and in full view of the subject, he slipped the candy under the black cup. Then, while the subject watched, he displaced the cup slightly and permitted him to retrieve the candy. On subsequent trials the displacements were gradually increased until the relative (left v. right) positions of the two cups were varied. All the while the subject fixed his attention on the cup under which the candy had been placed. When the writer then returned to the standard procedure, the subject quickly learned the black-white discrimination and then, within a relatively short time, learned the new orange-green discrimination. In effect, he had to learn to attend appropriately and become oriented to the procedure as a prerequisite for learning the color discrimination problem.

The need for a pre-training procedure for the development of a prerequisite attention was clearly brought out in a recent study of five-choice spatial delayed response performance (Davenport & Rogers, 1968). The subjects were adolescent chimpanzees reared for their first two years of life in impoverished and enriched environments. The pre-training procedures were designed to overcome the distractability and great difficulty in bringing to bear task-oriented behaviors on the learning and performance of the environmentally deprived animals. Although their pre-training procedures were to a large extent successful, it is suggested that Itard's procedure also might profitably have been tried out in this context.

[11]That the philosopher Condillac may have had a positive influence on the development of Itard's clinical acumen is suggested by the following passage:

> The appreciation of the mental state of our savage is more difficult than one would expect. Daily experience and acquired ideas tend to lead the judgment astray. Says Condillac in a very similar case, "If the habit we have formed of assisting ourselves by signs did not prevent us from noticing all we owe to them, *we should only have to put ourselves in the place of this young man in order to understand how little knowledge he could acquire;* but we always judge according to our own situation" (Itard, p. 49).

We find a related message in Bijou & Baer's warning against the pitfalls of phenomenology (1965, pp. 149-50).

[12]Kephart noted the following:

> Where variation is implied in the classroom activity, he will take the variation out and reduce the lesson to a rote memory drill. A constant task of the teacher of such children is that of insuring that the child does vary the task and of preventing him from developing solutions to problems based on high degrees of skill in rote memory activities. There is constant battle to avoid skilled response in the interest of generalized solutions to problems. If this battle is not won, the child may learn that

$2 + 2 = 4$ with great precision and be able to respond with great speed
but not know that 2 (1968, p. 55).

$$\frac{+2}{4}$$

[13]The interruption occurred because, in response to the increasingly demanding discrimination training program, Victor lapsed into episodes of
violent behavior.

> On such occasions he ran away and in a destructive mood bit the sheets,
> the blankets, and the mantelpiece, scattered the andirons, ashes and
> blazing embers, and ended by falling into convulsions which, like those
> of epilepsy, involved a complete suspension of the sensorial functions. I
> was obliged to give up when things reached this frightful pitch; but my
> acquiescence only increased the evil. The paroxysms became more fre-
> quent, and apt to be renewed at the slightest opposition, often, even
> without any determining cause (p. 43).

In the fashion of a twentieth-century behavior therapist, Itard pointed out the
dangers of reinforcing such behavior.

> I foresaw the time when all my care would result only in making an
> unhappy epileptic of this poor child. A few more fits and force of habit
> would fasten upon him one of the most terrible and least curable of dis-
> eases. It was necessary then to find a remedy immediately, not in med-
> icines which are so often fruitless, nor in gentleness from which there
> was nothing more to hope, but in a method of shock. . . (p. 43).

This "method of shock" was applied as follows:

> The occasion soon offered itself in the instance of a most violent fit, which
> was, I believe, caused by our resuming the exercises. Seizing the moment
> when the functions of the senses were not yet suspended, I violently threw
> back the window of his room which was situated on the fourth story and
> which opened perpendicularly on to a big stone court. I drew near him
> with every appearance of anger and seizing him forcibly by the haunches
> held him out of the window, his head directly turned towards the bottom
> of the chasm. After some seconds I drew him in again. He was pale,
> covered with a cold sweat, his eyes were rather tearful, and he still
> trembled a little, which I believed to be the effect of fear. I led him to
> his cards. I made him gather them up and replace them all. This was
> done, very slowly to be sure, and badly rather than well, but at least
> without impatience. Afterwards he went and threw himself on his bed
> and wept copiously. This was the first time, at least to my knowledge,
> that he shed tears. It preceded the occasions of which I have already given
> an account, when the grief at leaving his nurse or the pleasure of finding
> her again made him weep (p. 44).

Severe tantrums are common among autistic children (Lovaas, Schaeffer &
Simmons, 1965b). Itard, like Lovaas, eliminated the tantrums by means of
punishment. Yet Itard's technique was more complex in that he not only thrust
Victor out of the window, he also pulled him back to safety, thereby "rescuing"
him. Perhaps the rescue aspect, which is more in line with escape-avoidance
than with simple punishment, contributed to the unexpected appearance
of crying.

[14]Later, Itard proceeded from matching letters to matching words. He
pointed to a word written on one blackboard and required Victor to find its

counterpart, located in a reordered list on a second blackboard. When Victor mismatched words due to a superficial similarity of appearance, Itard, using a pointer, forced him to compare them on a letter-to-letter basis. Eventually, Victor could identify an error at a single glance whereupon he would immediately correct it.

[15]Substitute "redundant cues" for "accessories" and then reread Trabasso (see page 29).

[16]As revealed in the next quote, the list also included "book," the word-object combination on which Itard based his subsequent discussion of generalization.

[17]In terms of Kephart's approach, this would be dealing with the problem at too high a level. During the 1950s Kephart came to recognize a similar overemphasis on the visual perceptual level in Strauss' training program. *The Slow Learner in the Classroom* (1960) was Kephart's initial statement regarding the necessity of attaining a prior foundation on the motor level.

[18]Victor's developing the notion of an identity of uses and functions could have stemmed from the earlier matching exercises. In matching a key to its outline, could an implicit equation have developed? That is, by relating two similar, but not identical, shapes as equal, Victor was rewarded. When he equated knife and razor, he may have been following the same procedure. This was the only process Victor had on which to fall back. Actually, at this point Victor was ignorant of "uses." The visual S^Ds relating knife and razor were the only ones with which he was familiar. He was able to differentiate the two objects for the first time when he subsequently was exposed to a whole new set of S^Ds through practical manipulation of the objects.

[19]It is interesting to relate this anecdote to a problem-solving experiment by Sanstad and Raaheim (Krech & Crutchfield, 1958, p. 389), in which the solution depended upon using familiar items in unfamiliar ways — using a nail as a "hook" or newspapers as a "tube." As with Victor, the subject, unencumbered by the conventional meaning of those objects, might be better able to solve the problem.

[20]In their discussion of the results of speech training through *programmed conditioning,* Gray & Fygetakis (1968) distinguished two levels of response generalization. At the first level, the language deviant child exhibits a carry-over of learning to different but appropriate language situations. For example, some children who originally spoke only in fractional sentences ("mommy home") learned the appropriate use of the missing "is" and eventually used it correctly in spontaneous speech involving new sentences. At the second level of generalization, the child, in the absence of specific conditioning, spontaneously generated new language constructions. For instance, following specific training on the "is" construction, some children began spontaneously, and for the first time, to combine "is" with the word "what" to ask questions (*"What is that?"*). The demonstration of such learning effectively refutes the position taken by some cognitive theorists that the operant conditioning approach to language training yields only an automatic, parrot-like speech.

[21]For a similar approach to testing generalization, but in the context of imitation training rather than that of reading, see page 100.

chapter 2

Edward Seguin And The Physiological Method

Despite the belief, shared by Itard and Esquirol, that idiocy was not subject to treatment, by the 1840s Seguin had demonstrated the efficacy of his methods. A physician and a student of Itard, he incorporated Itard's techniques into his own system and then fitted them into a broader context.[1] As Talbot (1964) points out, many of the profoundly retarded present behavioral deficiencies with which Itard did not have to deal in his work with Victor. For example, having previously adapted to a feral life, Victor did not exhibit a total lack of purposive movements. The existence of such critical differences in initial adaptive levels contributed importantly to the evolution of Seguin's system and the extensions beyond Itard's original work.

Seguin translated his educational philosophy into an explicit developmental program beginning at the most profound level of impairment and extending through the level of responsible functioning in society. In terms of breadth and continuity, his system remains a rare achievement. His program dealt with issues that have aroused much controversy on the present scene. For example, an understanding of his approach to dealing with problems of behavioral control should help clarify the ethical issues involved in this much-debated topic. His specific techniques are not only ingenious but, in many instances, are directly applicable to today's training problems. Seguin was provocative and innovative; a dedicated and effective clinician who courageously faced the task of training even the most profoundly retarded. He worked with flexibility and ingenuity. He was fully immersed in the data of experience, yet intimately acquainted with the practical problems of instituting and sustaining long-term training of the retarded. To a much greater extent than most contemporary therapists, he used the natural consequences of actions to teach appropriate behavior. A unique feature, conspicuously absent from much of the contemporary writing on sensory education, is his discussion of the planned, purposive use of the teacher's interpersonal influence on the child. This is a much ignored critical variable that calls for urgent study. Let us now consider Seguin's attitude toward the phenomenon of curiosity.

> One of the earliest and most fatal antagonisms taught to a child is the forbidding of using his hands to ascertain the qualities of surrounding objects of which his sight gives him but an imperfect notion, if it be not aided by the touch; and of breaking many things as well, to acquire the proper idea of solidity. The imbecility of parents in these matters has too often favored the growth of the evil spirit. The youngest child, when he begins to totter on his arched legs, goes about touching, handling, breaking everything. It is our duty to foster and direct that beautiful curiosity, to make it the regular channel for the acquisition of correct perceptions and tactile accuracy; as for breaking, it must be turned into the desire of preservation and the power of holding with the will; nothing is so simple. . . . (Seguin, 1907, p. 143) [2]

The above passage, echoed almost 100 years later by Kephart (1960), reveals the essence of Seguin's educational philosophy: *"beautiful curiosity" is the motive and the vehicle for knowledge.* It is to be carefully nurtured and directed in the sense of being channeled, not forced into a rigid mold. Punishment of the child for breaking objects may generalize to all aspects of tactile exploration. Without thwarting spontaneity and curiosity and restricting learning, the child must be taught to preserve objects. Translating these goals into concrete action may not be as simple as Seguin suggests, but it can be done, as the following anecdote demonstrates.

> Once a very excitable child, eighteen months old, touching, breaking, throwing everything he could, seemed really ready, if he had been once punished for it, to become possessed by the old intruder; but it was not our plan. We bought unmatched *Sevres* cups and Bohemia glasses, really splendid to look at, and served the child in one of them, after showing him the elegance of the pattern, the richness of the colors, everything which could please and attach him to the object. But he had no sooner drunk then he threw the glass away. Not a word was said, not a piece removed from where it fell; but the next time he was thirsty, we brought him where the frag-

ments lay, and let him feel more thirst before we could find another glass equally beautiful. Some more were broken in the same petulant spirit; but later, he slowly dropped one, when at the same time, he looked into our eyes to catch signs of anger. But there was none there, nor in the voice; only the composure and accent of pity for the child who would willingly incur such a loss. Since then, baby took good care of his cups and glasses, finer than ours; he taught his little fingers how to embrace with security the thin neck of one, the large body, or the diminutive handle of others. In practising these so varied handlings, his mind became saving and his hands a model of accuracy. (pp. 143-44)

In the above situation, instead of branding the throwing and breaking as destructive behavior to be punished, Seguin interpreted them as means of exploring the nature of objects. But the child was at a point where he had to adapt to the use of glasses in the home. Seguin demonstrated a flexibly evolved, multifaceted strategy which serves as an excellent example of his teaching style. It also provides another demonstration of the analytic value of operant conditioning concepts. [3]

Seguin's philosophy of development emphasized spontaneity and curiosity as the touchstones of optimal growth. It is relatively easy to accept such an orientation in a world of normal children. But what of the world of the profoundly retarded — the idiot?[4]

A walk through one of the wards devoted to the profoundly retarded in a typical state hospital might readily convince one that he is viewing subhuman organisms. Some find it difficult to conceive of these individuals as human, much less the possessors of a latent capacity for spontaneity and will and the potential for learning. Yet Seguin conceived of such latent qualities. More importantly, he turned them into reality.

TRAINING WILLED ACTIVITY

To appreciate the magnitude of Seguin's accomplishment it is necessary first to visualize the behavior of the profoundly retarded. For example, instead of facing the problem of appropriately channeling the spontaneous action of the normal child, the teacher of mentally retarded or psychotic children is often faced with pervasive inaction. To account for this inaction, Lovaas[5] pointed out that, by doing nothing while seeming incapable of action, one may, in fact, *actively* control the behavior of others. Inaction may reflect a refusal to respond rather than an inability to do so. The only question is whether the teacher-therapist can meet the challenge of moving the child to purposive action. Seguin, even before the middle of the nineteenth century, understood the psychological basis of this behavioral deficit. He referred to this phenomenon as *negative will*. Although Skinnerians eschew the concept of "will" (Reynolds, 1968), the behavioral importance of this phenomenon as an obstacle to training is not to be doubted. Seguin described negative will as follows:

> . . . in negative immovability resides the power to nearly neutralize any external inducement or any internal motive to action. This immovability is therefore the first expression we meet with of the radical elements of idiocy, the negative will. Henceforth we shall find many and the most varied incapacities, all doubled, made nearly indomitable by the silent protean "I will not" of the negative will. (p. 71)

An enlightening example of negative will was observed by this writer in the course of a training session with a profoundly retarded child (IQ 19). This boy had failed to learn one of the first "lessons" in a self-help skill program (Bensberg, 1965): response to the command, "Come to me." The attendant-teacher stood facing him with a spoonful of his meal held about an inch from his mouth. He did not respond to the command. But, more significantly, he gradually began to lean backwards, whereupon the attendant followed him with the spoon. The child, while standing in place and seeming to do nothing, was actively controlling the teacher. The writer subsequently instructed the attendant to "freeze" in place so that the child would have to make the necessary movement. Before he moved in response to the command, the child missed a couple of meals. But once he moved that one inch under the control of the attendant he made rapid progress through subsequent and increasingly complicated training steps.

Sometimes, when the teacher forces the issue of control, the idiot manifests a complicated behavior repertoire, the very existence of which may be totally unsuspected. Such a development will be revealed in the anecdote regarding the training of a boy with an IQ of 12 (see page 89).

Because he frequently dealt with children who either refused to move or were incessantly in motion, Seguin thought it necessary to teach regular and effective movements that were under the pupil's conscious control. Among behaviors needing correction, he described various forms of repetitive, self-stimulating activities familiar to anyone who has worked with severely retarded or autistic children. He recognized that such self-stimulation provided a great deal of reinforcement. For example, describing "automatic movements" he observed:

> In automatic movements, the child uses one part of himself, one finger or one eye, as if it were an automaton whose recurrent movements produced his beatitude. (pp. 71-72)

Although he devised specific remedies for each kind of *disordered motion,* he sought first to eliminate them incidental to the training of orderly movements.

Especially among those children with disordered movement it was essential first to establish *positive immobility.* Seguin sought to bring the unwanted action under control and to develop in the child a readiness to respond in a purposeful manner. In the following passage we see how he achieved control over a disordered motion. The technique is an application of escape-avoidance conditioning that is the obverse of the "frightened grasp" in which the child spontaneously grasped the ladder to avoid falling (see page 90).

> If the immobility of the whole child cannot be enforced at once, we may seat him before us, half mastering his legs between our knees, concentrate all our attention upon the hands, and eventually upon the one most affected. To accomplish our object we put the quietest hand on the corresponding knee, whilst we load the delinquent hand with a heavy dumb-bell. Useless to say that he does not take hold of it and tries to disengage his hand; but our fingers keep his so bound around the neck of the dumb-bell that he does not succeed. On the contrary, we take care to let the weight fall more on his hand than on ours; if he does not carry it, he supports it at least. Supporting the burden, the more he moves to remove it the more he feels it; and partly to escape the increase of the burden, partly by fatigue, his loaded hand becomes still; that stillness was precisely our object. (p. 73)

Here, under the condition of an enforced grasp, spontaneous movement resulted in an unwanted muscular effort which was removed by a voluntary inhibition of movement. It is interesting to note that, in the latter instance, escape-avoidance conditioning does involve making a *choice*: one can elect to continue moving the hand if one is willing to pay the price of the burden. Once the child's hand was motionless, Seguin set it free opposite the other hand and sought to suppress further unwanted movements through his own vocal, facial and gestural cues. Once established, willed immobility was invoked prior to and at the close of every movement exercise. Also, it served as "transition and as repose between the various modes of active training" (p. 74).

Negative will was manifested in various ways. With "inert," immobile children Seguin began with various forms of passive exercise. But if this approach failed, he utilized another escape-avoidance strategy.

> [If], after all our passive exercises, he cannot yet stand erect and ready for a walk on a level floor . . . [then] we raise him on two blocks

or steps as narrow as his feet, and even we let him fall, being at hand
to prevent an injury, but not to blunt the emotion, and to restore him,
if needed to his up-isolation. There he must stand and stand firmly
too, having to react with an energy unknown to himself against the
vacuum around, which invites him to a fall. To resist the attraction
of the void, he must strain his muscles in readiness for any emer-
gency; he is anxious, he does not know exactly why, nor what to do,
nor what not to do; but his strength is gathered, and if we have in
front of him some other steps, and if we help him a little with our
hand or finger at first, he will try, in the prospect of escaping the isolation, to pass one foot on the next step, on another, and on another,
anxious, crying, but walking in fact for the first time. Left on a floor,
he would have slid his feet very likely, but not walked all his life.
(pp. 74-75)

Once walking and balance were acquired, Seguin concentrated on correcting those peculiarities of gait that "bespeak idiocy." In correcting this
problem, his use of footprint forms foreshadowed Kephart's later development of the "stepping stones" technique (Kephart, 1960). It is characteristic of Seguin that he could identify an intellectual component of this task.
Training was, simultaneously, motor and intellectual.

The act of directing each foot on each form is one of the best exercises for limbs which have previously escaped all control; but what
a superior exercise it is for the head above, which has never suspected
its regulating power: to walk among so many difficulties is to
think. (p. 76)

When Seguin had developed "steadiness of the foot" and of the body he
turned to training "accuracy of the hand." Seguin described the hand as
"the best servant of man; the best instrument of work; the best translator
of thoughts" (p. 82). The full scope of Seguin's concept of training is
nowhere better seen than in the education of the hand — the development
of *prehension*.

When we say prehension, we mean the complex action of taking,
keeping, losing hold; otherwise, to seize, hold and to let go: those
three terms are the beginning, the object, and the end of the act of
prehension. This act, so simple for us in its trilogy, is either impossible to or incidentally performed by the idiot. It requires for its mere
material accomplishment the concourse of contractile nervous and
willed functions. This concourse, far above the understanding of
many men, is certainly above the average ability of our pupils, who,
far from entering willingly, as the occasion offers, into new contacts, find in themselves more energy to avoid than would be neces-

sary to meet them. Considering the gravity of this infirmity, as shutting the being out from any intercourse and creating the most positive isolation, the task of teaching prehension can never be commenced too soon. Even the impossibility of standing on the feet must not be a cause to delay the improvement of the hands, since we see babies seize with their contracted fingers before they can use their feet to stand. (pp. 77-78)

Seguin's first task was to evoke active grasping. This he did through the ladder technique in which the child actively grasped the rounds to avoid falling (see page 90). By sensitive and judicious use of positive reinforcement, Seguin converted the "frightened grasp" to a voluntary one; for instance, by placing cool apples in the child's hands. Effecting the transition to voluntary grasping was of primary importance. Thus,

> . . . as soon as a function begins to be accomplished mechanically, we set it in action for purposes and objects more and more intellectual, trying to leave no gap in the series of progress till the *function* is thoroughly elevated to the rank of a *capacity*.* [6] (p. 79)

The relationship between function and capacity in Seguin's system closely parallels Kephart's distinction between motor skill and motor generalization (see page 121).

Seguin warned against an excessively or overly prolonged use of the ladder technique.

> From a heavy prehension, the child must pass to a light one; from a long one to a short one; and we must remember and apply the principle, to teach the prehension of bodies of every form and weight in its three modes — seizing, keeping hold of, and letting go. (p. 81)

Seguin's three modes of prehension are later echoed in Kephart's discussion of the development of "reaching, grasping, and releasing" (Ebersole, Kephart, & Ebersole, 1968, p. 68). In the following quote Seguin described the emergence of *handling* from *prehension*. [7]

> We prehend everything about in the same manner, but we certainly handle everything in a special manner, a glass, an axe, a pen, a spade, etc.; prehension is more physical, handling more intellectual; prehending done passively has only one object, obedience; or done actively, is for the direct use of the child; but handling is, we may say, always a willed action having reference to things, to persons, to feelings, and to combinations of these innumerable. (p. 81)

The transition from *physical* prehension to a more *intellectual* handling was demonstrated in some Russian research reviewed by Zaporozhets

(1965). Movie films were used to record manual movements (i.e., "acquaintance actions") of children in the process of tactually examining an irregular form screened from sight. The child was later required to identify it from among several objects presented visually. From a comparison of the actions of these intellectually normal children in different age groups, it was possible to characterize stages of development in tactile movements. The three-year-olds' movements were more similar to catching than to touching. Four-year-olds started to acquaint themselves with the object more actively by using the palms and the surfaces of the fingers. Fingertips were almost completely passive and usually only one hand was employed. By age five, children were observed touching the figure with both hands, confining themselves to its specific features. It was not until age six that children were observed tracing the whole outline of the figure with fingertips. The systematic development of "acquaintance actions" was correlated with the increased accuracy of visual identification of the tactually explored object. In a later study, younger children were taught to use the more mature forms of tactual acquaintance actions — with a corresponding improvement in perception. These findings provide a concrete, experimentally delineated frame of reference for Seguin's conception of the "intellectualization" of the hand. They are also consistent with Kephart's training program.

According to Seguin, "as soon as an idiot begins to prehend and to handle, he must be made to work" (p. 81). He observed:

> When we impose this rule we know what obstacles are to be encountered. His hand is clumsy and weak yet, his movements have no regularity nor steadiness, his mind does not offer to the organ of execution any object worth doing, and what he begins under our orders he drops through unwillingness. Even when his will begins to harmonize with ours in any undertaking, his synergy is soon exhausted, and as a sign of his weakness we may see his forehead or hand becoming covered with heavy drops of perspiration at the beginning of a thought or of an action. (p. 81)

Even the simplest of work, such as wiping dishes or picking up stones in the field, was considered better than nothing.

To prehension and handling, Seguin added a third element, *aggression.*

> The hand displaces and combines objects by prehension; it acts on the surfaces as in polishing, drying, etc., by handling; it acts on the substances proper, as in carving, cutting, hammering, piercing, by aggression.

He explained the importance of this factor as follows:

. . . a third element is to be introduced, the aggressive power of the hand over the substances to be worked—power whose use is entirely repugnant to the inoffensive nature of most idiots. This most important use of the hand, its aggressive capacity, is generally assisted by adjuvant instruments. It alters the surrounding bodies into likenesses of some ideal, which must preëxist in the mind; it consequently transmutes what is a mode of thinking into a mode of being; it works equally the ever similar wooden doll of the Cretin of the Alps, and the latest improvement in steam or electricity. (p. 82)

Seguin prescribed a series of exercises to train and prepare the hand "for every possible aggressive work on matter:" exercises such as winding up cords, pulling ropes, and placing geometrical blocks into the recesses of a formboard.

In order for the child to achieve an active, spontaneous level of functioning, a fourth ingredient must be added to prehension, handling, and aggression: *imitation.*

So far we have tried to make our pupil learn to act and walk; either by the passive process, somebody or something moving him; or half actively, of himself doing that which he could not help doing under the permanent pressure of our command. But the passive or quasi-active process cannot last forever, and the active one is very slow and intermittent. Between them nature has contrived an agency whose spring is magical for good or for evil; it is neither entirely passive nor entirely active; its initiation is passive, its performance is active; its modes are prescribed, its execution voluntary; and its performance admits of protracted reflex spontaneity — we have described the power of imitation. (pp. 88-89)

For training purposes Seguin classified imitation as personal (he raised an arm and the child did likewise) and objective (he set a book upright on the table and the child repeated with a second book). Imitation training started on a one-to-one basis and if the child, as was typical, failed to respond, he was put through the desired movements. The point was to make him aware of the movement patterns, even if passively. Then, even before active imitation was achieved, the child was placed in view of a group of children "smartly imitating movements monitored to them" (p. 90). This served as his initiation.

Seguin's training sequence strongly resembled those later developed by Baer, Peterson & Sherman, and by Risley (see page 96). One major difference lies in the fact that the modern investigators depended on primary reinforcement to instigate imitation while Seguin did not. Seguin's strategy was to work one-to-one with the child in a quiet, isolated, drab and monotonous closet-like room under conditions of concentrated attention. His success in working under these circumstances suggests that sensory restriction maximized the possibility that imitation would occur spontaneously. Of course, it is likely that he did socially reinforce appropriate movements. In any event, it is possible that Seguin made a more thorough-going use of imitation than did his twentieth-century counterparts. Once imitation was established in one-to-one sessions, the child was moved into group training. When new exercises were practiced, requiring numerous corrections and repetitions, an assistant corrected wrong movements from behind the child.

One critical difference between Seguin's imitation training and contemporary efforts such as those of Baer, Peterson & Sherman (1967) might lie in the fact that Seguin initially put the non-imitating children through the movements himself. Yet an actual description of Baer's procedure suggests that the differences in the two approaches might be much less than one would originally suppose.

> The first response of the program for Subject 1 was to raise an arm after the experimenter had raised his. The subject was presented with a series of arm-raising demonstrations by the experimenter, each accompanied by "Do this," to which she made no response. The experimenter then repeated the demonstration, reached out, took the subject's hand and raised it for her, and then immediately reinforced her response. After several trials of this sort, the experimenter began gradually to fade out his assistance by raising the subject's arm only part way and shaping the completion of the response. Gradually, the experimenter's assistance was faded until the subject made an unassisted arm-raising response whenever the experimenter raised his arm (Baer et al., 1967, p. 408)

When compared with Skinner's explanation and examples of shaping (see page 10), it is apparent that Baer and his colleagues used a procedure that represents an extension of the classical shaping procedure. It is certainly more practical to raise the subject's arm and then reinforce the imposed movement. One could shape arm raising following Skinner's approach as exemplified in his shaping the dog to hold its head much higher than usual (see page 10). But is would be much less efficient.[8] The revised procedure has great advantages, but it also appears not to be so very different from Seguin's.

When emphasis was on the correction and more rapid performance of previously mastered movements, Seguin used the more proficient children as models for the others. He emphasized the great reinforcing power of the group situation — "its contagious power."

Seguin sought to establish "mimical generalization," the equivalent of generalized imitation (see page 96). The ultimate payoff of imitation training was described as follows:

> . . . after months of alternate individual and group-training, in fatigue, often in despondency, we see them with joy, not only imitating the physiological exercises, but carry their new powers of imitation into the habits of life; trying to eat, dress, stand as we do before them, proffering their services to weaker children, as we tendered ours to them; and finally doing by the influences of habit, what more gifted children do only under compulsion. (p. 92)

MORAL TREATMENT AND BEHAVIORAL CONTROL

The course of action whereby Seguin moved from negative will through willed prehension and generalized imitation has been reviewed. However, we have as yet but a partial picture of how Seguin developed behavioral control in the direction of self-determination. There remains to be described how physiological training was blended with moral treatment. In the latter, Seguin looked at how the teacher directly interacted with his student. He defined moral treatment as follows:

> . . . moral treatment is the systematic action of a will upon another, in view of its improvement; in view for an idiot, of his socialization. It takes possession of him from his entrance in to his exit from the institution; from his opening to his shutting his eyes; from his acts of animal life to the exercise of his intellectual faculties. It gives a social meaning, a moral bearing of everything about him. The influences destined to give more impulse to the very life of the idiot come upon him from prearranged circumstances, from prepared association with his fellows, and, above all, directly from the superior will which plans and directs the whole treatment. (pp. 148-49)

Seguin's phrase, "the superior will which plans and directs the whole treatment," has implications that directly bear upon a current controversy relative to the ethics of behavioral control.[9] In any event, Seguin met the issue head on. From the outset he declared his intention to control and direct behavior from the vantage point of the "superior will." This could, indeed, suggest the very worst kind of authoritarianism. Yet in his use of authority is found a superb expression of how strength, humility, benevolence and singularity of purpose can subserve the cause of individual development. As in the previous discussion of physiological education, the continuity of Seguin's conceptualization of developmental training will, hopefully, be evident. In fact, it is in the context of moral treatment that we arrive at the end of a journey, i.e., that "bifurcation of the road" leading either to a "reflex" or a "self-regulating" life, a journey which began with the "frightened grasp."

The basis of moral training was *authority*. In the following, Seguin stated clearly and directly his conception of authority and how it was to be utilized therapeutically.

> . . . authority is, like obedience, a mere function, whose existence is provoked by corresponding incapacities, ceases when its object is accomplished, and is no more inherent to the individual who happens to exercise it, than his coat is adherent to his cellular tissue. This mild view of social equality and of functional inequality fits exactly the exigencies of the moral treatment of idiots. (p. 152)

Seguin's humility in the use of authority is also revealed in the following:

> Our authority over them . . . need not present itself in its historical features of absolutism, but assumes more tender forms as soon as it is firmly established. (p. 153)

It should be stressed that *personal authority was only an instrument*. In fact, Seguin preferred environmental manipulation to the exercise of personal authority. He warned against reliance on punishment and the unnecessary use of repression. He pointed out clever, game-like alternatives to the latter:

> A child could not be forced to stand motionless, even were his legs bound, who remains perfectly still in a circle traced with chalk around his feet. (p. 149)

Rewards of all kinds were to be used discriminatively. Seguin also emphasized the facilitating potentials of time, place, surroundings, and need. For example:

> The time to command an action, or incite to it, must be not only favorable, but the most opportune: as for instance the exercise of nomination of food must not only take place at meal times, but before the appetite begins to be satisfied. . . . (p. 150)

He sought also to exploit fully the possibilities of modeling and imitating other children. Thus,

> What we cannot command, another child will incite; what we cannot explain to a child, he will imitate from another; what a group cannot do after our command, will be done after the example of a small child. (p. 151)

As seen in the following, he employed modeling and imitation in a highly differentiated and flexible fashion.

However incapable we consider idiots, they can be made to act efficiently one upon another, if we know how to appose the vivacious to
the immobile, the loquacious to the mute, the imitative to the care-
less, the affectionate to the indifferent. This apposition of children in
view of their reciprocal advancement, ought to take place in various
ways, according to the object desired; by groups of equals, by series
of one capable and several incapable, and *vice versa*, by pairs of two
extremes in aptitude, by one commanding the other from outside
their ranks, by several correcting the vicious expressions or attitude
of the whole files, etc. (pp. 151-52)

Seguin's use of authority was pervaded by a quality of selflessness. He
sought first to create optimal conditions for performance, thereby encouraging the appearance of a spontaneous response. He tried to encourage
and tease out a manifestation of latent potentialities for self-direction. It
was only when such a strategy failed that he directly entered the picture.
Yet, as with every other instrumentality, he would use himself to max-
imum effect. Like the skilled surgeon who first exhausts every alternative
treatment possibility before deciding to operate, when Seguin finally did
pick up the scalpel of authority he used it surely and incisively.

In the following quote he pointed out an incidental benefit of one child's
training another that was echoed in a study by Whalen & Henker (1969).
His was a nineteenth-century version of their "therapeutic pyramid."

In these multiform operations of the simultaneous training, the child
who teaches another in a certain sense teaches himself more by the
reflex action of his will upon his own understanding; though it is
quite certain, besides, that very many things are taught from child
to child that we could not at all, or not so well inculcate ourselves.
(p. 152)

In a statement that might place him among the ranks of behavior therapists, Seguin identified the origin of the resistance to learning and acceptance of responsibility encountered so frequently in idiots:

This struggle would hardly be noticed if the moral treatment were
carried on by the parents from the beginning. But far from this;
when an utter neglect does not prevail, a mawkish sensibility opposes
itself to any effect at improvement: "The child is naturally miserable
enough, do not contradict him," says the mother. And the child, as
low as we can suppose him, takes heed of that sickly feeling, and will
never do anything until he is kept for a long time away from this
deleterious tenderness. We have seen idiots, after a year of obedience
and contentment, relapse into their anti-social habits at the sudden
reappearance of the weak-hearted person who once indulged their

idiot propensities, and the same children resume their orderly habits
at her exit. (p. 153)

Seguin provided an "analysis of the elements of command, as it must
be used with idiots." From an operant conditioning viewpoint, his analysis
can be conceptualized in terms of the myriad discriminative stimuli associated with the direct expression of dominating behavior. Consistent with
his entire philosophy of behavioral control, direct intervention was employed only as a final resort. As he pointed out, "how many things our
attitude alone will command." For example:

> The way in which we stand in front of a pupil is not indifferent;
> and our foothold tells pretty well the degree of our determina-
> tion. (p. 155)

In the following statement he alludes to the complex set of S^Ds involved
in the act of command.

> . . . command is expressed by attitude, corroborated by gesture,
> animated by physiognomy, flashed by the look, made passionate by
> the voice, commented upon by the accent, strengthened by the
> articulation, imposed by the emphasis, and carried by the whole
> power of the stronger on the weaker will. (pp. 157-58)

The S^Ds are diverse and of a subtle character; they must form a consistent overall impression. Seguin indicated this in his comments regarding
the relationship between the attitude conveyed in the expression of the
eyes, "the passionate center of the physiognomy," and other physical
signs: "all the other parts coordinate their expression to the eyes." The
extent to which Seguin used the "look" to control behavior at a distance
is revealed in the following passage:

> The influence of this organ [the eye], as an instrument of moral
> training, cannot be overrated, whether we consider it from the mas-
> ter's or from the pupil's side. For if the look of the former is alter-
> nately inquiring, pressing, exacting, encouraging, caressing, etc., the
> look of the latter is avoiding, opposed, submitted, irate or grateful,
> borrowing its expressions from feelings incited by the former. To
> obtain this result, the master's look must have taken possession of the
> other, have steadily searched, penetrated, fixed, led it. . . . (pp.
> 154-55)

Seguin's technique of command can be interpreted as still another
variation on escape and avoidance conditioning. The child follows the
command to avoid the seemingly inescapable, overpowering, domination

anticipated as the result of a failure to respond. What differentiates this from the "frightened grasp" of the ladder technique is what might be described as the "credibility" of the negative consequence. The child instinctively fears the height which is unambiguously threatening. In contrast, interpersonal assertiveness often contains contradictory S^Ds; for example, a harsh tone and an angry look, when correlated with a hesitant approach, may belie resoluteness. Even idiots know this. They learn it after winning many "poker hands" in the game of behavioral control with parents. On the other hand, when faced with an unambiguous set of S^Ds for resoluteness, the idiot often behaves appropriately. Thus,

> . . . whatever may be their low condition, they understand our meaning, can measure the opposed forces, and will behave accordingly. (p. 159)

While identifying the source of power in command, Seguin simultaneously warned against employing it rigidly or excessively.

> This power, as expressed here in the abstract, would be the most wearisome attribute of its possessor, and the heaviest burden on children, if it were not incessantly modified by circumstances, and by passing from one person to another; passage in which it loses its tension for the master, and its grim appearance for the child. Moreover, for reasons easily understood, and insisted upon afterwards, the moral power of command must not be always exercised immediately, directly and from man to man; but by a law of descending gradation, it becomes from immediate, mediate, contingent, negative, etc. It is also modified by habits, studies, moral progress, etc. (p. 158)

It is Seguin's contention that the person giving the orders must establish certain priorities. To insure obedience, and therefore the success of the treatment, he must determine which orders the child is capable of following: "Our first orders . . . must be chosen from the class of the things which can be made to be" (p. 161).

But even as he insisted on control, he devised ingenious strategies for eliciting the desired behavior without a struggle. For example,

> . . . we must not order, at first, a child to open his mouth, for what power on earth can make him open it if he will keep it closed against your order? But, on the other hand, what opposition can he offer to our command not to scratch his face, if we occupy his hands at a distance, at the same time that we forbid him to do it? Consequently, let us only command at first that which we have the power of enforcing; and when the child shall feel, after a succession of such commands, that he must obey, we surreptitiously introduce others of a

more arbitary nature, to which he submits himself without noticing their difference from the first; and soon he obeys any order of ours, not because he cannot avoid it, but because he feels that he ought to do it, and finally, because he likes to please us in so doing. (p. 161)

Although the behavior of non-scratching was indirectly elicited, it was nonetheless appropriate behavior which could be reinforced. With repetitions, the command developed into a discriminative stimulus for a behavioral sequence ending in reinforcement. In this way, the command came to "control" the behavior of not scratching. As it did gain control, it was possible to fade out the activity that occupied the patient's hands.

LEVELS OF COMMAND

Seguin described *immediate command* as "the most stringent, sometimes painful." He had reservations about this form of control because it "must be too often supported at the start by coercion." Even at this level, while trying to leave no room for the child to evade the command, he rejected the use of corporal punishment. Thus,

> . . . to command immediately means to command without the mediation of anything or anybody; means to employ the forms of command which can directly touch the child, and take an anticipated direction of his contingent doings. For instance, if when ordering an immobile idiot to move the dumb-bells, we stand in front of him, near enough, and in the most immediate conditions, he will do it. . . . (p. 159)

Since, when repeated from a greater distance, the command failed to elicit the response, Seguin concluded:

> Here, evidently, the propulsor of the child was outside of him; felt only by immediate contact and adaptation of our faculties to his organs, and impotent at a greater distance. (p. 160)

Once again, he warned against using immediate command incessantly or repetitiously.

In his association with the Pacific State Hospital token economy program, this writer (Ball, 1969a) received several practical lessons on the topic of immediate command. In this program, mildly retarded adolescent girls earned tokens for appropriate behavior. Overall, the program has been a genuine success. Yet, it has had only limited success with one specific kind of patient, the physically strong, well coordinated, borderline retardate, frequently diagnosed as sociopathic, who comes from a high delinquency, usually ghetto, area. Such individuals are hospitalized, not because of retardation but because of antisocial behavior. The writer's (unplanned) use of immediate command occurred under the following circumstances: One afternoon he observed Susan deal aggressively with another patient during a volleyball game. He beckoned to her and she refused to comply. Sensing a confrontation, the other patients moved to the sidelines. Concerned over a loss of authority that might generalize to the entire staff, the writer approached the girl and, ignoring her threatening stance, grasped her firmly but not painfully by the arm. She responded, "You can't touch me," but did not physically resist. He then led her across the courtyard, stopping next to a bench. When he ordered her to sit down she again refused. By exerting a firm pressure on the arm he maneuvered her into a sitting position. Once again, despite a menacing refusal, she complied without resisting.. The writer later learned that, following the incident, she enthusiastically remarked, "He really meant it."

Unfortunately, despite the successful outcome of this particular inter-action, the token economy program had only limited success with this girl. As the staff reflected on the case of Susan, it became evident that she could "walk through" the program without fundamentally being influenced by it. The underlying reason may well have been that, more so than any other individual on the ward, she was a master of the art of manipulating her peers. The ghetto teaches not only the art of violence in its many forms, but also, as a corollary, the art of intimidation. The ghetto child experiences an unending series of intimidations, some backed up by violence, others not. In this classroom of the streets the ghetto child, retarded or not, learns to detect those cues of physiognomy that do, in fact, presage violence. He also learns to simulate these cues to great effect. Susan effectively controlled the behavior of other patients through such intimidation and could thereby obtain many tangible reinforcements. It seems likely that, for her, the very act of intimidation became reinforcing to the extent that it was a means of environmental control.

Susan was placed in an environment in which only appropriate behaviors were reinforced. Whenever possible, inappropriate behaviors were ignored. With few exceptions (such as the above) no attempt was made to control her physically. When her behavior was inappropriate, the staff withheld tokens. Yet, even as she temporarily lost these reinforcers, she continued to reap benefits beyond the continuous control of the staff. That is, she succeeded at extortion and also enjoyed the sense of power derived from her control of other patients through intimidation. Unlike the other girls for whom the tokens were a major source of reward, she operated in a dual system of reinforcers, one of which remained almost completely under her control. In his encounter with Susan, the writer neutralized her intimidation strategy, but only momentarily.

In Seguin's system, control was significantly attenuated at the level of mediate command, described as follows:

> The mediate command is one given in such circumstances that the child can disobey it if he choose; as across a large table; from one end of a room or garden to the other; in the middle of a group of other children; when that command interrupts a more pleasing occupation; or when it must be obeyed after a certain time has elapsed. Thus, in the mediate command, there is a medium of space, time, object, or person between us and the child: and moreover, that medium may be temporary or permanent, insignificant, effective, or absolute, representing the degree of trust which we can repose in the good faith and good-will of the child; it embraces a wide range of relations. (p. 160)

From the mediate command Seguin moved to still milder forms of command. These took varied forms conformable to varied circumstances. In the following quote, note how command was used to develop "consciousness" and how Seguin remained concerned with spontaneity. It reveals the end result toward which he labored: authority that became "no more than a watching kindness."

> . . . the milder form of command, postponed to make room for his explanation, will be resumed. The most comprehensive form is the contingent, conditional, or even simply optional, which may depend upon actions of the child, or of others, present, past, or future events; taste, and contingencies calculated to leave more room for deliberation in obedience. These pre-arranged conditions must be simple, and immediately precede the required action; but later some interval may be left between them, and more time allowed for remembrance and reflection; more to evoke and draw conclusions, and more to think before acting, to favor the rise of consciousness. In this degradation of the original command, the passiveness of primitive obedience has made room, little by little, for the judicious execution of orders; this is not spontaneity, but discriminative obedience.
>
> At this time, other forms of command succeed; negative, that which results from not leaving any room for disobedience, letting circumstances themselves impose the order; silent, when the simple presence of the master, near or distant, is sufficient to renew the vividness of the past orders; imitative, when the preconcerted action of other children carries with itself an implicit command to do the same; attractive, when showing the pleasant result of an act, we make our child venture to do the same; but at this extreme limit of mitigation,

command loses its name with the remnant of its harsh features; and
authority is no more than a watching kindness. (pp. 161-62)

Seguin pointed out that command is "alleviated . . . by the variety of its
modes of application." He warned against "protracting sittings" and rec-
ommended a "rotary system" involving continuous changes in activity and
in attending adults. According to Seguin, "this variety in the manner of
handling idiots precludes monotony and aggravations" (p. 162).

Even at the point at which authority reduces to "watching kindness,"
Seguin felt that his work was not done. Rather, a crucial point had been
reached. Thus,

> . . . we have come to the *bifurcation of the road** leading to passivity
> or to spontaneity, whence our pupil may start for a reflex life, whose
> spring shall be in others' hands, or for a self-regulating life, whose
> spring is within his conscience. (p. 163)

To achieve a self-regulating life, long before eliminating the active
forms of command, Seguin began to introduce "incitations to spontaneity." With these "gentler forms of inducement" he hoped eventually to
achieve "earnest self-government." He described the strategy as follows:

> Henceforth, we do not command, we incite; we put the child in con-
> tact with motives, and he moves; we create for him, in the artificial
> atmosphere of the institution, the same relations which impel men
> of the world to action, and he acts; we present to him attractions,
> and he is attracted in the measure of his attractability. Hence, he
> desires, tries, plans, succeeds, fails, gets elated or discouraged, loves
> and feels of his own free will, as he would under the incitations,
> apparently accidental, of social life; the only difference being that
> we have prepared and graduated to his proportions the contacts to be
> encountered, or the obstacles to be overcome, whilst, in ordinary
> social life, such earthly providence is not to be expected. (p. 164)

He added:

> The relations of money to food and to labor are to be presented to
> such of the children as can understand them, in the most practical
> form; their own books establishing the balance of their accounts with
> the institution; each child credited with the value of his work, and
> debited with his expenses. When they have followed a class of
> pricing . . . for usual objects, with critical observations on the qual-
> ities requisite in each, such as shoes, books, gloves, needles, etc., we
> send them to make experimental purchases with their own earned
> money, and let them and the other children debate together the re-
> sult of these foreign operations. (p. 167)

The above quotes could serve as an apt description of the goals of a modern-day token economy program. To be successful, behaviors developed in a token economy program must be keyed to the reinforcers normally available in the community. The patient learns the value of earning and saving money in the miniature capitalistic society of the token economy ward. At Pacific State Hospital, the ward "store" provides items to be purchased with tokens. If the resident progresses adequately in the token economy program, she is enrolled in a community-based sheltered workshop and earns money which can be spent in community stores. If she has sufficient ability, she may eventually be placed in industry and earn a regular salary. As Seguin suggested, she is geared into community life in graduated fashion, but the reinforcers are those that "impel men of the world to action."

Additional incitations to spontaneity included applications of modeling and imitation involving carefully tailored pairing of the more able with the less able children. He created the opportunity for them to perform charitable acts for others, and by sending them to selected community activities and institutions, such as churches, museums, and theaters, he sought to develop "a desire of mingling with the yonder world; pregnant curiosity, which is itself one of the mainsprings of life." He tried to engineer social contacts with the extra-institutional world in pursuit of "concert, harmony, and affection," but when such contacts were painful, he was on hand to soothe "sore feelings."

In the final analysis, Seguin felt that "those alone that love them are their true rescuers" (p. 171). Such love, readily communicated, had a major impact on the lives of his patients. As he wrote:

> To make the child feel that he is loved, and to make him eager to love in his turn, is the end of our teaching as it has been its beginning. If we have loved our pupils, they felt it and communicated the same feeling to each other; if they have been loved, they are loving in all the degree of human power conformable with their limited synergy. (p. 170)

Let us conclude our consideration of moral treatment with the following question: Is compassion an end in itself, or is it a vital raw material that we must mold and shape into a creative instrument of good? The answer is provided by Seguin who shows that we must use compassion discriminatively, wisely and selectively. For it is unfortunately true that in certain special circumstances we can literally destroy with kindness and concern if applied at the wrong time and in the wrong place. Pioneering experimental work by Lovaas, Freitag, Gold & Kassorla (1965a) on self-destructive behavior has conclusively demonstrated this point. There are lessons in self-discipline that are difficult to learn. It is perhaps one of the characteristics of the great therapist that he is selective in his expression of love, that he can control and orchestrate his actions and expressions of feeling.

SENSORY TRAINING

In the midst of his discussion of physiological education, Seguin pointed up the need for sensory training. Such training was believed necessary to overcome deficiencies in transmission of sensory input to the central nervous system. He was concerned about diagnosing "the point or points where lies the deficiency of a nervous function," that is, the "centripetal nerves" or the "sensorial ganglia." These notions can be dismissed as an outmoded neurology. It does not follow, however, that his training techniques, the validity of which does not hinge upon such diagnostic speculation, can likewise be dismissed. They should be evaluated in their own right. An example of how Seguin evaluated and treated such a disorder in the transmission of sensory input is as follows:

> The occasions for the special trainings of the peripheric organs of touch are of frequent occurrence; they being so often under and above the normal standard of sensibility.
>
> Once we had a girl, seven years of age, much afflicted; for, besides her idiocy, which was superficial she could not stand on her weak legs. Her sensations of sight and hearing were good, those of smell and taste rather fastidious; those of the tactile order, instead of being concentrated, and intellectualized in the hands, were rather running wild through her frail crippled body, which could stand almost no contacts, or was seeking for those of an enervating order, making her a very nervous, tiresome, and often miserable child; against this tactile infirmity, which was tending rapidly, in our judgment, towards a more specific nervous affection, we instituted a series of tactile experiments drawn from collections of everything that could be handled; her eyes were shut, her hands ready, the things given to her and named by her, in a continuous and contrasting succession; attention of the touch, that is to say, protracted tactile exercises, gave a new direction to her feelings, she became more quiet and could use her once useless hands after a short time for ordinary purposes.[10] (p. 98)

Seguin considered touch the most general sense, the others being "mere modifications of it." He emphasized that "each sense must be taught as a function, and taught besides as a faculty." He limited his consideration of touch to the following two aspects:

... as a receiver of sensation constituting the touch proper, the other as seeker of sensations deserving the name of *tact*.* [11] By the first we perceive that we are touched by somebody; by the second, we seek for certain characters or properties of bodies. In the exercise of the former we are to a certain extent passive, ready or not to receive the coming impression; in the exercise of the latter we are essentially ready and active. This does not constitute two senses, but two *modi operandi* of the same sense: the like remark obtains for the other senses. ... (p. 96)

The procedure utilized in the above example concerning treatment of the child with a tactile infirmity emphasized training in "touch proper." Tact, on the other hand, focused on acquiring information. *Passive perception* corresponds to what the Russians describe as the orienting reflex and *tact* is the equivalent of their orienting-exploratory reflex. Like Seguin, they actively train orienting-exploratory behavior (see page 127).

Seguin again contrasted *function* and *faculty* in his analysis of the sense of hearing; that is, he distinguished a passive mode, hearing, from an active mode comprising auditing and listening. He promoted the transition from function to faculty as follows:

As soon as the child shows signs of sensibility to music, these various experiments must be made pleasant enough to transform the simple function of hearing into the capacities of auditing and listening. One, auditing, is developed by giving continuity to the tunes as if they were discoveries; the other, listening, is created by breaking the continuity of the tune at its most interesting accent-point where in language we place the mark of interrogation; leaving the ear of the child hearing yet, and listening, as if thirsting for more. (p. 106)

What makes the above especially interesting is that it is directly translatable in terms of the orientation reaction. As noted previously (see page 13), the OR can be evoked by a change in environmental conditions. Lynn (1966, p. 11) cites the work of Soloveichik (1928) who evoked an OR by changing the order of stimuli habitually presented in a specific sequence. Here is the exact counterpart of Seguin's giving "continuity to the tunes" and then "breaking the continuity ... at its most interesting accent point." Leaving the ear thirsting for more connotes at least a short-term persistence of the OR.

Seguin also spoke of developing attention through the sense of smell. In the following passage, he deals with attention in the context of an instrumental response. The passage is also of value as an illustration of Seguin's pervasive interest in spontaneity.

In the first place, in the blank condition of their mind, anything desired by the taste or smell, even the most vulgar, which can make an
impression must be welcome, as the first object likely to exercise
attention, and to be compared with the next. In the second, if the
child does not care for anything but a few objects whose taste and
smell we taught him to like and wish for; well, there are our first
levers, there are the characters of our drama, let them speak. A smell
attracts the attention of the child; his hand, which has never held
anything, brings the perfumed flower to his nose, or oftener to his
mouth, very frequent and curious confusion of the two senses; let
him do; do not disturb this first intention, this first desire followed by
a voluntary action, and its rewarding pleasure, even if he eats the
flower, instead of smelling it. (p. 101)

Seguin differentiated between *passive vision* (function) and *active
vision* or *look* (faculty) as follows:

Idiots, even seeing quite accurately, seem to experience various difficulties in looking at, in directing, or concentrating their willed regard in some direction or at some distance; generally their look,
when they have any, does not seem to go or stay where they wish,
and appears thrown at hap-hazard. The voluntary functions of this
sense are always defective. They see, but look badly or accidently,
and use their sight only for hunting the things they crave for; some
even, when asked to look at something, shut their eyes firmly when
trying to obey. [12] In fact the sight is, of all our senses, the most intellectual, and the one whose anomalies are the most varied and the
most connected with intellectual disorders in idiocy. (p. 112)

Seguin described an active avoidance of eye contact, a phenomenon he
might appropriately have referred to as a manifestation of negative will
in the field of attention. For the more extreme cases, his training approach
was both direct and energetic.

Of all the things, if there be any, which can penetrate the glassy or
tarnished eye of our pupil, it is our own look: the looks call for the
look. We keep the child seated or standing, in front or close to us,
alone, no noise, no company, not much of light nor of darkness; our
feet ready to immobilize his feet, our knees his knees, our hands his
head and arms. We search his eyes with our intense and persevering
look — he tries to escape it; throws his body and limbs in every direction, screams and shuts his eyes. All this time we must be calm and
prepared, correcting eccentric attitudes and plunging our sight into
his eyes when he chances to open them. How long will it take to succeed? Days, weeks, or months; it depends upon the gravity of the

case, upon the help received from the general training, and from other means of fixing the attention of the eye soon to be exposed. But the main instrument in fixing the regard is the regard. When this does succeed, as soon as our look has taken hold of his, the child, instead of taking cognizance of phenomena by the touch or smell, uses concurrently, and after a while exclusively, his newly acquired power. At that time the voice and commands will be better understood, and need not be uttered so loud, since besides hearing, the child now looks at us, and understands also the meaning of our words by that of our physiognomy. (p. 113)

A modern-day counterpart of the above is Zaslow's (1967) *rage reduction* technique for the treatment of autistic children. It is described as follows:

> The rage reduction technique has three essential purposes: to demonstrate to the child that the therapist or *E* can essentially control:
> 1. The child's orientation in space (i.e., front, back, up, down).
> 2. The attempts of the child to disengage from human contact.
> 3. Local motor reactions of parts of the body, e.g., forcing the head and turning the child's face towards the *E*'s face, attaining mastery over positioning of the hands, and even holding the mouth and manipulating the mouth region when the child tends to stimulate himself with meaningless sounds.
>
> In this manner, the child begins to realize that any attempt at aversive movements or motoric resistance is useless and that the *E* is totally and consistently in charge of the child's gross bodily actions. At a later point, eye contact can even be forced by the *E* holding the child's head and looking closely and directly into the child's eyes. Should the child try to avoid eye contact by rolling his eyeballs, the *E* relentlessly maintains eye contact by moving his head in a manner that prevents loss of eye contact. (Zaslow, 1967, p. 15)

In both Zaslow's and Seguin's procedures a tremendous amount of control is exerted over the child. When this kind of domination is related to the earlier discussion of immediate command (see page 64), it gives rise to the following question: Did Seguin differentiate between control and coercion? Seguin exerted tremendous control when he felt it was called for as when, in physically manipulating the child, his "look has taken hold of his." His comment that the child subsequently "understands also the meaning of our words by that of our physiognomy" ties in with the previous discussion of cues exploited by Susan, a sociopathic resident of the token economy ward. Susan's version of command was coercive. There was always the implied threat that failure to respond to her cues for social control would precipitate violence. Yet Seguin was also a master of the art of command. How did he accomplish it if he did not resort to corporal punishment? A suggested answer can be found by analyzing his technique for gaining eye contact. As both Seguin and Zaslow indicated, some children strenuously resist all attempts at establishing eye contact and gaining physical control over their actions. Physical resistance is reinforced because it removes an aversive stimulus (human control). The S^Ds attached to this avoidance behavior consist of that complex of stimuli, varying from gross motor components to subtle aspects of facial expression, which constitutes the sequence of events signalling another unsuccessful attempt by an adult at establishing control. Seguin and Zaslow could have gained control over the struggling child by inflicting pain and forcing a submission based on fear. This is unlike what they actually did, although they continued to manage him physically throughout the course of the struggle. Yet over a period of time, sustained exertion becomes an aversive experience to be escaped. Finally, perhaps out of sheer exhaustion, when the child's struggle ceased and eye contact was established, the controlling grip was relaxed. Both the escape from the fatigue arising from a sustained struggle and the adult's relaxation of control probably served to reinforce the child's relaxation in the adult's presence. The therapist, with his calm but persistent manner (so unlike that of distraught parents), presented a new set of discriminative stimuli to the child. These S^Ds became associated with cessation of resistance and served to cue relaxation in his presence. That they were more effective than mere words was suggested by Seguin when he noted, ". . . besides hearing, the child now looks at us, and understands also the meaning of our words by that of our physiognomy." Words acquired stimulus control by virtue of their association with prior stimulus control acquired by non-verbal physical cues, especially those of facial expression. The child learned that Seguin and Zaslow meant business, not in the sense of inevitable punishment, but of inevitable control.

In many aspects, the process resembles that of humanely breaking a horse. If that comparison is unpalatable, it should be noted that gaining complete behavioral control was a first and essential step in Anne Sullivan's training of Helen Keller. Thus, three days after arriving at the Keller home, she wrote, "The greatest problem I shall have to solve is how to discipline and control her without breaking her spirit" (Keller, 1965, p. 178).[13] Two weeks later Sullivan recorded:

> The great step — the step that counts — has been taken. The little savage has learned her first lesson in obedience, and finds the yoke easy. It now remains my pleasant task to direct and mould the beautiful intelligence that is beginning to stir in the child-soul. (*ibid.*, p. 184)

Seguin found that once he had established and controlled eye contact, vision came to predominate over touch and smell. He implied that this occurred in the absence of formal sensory training. If this did occur, it might suggest that, analogous to Ball's and to Porter's conditioning an orientation reaction to sound in blind subjects, Seguin conditioned a visual OR that generalized to the environment.

When such active resistance was not evidenced, Seguin used a dark room which "is made the theatre where light will appear at intervals" (p. 114). In the same room he elicited attention through the use of small "fire-works" and a kaleidoscope. Seguin also employed another variation on escape-avoidance conditioning. This was through use of a "balancing-pole" held horizontally to the ground and thrown briskly back and forth between teacher and pupil. Wandering attention could result in an uncomfortable physical reminder.

Seguin believed that "attention once fixed, is fixable; discrimination and will once acting upon our series of phenomena will act upon others" (p. 101). Thus, once attention or "voluntary sight" was partially trained, Seguin would quickly apply it to an educational purpose, for instance "to make him [the pupil] appreciate the properties of bodies" (p. 115). He trained for color discrimination, appreciation of the size of bodies and the distance between objects, and an appreciation of plane surfaces. But he was much more concerned with training an appreciation of shape. The rationale for such training continues essentially unaltered to the present day.

> Our appreciation of the shape of everything in nature has its foundation in the knowledge of a few typical forms to which we refer as matrices for comparison. The simplest of them are circles, squares, triangles, etc., adapting themselves to their corresponding forms and to no others. The child, by contrasting the differences, must find the similarity of these shapes. The same comparison must be established between solid forms and those only painted, and between these types and the objects of daily use, similarly if not identically shaped. (p. 115)

Later, he added:

> By striving to give at the start correct perception through a sense, we insure correct impressions to the sensorium, impressions which will be the premises of sound judgment for the mind. What is called error, scarcely ever depends upon false conclusions of the intellect, but mostly on false premises gotten from incorrect perceptions; so that the faculty of judging is not so often the culprit, as is the function of observation; what is badly seen is wrongly judged of; and

our future is too often the stake we pay for the error of our senses. (p. 129)

He also observed,

> . . . children are found whose idiocy being due to deficiency of per-
> ception more than of understanding proper, take in the course of
> their training a healthy mental growth, capable of being applied to
> many objects of learning, mathematics among others. These children
> are easily distinguished from puny prodigies by a general, not a spe-
> cial adaptation of their newly acquired faculties. They were affected
> with extensive paralysis and contractures; or deprived from birth of
> steadiness of touch, or sight, or of hearing; or simply they were
> arrested in their development by superficial idiocy. (pp. 132-33)

Seguin used domino-like blocks for his initial training exercises in form perception. His procedure was based on objective imitation (see page 57).

Much as Kephart eventually did, he initially intensified the tactual-kinesthetic aspects of his training exercises. He believed that this would facilitate learning and enhance the child's active, purposive participation in the task. Children were given plastic substances (e.g., clay) to mold into simple shapes, and soft wood to be whittled to certain marks. The follow-ing stepwise procedure for training appreciation of shape corresponds closely to what Kephart later developed in the context of chalkboard training (Kephart, 1960, pp. 185-92). Seguin's cardboard pattern can be equated with Kephart's "template."

> The scissors are among our favorite instruments. Patterns of card or
> wood are given, and their likeness cut out from rags or newspapers:
> firstly, by application of the pattern on the paper; secondly, by the
> standing of the pattern in front of the child; thirdly, by its mere
> presentation to the sight and withdrawal; and fourthly, by the
> nomination of the shape that is to be reproduced from the image
> evoked by the command. (p. 120)

Using objective imitation, Seguin gave extensive blackboard training in the production of simple straight lines which were eventually combined to form simple figures such as the triangle. With the attainment of curved lines, the two kinds of lines were combined to produce an unlimited variety of figures. In the course of drawing these figures the child, without realiz-ing it, produced various letters of the alphabet, so that "the child writes already by imitation without suspecting it" (p. 123). This is precisely the build-up to writing later employed by Kephart. Drawing by imitation was then set aside to allow for imitative drawing of letters. In a fashion followed later by Kephart (1960) and Fernald (1943), each letter was drawn "as a whole, without analyzing its parts" (p. 123). Another parallel to Kephart was the following:

> Contrarily to school practice, and agreeably to nature, our letters are to be written before being read. (p. 123)

Seguin referred to memory and imagination as "the two most general faculties." To train memory, he directed the child's attention to an event under three circumstances: at the time it took place, after it was accomplished, and at the time it was to be recalled. As objects of recall, Seguin initially emphasized meaningful events that were sensorily vivid and related to instinctual needs (cold, pain, fatigue or hunger). In line with the principle of comparison, which he believed basic to all sensory education, he presented impressions in contrasting pairs; for instance, the thing most liked versus that most dreaded. In addition, the item to be recalled had to be something that the child would do again or that would have some bearing on his future conduct. An appropriate memory performance could, to a certain extent, be elicited by a careful selection of time and circumstances, e.g., "as when the hands nearly freeze, we ask what may keep them warm; the recollection of mittens or of a stove will suggest itself to the dullest mind" (p. 136). To ingrain the memorial impression of more abstract notions such as "the value of time, money, food, fuel, clothing, light, home, labor," these concepts were associated with "his own comfort and duties, with the happiness and misery of others" (p. 137). Seguin then sought to transcend recollections founded on basic physical needs and "convert the physical into moral impressions, and to develop the sense of kindness, of justice, of the beautiful. . ." (p. 137).

NOTES

[1] Leaving France for political reasons in the middle of the nineteenth century, Seguin came to the United States, and here continued his pioneering work. He is credited with founding the American Association on Mental Deficiency. For an excellent historical treatment of Seguin's work, see Talbot (1964).

[2] This and all subsequent references to and quotes from Seguin's work are taken from a single source: E. Seguin, *Idiocy: And Its Treatment By the Physiological Method* (Columbia University Teachers College, 1907; originally published 1866).

[3] Within an operant conditioning framework, Seguin's strategy can be interpreted as follows: (1) He attempts to establish the glass as a positive rein-

forcer by interesting the child in its "elegance" of pattern and color. Breaking the glass would then involve the loss of a positive reinforcer. (2) The child drinks and then throws the glass away. It was not yet sufficiently established as a reinforcer. The glass was valued only insofar as it permitted retention and transport of a *primary* reinforcer, water. Seguin lets the glass fall and break without reaction. In effect, he meticulously avoids the introduction of social reinforcement contingent on the glass-throwing. (3) Seguin waits until the child is again thirsty to return to the broken glass and until he is even more thirsty before getting another glass. This is a superb example of allowing the child to experience a natural consequence from his environment; that is, if you break the glass you lose the means of obtaining water. (4) At this point, having had no success, Seguin identifies the child's "petulant spirit" for what it is: a conditioned operant sustained through social reinforcement. The child, lacking the usual social reinforcement associated with glass breakage, cannily begins to test out the sequence ("He slowly dropped one, when at the same time, he looked into our eyes to catch signs of anger"). Yet Seguin knew precisely the reinforcement he sought and carefully withheld both facial and vocal expressions of anger. It was the withdrawal of social reinforcement from the act that finally brought it under control. This does not, however, deny the possible contributions of previous strategies to the ultimate control of the behavior. In the child's subsequent careful preservation of the glasses we see that they eventually did become positive reinforcers. Now, to avoid the loss of the reinforcer, the child *teaches himself* how to hold on. Just as imitation, when feasible, is more efficient than shaping, so also, in many instances, is self-education. (5) The child has achieved a self-taught skill — "his hands a model of accuracy." But Seguin feels he has also acquired an important attitude, generalizing beyond the specific learning activities — "his mind becomes saving." Even at this tender age there is an opportunity for character training.

Assuming that pattern and color were, in fact, mildly reinforcing for the child, step (1) above could be described as a special case of *reinforcer exposure* (see Ayllon & Azrin, 1968, pp. 103-13). However, at that point, preserving this source of visual reinforcement was outweighed by other reinforcing aspects of the object, realized through its destruction.

[4]"Idiot" has been abandoned as a descriptive term. Seguin usually employed the term in reference to profound intellectual impairment. Yet, "mild idiocy" was used in reference to educable retardates. He devised various subclassifications of idiocy which, though of historical interest, need not concern us here.

[5]I. Lovaas, personal communication, December 15, 1968.

[6]"Capacity" corresponds to his later use of "faculty" in the context of sensory training (see page 69).

[7]In Kephart's terms, prehension is a motor *skill*; handling, a motor *generalization*.

[8]See Fuller (1949) for an example of how a classical shaping approach was used to train a vegetative retardate to lift his arm.

[9] See the February and July, 1968, issues of *Hospital and Community Psychiatry,* and Vogler & Martin (1969).

[10] It is interesting to see how Seguin's neurological constructs influenced his thinking about the child's behavior. His references to a "tactile infirmity" and his speculation about "a more specific nervous affection" reflect the use of neurological constructs to interpret this disorder. In present-day parlance, Ayres describes what seems to correspond to Seguin's tactile infirmity in terms of a "defensive reaction" to direct tactile stimulation. The hypothetical construct she employs to explain the infirmity is an "imbalance of the excitatory-depressant homeostasis which the stimulation may be increasing instead of decreasing" (Ayers, 1968, p. 52). Looking inside for explanations may lead one to ignore what is going on around the child. For example, Lovaas, *et al.,* (1965a), in an experimental *tour de force* that refuted the psychoanalytic interpretation of headbanging, clearly revealed the degree to which it was under *environmental* control. Yet, sometimes people do the right things for what may be the wrong reasons. Assuming the above-mentioned child's tactile infirmity was an active and strongly reinforced mode of manipulating other people, Seguin's treatment approach nonetheless made sense from a strictly reinforcement-theory point of view. The procedure of having the child palpate objects with his eyes shut placed the activity in a game context. Presentation of a succession of objects provided reinforcing novelty. Further reinforcement was provided through the attention and interest shown in her performance. Assuming that her infirmity actually represented an active rejection of stimuli as a means of controlling the environment, it appears that Seguin not only removed the usual S^Ds for such negativism and promoted desensitization of emotional responses to tactile activity, but he also provided a host of new reinforcers for active touching. Ayres' training program would provide similar input. An unanswered question is whether or not the job could have been done more efficiently through a straightforward shaping approach.

[11] "Tact" is similar to the previously discussed concept of "capacity" (see page 55).

[12] Both Bruner and Kephart have described this phenomenon (see page 155).

[13] H. Keller, *The Story of My Life* (New York: Airmont Publishing Co., 1965). All quotations from this book are used by permission of the publishers.

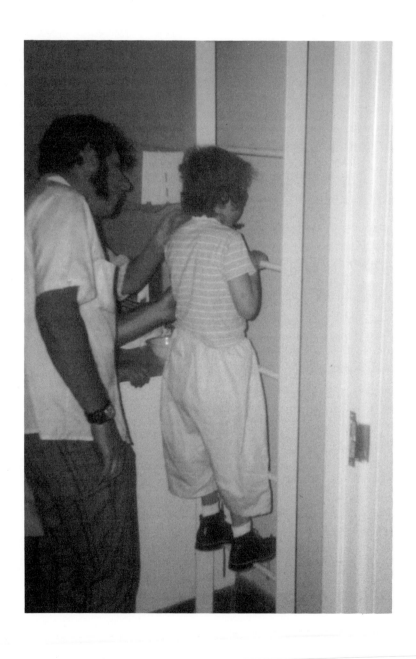

part 2

Threads of Continuity

chapter 3

Treatment by Escape-Avoidance Conditioning: Historic and Contemporary Applications

As in other fields of endeavor, there has been a seeming information explosion in the literature on the treatment of atypical children. If this voluminous output reflected a corresponding increase in basic knowledge, the task of organization and the search for continuity would be even more formidable than it already is. Yet, the so-called explosion is more in the realm of words than in original and meaningful contributions. Where real agreement may exist among various authorities, it is obscured by idiosyncratic terminologies or theoretical squabbles; historical continuities in the development of a methodology or treatment concept are ignored (see Doll, 1967, p. 5). Steps must be taken to highlight such unifying themes and to reveal areas of agreement and connectedness.

Relative to historic contributions, reviewers of therapies specifically derived from conditioning principles cite Watson & Rayner (1920) as the earliest reference. This historical orientation is correct only in a restricted sense, for at least one variety of conditioning, i.e., escape-avoidance, was skillfully and subtly applied to the treatment of atypical children long before it was scientifically identified and formally labeled. In fact, both Itard and Seguin evolved treatment applications of escape-avoidance conditioning many years before the *births* of Watson, Thorndike, or Pavlov.

The purpose of this chapter[1] is to apply escape-avoidance conditioning as a construct which reveals continuity in diverse contemporary approaches; that is, the operant (Lovaas) versus the cognitive (Kephart), and the contemporary versus the historic. The latter approaches embrace Itard, who began his therapeutic work with Victor, a feral child, discovered in 1799, and his pupil Seguin, who, in the 1840s, emerged as a pioneer in the treatment and training of retardates.

A young child, while playing on a rocky field, gets a pebble in his sandal. He stops playing to extract it. The act is learned because it removes the aversive stimulus, discomfort. This is *escape conditioning*. The next time he goes to the field, to avoid a recurrence of the incident, he wears tennis shoes which prevent entry of additional pebbles. Since he has learned to prevent a recurrence of the discomfort, *avoidance conditioning* has also occurred. In this case, the absence of the foot discomfort is the reinforcement. Of course, after a period of time the child may forget the experience and revert to wearing sandals. A repetition of the negative reinforcement would suffice to restore the wearing of tennis shoes.

A common laboratory procedure for escape and avoidance conditioning (Seligman, 1969) involves a two-compartment box in which an animal learns to escape an electric shock simply by jumping across a barrier from an electrified section into a non-electrified section — escape conditioning. The procedure usually involves an S^D, such as the dimming of lights ten seconds prior to the shock. To prevent being shocked, the animal learns to jump from the hot side as soon as the light goes on — avoidance conditioning.

Lovaas et al. (1965b) have adapted the classical laboratory procedure to their experimental-therapeutic work with schizophrenic children. They argue that escape and avoidance conditioning play a key role in child rearing. Pain reduction causes the person associated with it to become a positive reinforcer. Thus, to a large extent, the development of an interpersonal relationship between infant and mother stems from her continually rescuing him from anxiety, pain and distress.

Interpersonal responsiveness is precisely what schizophrenic children lack. Lovaas reasoned that by setting up an intensified, more specifically controlled, laboratory version of the escape-avoidance situation, interpersonal responsiveness might be promoted. His procedure involved placing a child, barefoot, on an electrified floor. During the initial trials one experimenter oriented the child so that he faced the second experimenter and then pushed the child toward the second experimenter. The child learned that the shock, once activated, would be terminated when he sought the company of the second experimenter seated facing him a few feet away.*

It was apparent that the people associated with shock termination did actually acquire positive reinforcing properties. The children, previously unresponsive to any form of social stimulation, worked hard merely to observe the attending adults. Furthermore, a number of generalized changes, completely incidental to training, were observed: increased physical contact with adults, enhanced responsiveness, affection seeking and dependency, and the appearance of "social" smiling.

This procedure may seem cruel and inhuman, or, at the very least, controversial. Yet the results are amazingly paradoxical and can be appreciated fully only by viewing Lovaas' film. The writer had fully expected that, upon learning to avoid the shock, the children would run across the electrified floor in a frightened, cowering, even panicky fashion. But the opposite was true; they were smiling and relaxed, and moved in a carefree manner. With successful avoidance, it is expected that fear would be extinguished. But why was happiness expressed in the very movements involved in avoidance? One explanation entails the developing effectiveness of the second examiner as a secondary positive reinforcer. Specifically, the learning sequence may have been as follows: (1) the adult becomes a secondary positive reinforcer through association with escape from pain, (2) successful avoidance results in the extinction of fear of the situation, and (3) the newly acquired secondary reinforcement of the adult positively rewards the movements involved in what was previously an escape sequence. As a consequence, the sequence takes on a positive emotional tone.

Recently, under Kephart's direction, Miles (1969) developed a program of aquatic activity for children with learning disabilities. He emphasized the development of balance, directionality, space and time perception, body image and flexibility, as some of the major benefits derived from the program. Although he does not mention escape-avoidance conditioning, many aspects of his program are readily interpretable within this framework. Features of such conditioning are most evident in a special program of experimentation following a period of *gradual* adaptation to the swimming pool. At this point the trainer begins "launching" the child first by asking him to stiffen his leg and then throwing him in the air by lifting on his foot. He is thrown in different directions and in different ways; sometimes he lands on his back, sometimes on his stomach. Each

---

*In Lovaas' hands this has been a creative and constructive procedure. This is *not* to say, however, that the writer endorses an uncritical, widespread use of this technique in situations lacking adequate scientific and ethical controls.

time, however, he must swim to the surface and to the nearby trainer who is ready to assist him if he encounters difficulty. Kephart points out that this is a completely unstructured activity. There is no right answer. The child must get out of the problem as best he can. Kephart observes, "When the child can play this game and enjoy it, he is well on his way to learning." He adds, "We have often said that, when a child is thrown up in the air in this way and voluntarily comes back for more, he is ready to learn to read." [2]

Psychological parallels between the Lovaas procedure and Kephart's swimming pool technique are immediately apparent. Like the electrified floor, working one's way to the surface of the water and the physical support and safety of the trainer invokes a primitive survival mechanism, in this case, escape from the threat of drowning. Both situations evoke active coping activities in children who were originally passive and non-coping: purposive, goal-directed running (Lovaas) and swimming (Kephart). Each circumstance, in effect, presented a problem-solving situation involving a question of survival. However, Kephart's children were faced with a more complicated problem of spatial orientation and adaptation than were Lovaas'. His statement that children who come back for more are ready to learn suggests that the active problem-solving, elicited in the context of escape-avoidance, becomes intrinsically reinforcing. This intrinsic reinforcing quality is perhaps a byproduct of the social reinforcement provided in the context of the "horseplay" with the trainer and also the fun that may be associated with first mastering an originally feared circumstance. In any event, it appears that the active problem-solving set may generalize to academic forms of learning. For example, such a set may overcome the pervasive and maladaptive attitude of futility so frequently encountered in retarded readers.

Despite the obvious similarities, the parallel between the Lovaas and Kephart procedures might appear to break down in terms of the child's relationship to the adult, in that Kephart initially said nothing about interpersonal factors. However, in a chance remark Kephart observed that he had more success with the technique than had a colleague. This writer requested details regarding the variations in the approaches utilized.

> Dr. X and I were using the "horseplay" technique in the swimming pool when we noticed that I was having more success than he was. We, therefore, analyzed what we were each doing. We discovered that when the child came up, Dr. X grabbed him usually around the chest and, holding him in the position in which he happened to be, established verbal contact. On the other hand, I grabbed the child by whatever was handy and immediately pulled him into a vertical position holding him close to me. After he relaxed, I then established

verbal contact. After this analysis, Dr. X switched over to my technique and noticed that he was more successful also.[3]

The key phrase is "after he relaxed." In other words, like Lovaas, Kephart allowed the child to experience fully a sense of relief at the end of his effort in the context of a strong, reassuring embrace. The child was given a chance to experience complete relaxation at the end of the escape sequence, thereby completing his escape both physically and emotionally. Dr. X, on the other hand, aborted rather than promoted this experience of reinforcement. No wonder the results were different!

Jean Itard evolved techniques that were unmistakably escape-avoidance in nature. Some applications were very simple and direct. For example, Itard exploited Victor's need to escape from coldness as a means of teaching him to dress himself. Thus, after awakening him in the morning he left him exposed to the cold but in reach of his clothes.

Another, more complex, application involved his escaping a potently aversive stimulation, that of an electrical shock. In this case, Itard saw this as an emotional stimulant of anger. He remarked that the emotional stimulants of joy and anger had beneficially activating effects. Regarding anger, he observed, ". . . sometimes . . . in the force of his passion his intelligence seemed to acquire a sort of extension which furnished him with some ingenious expedient in order to get himself out of trouble" (Itard, p. 17). What Itard seemed to say was that escape from an emotionally arousing, highly aversive stimulus, in a situation of optimum complexity, induced active problem solving. The amusing anecdote which follows clearly supports this position.

> One day when he was in my study sitting upon a sofa I came to sit at his side and placed between us a Leyden jar lightly charged. A slight shock which he had received from it the day before had made him familiar with its effect. Seeing the uneasiness which the approach of the instrument caused him I thought he would move it further away by taking hold of the handle. He took a more prudent course which was to put his hands in the opening of his waistcoat, and to draw back some inches so that his leg would no longer touch the covering of the bottle. I drew near him a second time and again replaced it between us. Another movement on his part, another adjustment on mine. This little maneuver continued until, driven into a corner at the end of the sofa, he found himself bounded by the wall behind, by a table in front, and at my side by the troublesome machine. It was no longer possible for him to make any movement. It was then that, seizing the moment when I advanced my arm in order to guide his, he very adroitly lowered my wrist upon the knob of the bottle. I received the discharge. (Itard, pp. 17-18)

Itard's observation regarding the "ingenious expedient" is consistent with known effects of escape-avoidance conditioning in the laboratory setting. Recently, Seligman (1969) demonstrated that dogs who first had received a series of unavoidable shocks, when later placed in an escape-avoidance situation, develop a markedly unadaptive, non-coping behavior. Instead of learning to jump across the barrier they settle down and take the shock — they appear to give up. Occasionally, however, one of these helpless dogs, after enduring three or four shocks, will jump over the barrier and escape the shock. According to Seligman, "a naive dog's first escape response reliably predicts that it will continue to escape the shock in *increasingly adaptive ways*"* (Seligman, 1969, p. 43). There is one striking parallel between the lack of adaptability in some atypical children and that of Seligman's dogs; that is, in both instances behavior became dramatically more adaptive in the escape-avoidance context. In terms of overt problem solving, animal and human alike do seem to acquire an "extension of intelligence."

As noted above, Itard's notion of an extension of intelligence is consistent with Seligman's observation of the increasingly adaptive behavior of those "helpless" dogs that learn to escape shock. To a surprising extent, Lovaas' autistic children, prior to training, behaved with an almost identical helplessness. Thus, in an incidental observation, Lovaas noted:

> When shock was first presented to S2 [subject #2] . . . he remained immobile, even though adults were in the immediate vicinity. . . . This immobility when hurt is consistent with observations of Ss when they were hurt in the play-yard, e.g., by another child. But after Ss [subjects] had been trained to avoid shock successfully in the experimental room, their nurses' notes state that Ss would come to the nurses when hurt in other settings. (Lovaas et al., 1965b, pp. 107-08)

In the above anecdote Lovaas emphasized the social aspect. The children did turn to the nurses for help. On the other hand, the shift in behavior from immobility when hurt to actively seeking relief can just as legitimately be interpreted in terms of a newly acquired adaptive behavior. Rubbing a bruised shin can relieve pain, quite aside from the social reinforcement incidental to the activity.

Itard related the appearance of Victor's ingenious expedient to the emotional stimulant (anger) aroused by the frustrating situation he (Itard) contrived. To the extent that a frustrating problem-solving situation was involved, his work has one point in common with some research by Maltzman (1960). Working with bright adults, Maltzman repeatedly presented a list of stimulus words and, each time, required different associations.

These associations became increasingly original. The enhanced originality generalized to an independent test of original thinking. Of course, it is frustrating to be forced to give new responses to the same stimuli. As a result, Maltzman's subjects grew "disturbed by what quickly became a surprisingly difficult task." Thus, the original responses occurred in the context of frustration and anger which, as Maltzman speculated, may have been a *self-reinforcing* state of affairs.

Working with an institutionalized profoundly retarded patient, this writer (Ball, 1966) also observed a manifestation of an ingenious expedient. The patient, a fourteen-year-old boy, had had several sessions devoted to shaping dressing skills. In a training session following one in which he manifested considerable frustration and resistance, he spontaneously removed his clothing immediately upon entering the room. Then, in response to the command to put on his trousers, he did something not previously observed; he picked up the trousers and placed them in a cubbyhole located along one wall about six feet above the floor. This was obviously something much more than a simple refusal to perform. It was a novel response never witnessed previously by the trainer. Like Maltzman's subjects, this patient had experienced a series of demands which he had found increasingly frustrating. Despite his limited intelligence (IQ 12), the concomitant anger did seem to evoke originality.

In discussing the swimming pool technique, Kephart indicated that an active coping and problem-solving approach, evoked in the swimming pool context, may transfer to academic learning. How such a transfer might take place is illustrated by Itard. In the midst of reading instruction Itard became aware of the abysmal concreteness of Victor's reading performance. He was bitterly disappointed, a fact clearly communicated to the boy who showed unmistakable signs of grief. Characteristically, Itard turned even this unhappy situation to his and Victor's advantage.

> I had often noticed that when such emotions had reached the point of tears, they formed a kind of salutary crisis that suddenly developed the intelligence which immediately afterwards was often able to overcome a difficulty that had appeared insurmountable some moments before. I had also observed that if at the height of this emotion I suddenly left off reproaching him and substituted caresses and a few words of affection and encouragement, I obtained an increase of emotion which doubled the expected effect. The occasion was favorable and I hastened to profit by it. I drew near to Victor. I made him listen to a few kind words which I spoke in such terms as he could understand and which I accompanied by evidence of affection still more intelligible. His tears redoubled and were accompanied by gasps and sobs, while I myself redoubled the caresses, raising his

emotion to the highest intensity and causing him, if I may thus express myself, to vibrate to the last sensitive fiber of his mentality. When all this excitement had entirely calmed down I placed the same objects again under his eyes. . . . (Itard, p. 74)

Victor returned to the task. Uncertain about how to proceed, he looked to Itard for some sign of approval or disapproval. But Itard maintained a blank expression. Thereby reduced to his own judgment, Victor actively resumed his efforts to deal with the present problem. In the end, he presented the sought-after object to Itard "with a radiant air."

The writer would interpret this as a sequence of two escape-avoidance situations, the first building up to and, to a large extent, even "setting up," the second. Strictly speaking, the first situation represents escape from an emotional crisis. As in Lovaas' example of the infant rescued from a crisis by his attending mother, the interpersonal response to Itard is emotionally intensified. Itard then allows Victor to calm down before entering the next phase in which he again presents Victor with a difficult problem. Victor searches for a cue in the form of an approving look. By withholding approval Itard communicates two facts: (1) that Victor must solve the problem on his own, and (2) that approval will be withheld pending such a solution. Because of the previously experienced rescue from distress in which Itard openly and generously comforted Victor, the suspense is rendered all the more poignant. This then evolves into another escape and avoidance situation: escape from the discomfort aroused by Itard's detachment, and avoidance of ultimate, overt disapproval. Solving the problem was the means of both escape and avoidance. It was the analog of Kephart's child's swimming to the safety of the trainer.

Seguin's applications of escape-avoidance strategies reached a rarely attained level of clinical virtuosity. It is especially evident in his use of a ladder to train the idiot who "cannot, or will not, use his hands" (Seguin, p. 78). With procedural precautions against an actual fall, Seguin placed the child on a ladder, with hands and feet appropriately placed on rungs. He then released his hold whereupon the child, to avoid falling, actively grasped the rungs. At a more advanced stage the child, on the inclined ladder, was made to grasp one of the highest rungs. The teacher then pushed the child's feet from their perch. A spirited contest then developed between the child, who attempted to regain the rung, and the teacher, who tried to prevent it. The next step was to dislodge one of the child's hands and direct it to the next lower rung. Seeking both rest and a secure location, the child grasped it readily. In this way, through successive rungs, the child proceeded down the ladder. There follows the carefully timed introduction of a peculiarly suitable positive reinforcement. Seguin quickly moved to convert this "unwilled prehension," produced by the avoidance training, to a useful, actively exploratory kind of prehension subserving intellectual development.[4] His technique for achieving willed prehension is explained by the following passage.

> We study him after coming from that ladder; he is seated, or stand-ing, or sitting piteously enough, looking at his hands slightly bruised, and heated by the process they have gone through. Do we intend to leave him there under such an impression? If we do, he will present more resistance to our next trial, and will not be blameable for it; for so far, we have taught him less how to prehend with his hands than how much to apprehend with his mind instructed by the sight and touch, the next similar painful contact; in fact, we have created less positive power than negative resistance to the series of manual exper-iments in which he was entering. On the contrary, on taking our child down from the ladder we do not leave him time to look at his hands, but extending them horizontally, we put on each a bright apple. He, partly to feel the coolness on all the burning surfaces, partly not to let the apples fall, will contract his fingers and get a circular, equable, willed prehension of them; quite a progress on the passive contrac-tion of the hands on the ladder's round.

He adds:

> As for the object, pleasure confirms the first consciousness of pre-hension gotten by force, and opens the organ to any unexpected per-ceptions; preparing the hand, so to speak, to think and to foresee for itself. (Seguin, p. 80)

SUMMARY

Lovaas was interested in escape-avoidance conditioning insofar as it enabled him to establish adults as social reinforcers.[5] He did not see it as an important means for developing new behaviors. With Itard, Seguin, and Kephart, however, the emphasis is completely reversed, and for this reason their work has important implications for the development of adaptive and coping behaviors. Relative effectiveness in producing such behaviors is an important dimension on which the various training programs can be compared.

Seguin's ladder technique produced the stereotyped and adaptively specific "frightened grasp" and nothing more. Adaptiveness entered the picture in the form of prehension, established after the fact by a quick transition to grasping positively reinforcing objects, in particular, cool apples. [6]

In Itard's successful evocation of the "ingenious expedient" (problem solving) by means of the Leyden jar, we see antecedents to the contemporary work of both Seligman and Maltzman. As with some of Seligman's animals, Victor learned to avoid the shock in a highly adaptive fashion. Itard's reference to an extension of intelligence coincides nicely with Maltzman's comments regarding the original responses which occurred in psychologically frustrating circumstances that his normal adult subjects definitely wished to escape.

Itard's Leyden jar procedure stimulated behavioral variability. Yet, among the individuals discussed in this book, Kephart proved unique in the extent to which he systematically evoked response variability. During the course of training the child is sometimes thrown on his back, sometimes on his side; each time he must reorient himself from a novel position and swim back to the trainer. The act of reaching the trainer then reinforces the novel escape sequence.

The idea of reinforcing novel responses in a swimming context takes on added significance when related to a recent study in the training of novel behavior in porpoises (Pryor, Haag, & O'Reilly, 1969; Pryor, 1969). The porpoise selected a "docile, timid individual with little initiative," had a large repertoire of shaped resonses. Its *spontaneous activity,* defined as "any movement that was not part of a normal swimming action of the animal," had never been reinforced. Training therefore involved such reinforcing. Over a series of thirty-two training sessions the animal's behavior became increasingly novel and complex. Several behaviors were recorded that have never been known to occur spontaneously in this species. Not only did reinforcing spontaneous activity result in the appearance of entirely novel *non-shaped* responses, but also it resulted in a reduction of the stereotyped behavior pattern ordinarily apparent during periods of non-reinforcement. The authors concluded:

> . . . by using the technique of training for novelty described herein,
> it should be possible to induce a tendency toward spontaneity and
> creative or unorthodox response in most individuals of a broad range
> of species. (Pryor et al., 1969, p. 661)

The basic methodological difference between Kephart and Pryor is that Kephart *evoked* behavioral variability in his application of escape-avoidance while the latter *selectively reinforced* variability in a free operant context. [7] Yet it can be argued that the two procedures are, in fact, closely related. [8] Of more significance is the difference in the organisms dealt with by Kephart and Pryor; children with learning disabilities are probably much more stereotyped in their motor behavior than even the least spontaneous porpoises. Thus, Kephart's swimming pool technique may be a highly efficient way to disrupt such stereotypy and to develop response variability — a variability that may then transfer to the context of formal reading instruction and may promote adaptability. Lovaas (1968, p. 119) recently expressed concern over developing training programs in spontaneity. As has been suggested, the training techniques developed by Itard, Seguin and Kephart in the context of escape and avoidance conditioning may be highly effective in accomplishing this goal.

Lovaas conducted the first truly *scientific* study of clinical applications of escape-avoidance conditioning. When viewed from the same scientific frame of reference, Itard, Seguin and Kephart point the way to additional and potentially powerful treatment and training applications.

A Cautionary Statement: Seguin warned that the ladder technique, used inappropriately, would punish grasping and thereby impede further learning. His warning is applicable to all escape-avoidance techniques: if used mechanically and insensitively, they may seriously hinder, rather than promote, adaptive behavior.

NOTES

[1] This material was previously published in the *California Mental Health Research Digest*, 1969, **7**, 165-75.

[2] N. C. Kephart, personal communication, May 1969.

[3] *Ibid*.

[4] There are parallels between the ladder technique and Colwell's (1965) method of teaching finger-feeders to spoon-feed themselves. Colwell begins by placing his hand over the child's, physically reinforcing his grasp. Then, guiding the spoon, he dips out some food from the bowl, brings it to the child's lips, and then releases his grasp. The hungry child, faced with the loss of food, clutches the spoon and, on his own, brings it into his mouth. For a similar, somewhat more complicated example, see Ayllon & Michael (1959).

An even more striking parallel to Seguin's ladder technique can be found in a study by Nissen. The subject, a chimpanzee deprived of tactual experience from infancy, behaved remarkably like the idiot who cannot, or will not, use his hands. And though Nissen's training techniques were relatively crude when compared to Seguin's, using essentially the same approach he successfully developed voluntary out of reflexive grasping (1951).

[5] Lovaas related his results to autistic children. Neither Kephart nor Itard worked primarily with austistics. Seguin, however, dealt with children with autistic features, some of whom were seemingly as unresponsive as Lovaas' subjects.

[6] Some applications of the Bobath "facilitation" technique for the treatment of cerebral palsy can be interpreted as escape-avoidance conditioning of early adaptive behavior. For example, voluntary reaching can be developed out of an elicited protective extension of the arms in much the same way as Seguin developed prehension from the frightened grasp. For a brief but excellent review of this approach, see K. Bobath & B. Bobath, The Facilitation of Normal Postural Reactions and Movements in the Treatment of Cerebral Palsy, *Physiotherapy,* 1964, **50**, 246-62.

After an initial failure with a standard operant conditioning method, Dean Alexander and I developed a training program based on Seguin's ladder technique and succeeded in teaching a profoundly retarded, blind and partially deaf child to voluntarily grasp and retain a spoon and then to feed herself with it.

[7] In 1968, Kephart described training methods that correspond even more closely to the Pryor technique than does the recently developed swimming pool procedure. A child may to told to move from one location to another in any way he pleases. Upon completion, he is given social reinforcement, asked to return and repeat the performance but with a different means of locomotion of his own invention, e.g., if he first walked he might elect to crawl on the second trial. On each successive trial, he must devise a new technique.

[8] This position is certainly consistent with the revised interpretation of avoidance behavior recently reported by Schoenfeld:

> It seems to me that because "aversive" responding is not different in either principle or process from the acquisition and maintenance of other tyes of responding, it is involved in the broader question of "reinforcement in general. (1969, p. 669)

chapter 4

Training Generalized Imitation: Variations on an Historical Theme

In the preceding chapter I pointed out that, while the formal history of behavior therapy dates back to the 1920s, conditioning principles, though not officially identified as such, were systematically applied therapeutically at least as early as the beginning of the nineteenth century. The same point can be made in regard to imitation training: although a scientific treatment of the subject awaited the twentieth century, imitation training, even in the most current sense, had clear-cut nineteenth-century antecedents.

The purpose of this chapter[1] is to relate some contemporary work on imitation training conducted by behavior therapists, especially Lovaas and Baer, to the historic contributions of Itard and Seguin.

Where appropriate responses are absent and both verbal and non-verbal controls over behavior are lacking, new behavior can be effectively shaped through successive approximations. This approach is especially appropriate in teaching basic self-help skills to profoundly retarded individuals (Bensberg, 1965; Minge & Ball, 1967). However, much learning, especially social learning, does not develop solely in this fashion. It is greatly facilitated by imitation. Operant principles can be applied to the framework of imitation, although some important theoretical extensions are required (Bandura & Walters, 1963).

It is important to differentiate the technical from the popular meaning of imitation. Thus, Baer & Sherman (1964) pointed out that a mere repetition of the behavior of a model does not guarantee that the similarity of the two behaviors was functional in producing that behavior in the observer. This is a subtle but critical distinction. For example, if a little boy sees his father obtain candy by pressing a lever on a vending machine and does likewise, we can only say that he learned that pressing a lever led to a tangible reward. The presence of the father, per se, was perhaps unnecessary. The child might have witnessed the sequence carried out automatically, as by an invisible operator, and then learned the response. On the other hand, if the child begins to duplicate the father's idiosyncratic gestures, his gait, etc., in the absence of any overt attempt to encourage or reward these duplications, we see generalized imitation. The child imitates because it has become intrinsically rewarding to "be like Dad." Stated more formally, imitation occurs *"when many different responses of a model are copied in diverse situations, often in the absence of extrinsic reinforcement"* (Gewirtz & Stingle, 1968, p. 375).

The effectiveness of imitation training in facilitating other learning was clearly revealed in a study by Baer, Peterson, & Sherman (1967) who worked with profoundly retarded children without spontaneous imitative behavior, either vocal or motor. Selectively using food as reinforcement, they taught the children a series of responses (raising the left arm, putting on a hat, etc.) identical to a prior demonstration by an experimenter. Initially, intensive shaping through successive approximations and fading[2] was required to induce a matching of the experimenter's responses. Gradually, however, the subjects began spontaneously imitating new responses without their first having to be trained. While most of these spontaneous imitations were reinforced, some were not. Responding to the latter items, called *probes,* persisted as long as some other imitative responses were reinforced. Verbal imitations were then incorporated into the patterns of motor imitations; for example, in one demonstration the experimenter said "Do this," rose from his chair, walked to the center of the room, turned toward the subject, said "Ah," and returned to his seat. The result was that a generalized tendency to imitate, initially achieved on a motoric-gestural level, markedly facilitated subsequent verbal learning: children who would not imitate sounds prior to training, imitated the entire sequence, including "Ah."[3]

Utilizing the same principles described above, Lovaas et al. (1966) taught mute schizophrenic children to speak by imitation. Verbal imitation was developed through a discrimination training procedure entailing six distinct steps. In step 1 the child was reinforced for any and all vocalizations, simply to increase their rate of occurrence. He was also reinforced for looking at the trainer's mouth. In step 2, an effort was made to establish speech imitation specifically in response to the adult's vocalizations. For example, the child was reinforced only if he vocalized, "baby," within six seconds after the adult said it. Step 3 included the additional requirement that the child actually match the adult's vocalization before receiving the reinforcement. Words were selected, the enunciation of which could be facilitated through the use of external cues or prompts, especially visual ones. Lovaas provides an example of the use of a prompt in teaching the "b" sound.

> The training would proceed in three stages: (1) the adult emitted "b" and simultaneously prompted the child to emit "b" by holding the child's lips closed with his fingers and quickly removing them when the child exhaled; (2) the prompt would be gradually faded, by the adult's moving his fingers away from the child's mouth, to his cheek, and finally gently touching the child's jaw; (3) the adult emitted the vocalization "b" only, withholding all prompts. The rate of fading was determined by the child; the sooner the child's verbal behavior came under control of the adult's without the use of the prompt, the better. (Lovaas et al., 1966, p. 706)

Using this procedure, additional sounds were added and the child was forced to discriminate them in order to be reinforced (step 4). Lovaas' training[4] then proceeded through what amounted to at least two additional steps. Thus, words and then phrases were introduced and finally the children were taught to use language appropriately.[5]

To test for the generalization of speech imitation (that is, that imitative behavior provides its own reward), Lovaas introduced Norwegian words which the children imitated without being rewarded. Rewarded English words were interspersed throughout the session. The children continued imitating with increasing accuracy despite the lack of reward for Norwegian words. Lovaas concluded that, as a result of the prior training, verbal imitation had become intrinsically reinforcing in the absence of such extrinsic rewards as food and praise. Generalized imitation was achieved. The significance of this feat stems from the fact that, prior to training, these children imitated nothing. Without imitation, the autistic child would have to acquire each speech sound through specific shaping — a task so monumentally difficult as to be unfeasible in execution.

Seguin's concept of *mimical generalization* is a nineteenth-century equivalent of *generalized imitation*. Thus,

> ... personal imitation, far from being the circular repetition of a few gestures, is the sudden, unexpected call into action of any organ that

can be moved by the will. This is the broad ground of our training in
education. . . . (Seguin, 1907, p. 90)

As do his twentieth-century Skinnerian counterparts, Seguin used generalized imitation as a modality for training in articulation. He worked to
accomplish the following:

. . . to transform or concentrate gradually the imitatory movements
of the whole body into the imitative mimicry of the organs of
speech. . . . (p. 109)

Like Lovaas, Seguin's initial concern was with the frequent emission of
spontaneous vocalizations. He took pains to reinforce such vocalizations
rather than to suppress them through premature attempts at modifying
them into speech sounds.

"At the start everything sounding like syllables is to be encouraged
first, and corrected afterwards" (p. 110). He added:

Our primary teaching must go through without touching this natural
speech, taking care not to substitute Greek etymologies for those of
passion, fearing to suppress in the speech of the child its higher element, spontaneity. . . . (p. 111)

Seguin's first lesson in articulation resembled Lovaas' procedure as
noted in the previous example of teaching the "b" sound. Perhaps it is best
characterized, however, as a combination of Baer, Peterson & Sherman's
approach with that of Lovaas. Thus, like Baer, Seguin established the
groundwork for imitation in a speech context through a course of non-
verbal imitation starting with gross motor movements.[6] Like both Baer
and Lovaas, he made use of what could be classified as prompts and fading. An important difference is that, unlike Lovaas, Seguin induced the
child to provide and then fade out his own physical prompts through imitation. Also, conformation of the speech organs preparatory to speech
was done without vocalization. Finally, the introduction of "Ma" or "Pa"
is more reminiscent of Baer, in his introduction of the "Ah" sound, than
of Lovaas.

At the first lesson appointed for the beginning of articulation, the
child is made to resume his morning and evening exercises of imitation without warning, explanation or ado; the movements are mostly
concentrated in the hands, the hands brought about the face, the
fingers put in and about the mouth. All the parts of the face are
moved in correlation with the fingers, and the mimicry is effected
with the double object, first: of giving the child an analytical sur-

vey by the touch, the sight, and the movement of the various parts involved in the act of speech, from without inwards; second, of making him execute silently after us the movements of the different parts employed in speaking. At this second stage of imitation, the hands have been withdrawn little by little, the teaching and the taught faces have come nearer, taken a better survey of each other, and their execution of mimicry has grown warmer, quicker, more correct. After this, all the organs of speech, the lips, tongue, etc., are moved freely in all directions and in every manner; and once, as if by chance, in the middle of the mute, mimical exercises, the lips being well closed, we part them by thrusting out an emission of voice which pronounces *Ma* or *Pa.* . . . (p. 108)

Like Lovaas, Seguin taught syllables "from the lips backwards, from the seen to the unseen" (p. 110).

Seguin's aphorism, "we sow and nature fecundates," reveals a patient, long-term view of the educational process. He differentiated between the limited range of cues for behavior existing in the context of formal instruction and those spontaneous, albeit uncontrolled, promptings from an enriched daily environment.

At whatever point of the vocal teaching we are engaged, it is important to remember that speech is such a spontaneous faculty, that it is not enough to teach it, to produce it. The chances are that what the child learns to-day, he will not show at once; but occasion will bring it out later; or what the child learned and did not show in private teaching will appear when he shall take his part in the group, and *vice versa;* and what private or group emission of voices cannot bring out, may flow from his lips without effort after some lazy looking on, and accidental hearing. . . . (pp. 110-11)

Itard's most complete statement regarding the use of imitation for training purposes occurred in conjunction with writing rather than with speech. He saw writing as "an exercise in imitation." He gave Victor chalk and attempted to induce an imitative copying of strokes on the blackboard, but without success. Itard then evolved a procedure for the training of imitation which, though less detailed, is strikingly parallel to that utilized by Baer et al., (1967).

Here then it was necessary once more to retrace our steps and to try and rouse from their inertia the imitative faculties by submitting them, as we had the others, to a kind of gradual education. I proceeded to the execution of this plan by practising Victor in the performance of acts when imitation is crude, such as lifting his arms, putting forward his foot, sitting down and getting up at the same time as myself; then opening his hand, shutting it, and repeating with his fingers many movements, first simple, then combined, that I performed in front of him. (Itard, 1932, p. 83)

As with Baer et al., these exercises were not an end in themselves; they were preparatory to a more significant educational objective. Upon achieving a satisfactory level of imitation, Itard switched to his immediate educational objective — writing.

I next put into his hand, as in my own, a long rod sharpened to a point, and made him hold it as if it were a quill for writing, with the double intention of giving more strength and poise to his fingers through the difficulty of holding this imitation pen in equilibrium, and of making visible, and consequently capable of imitation, even the slightest movement of the rod.

Thus prepared by preliminary exercises we placed ourselves before the blackboard, each furnished with a piece of chalk, and placing our two hands at the same height I began by making a slow vertical movement towards the bottom of the board. The pupil did just the same, following exactly the same direction and dividing his attention between his line and mine, looking without intermission from the one to the other as if he wished to compare them successively at all points.

The result of our actions was two lines exactly parallel. My subsequent lessons were merely a development of the same procedure . . . at the end of some months Victor could copy the words of which he already knew the meaning. (Itard, 1932, pp. 83-84)

Although they involved writing rather than speaking, up to this point Itard's procedures and objectives closely paralleled those of the Skinnerians. The following quote, however, reveals that he also used imitation as a vehicle to place Victor in a problem-solving situation containing conflictual cues.

In considering my experiments as a real course in imitation, I believed that the actions should not be limited to manual activity. I introduced several procedures which had no connection with the mechanism of writing but which were much more conducive to the exercise of intelligence. Such among others is the following. I drew upon a blackboard two circles almost equal, one opposite myself and the other in front of Victor. I arranged upon six or eight points of the circumference of these circles six or eight letters of the alphabet and wrote the same letters within the circles but disposed them differently. Next I drew several lines in one of the circles leading to the letters placed in the circumference. Victor did the same thing on the other circle. But because of the different arrangement of the letters, the most exact imitation nevertheless gave an entirely different figure from the one I had just offered as a model. Thence was to come the idea of a special kind of imitation which was not a matter of slavishly copying a given form but one of reproducing its spirit and manner without being held up by the apparent difference in the result. Here was no longer a routine repetition of what the pupil saw being done, such as can be obtained up to a certain point from certain imitative animals, but an intelligent and reasoned imitation, as variable in its method as in its applications, and in a word, such as one has a right to expect from a man endowed with the free use of all his intellectual faculties. (pp. 84-85)

In the above problem, a previously relevant set of cues was no longer applicable: those related to producing an exact replication of Itard's drawings Victor had to shift to another set of cues — connecting letters.

The circular letter-connection exercise can be considered a test of generalized imitation fulfilling the same function as did the non-reinforced Norwegian words for Lovaas. Although Victor had previously used letters in simple matching activities, the circle exercise placed matching in an entirely new context. With Lovaas, and also with Baer et al., the subject was presented with a discriminative stimulus (the item to be imitated) representing a slight variation from a series of S^Ds already presented and reinforced. For example, one subject trained by Baer et al., was reinforced for imitatively tapping his nose. But correct imitation of the next item, tapping the arm of his chair, was not reinforced. Imitation of these non-reinforced discriminative stimuli, occurring without the experimenter's intervening with shaping or fading procedures, was the criterion of generalized imitation. This is in contrast to Itard, who, in drawing a line connecting letters, presented Victor with a standard, unvarying S^D for a literal reproduction of his actions. Yet the task required a new response; that is, a line drawn in a different relative location and a different orientation. In making a new response to an old discriminative stimulus, Victor made a significant shift in imitation procedure. Although Itard's reporting was anecdotal and Victor cannot be equated with Lovaas' or Baer's subjects, the circle test would nonetheless appear to be an unusually rigorous test of generalized imitation.

Itard applied imitation in a final attempt at training speech, a capacity he described as "the most marvelous act of imitation." His emphasis on attention and imitation embodies the essentials of Lovaas' strategy. In laying the groundwork for imitation of movements of the external organs of speech by an initial imitation of grimacing, Itard used the *method of insensible gradation,* a technique which seems equivalent to the Skinnerian method of successive approximations. [7] Also, in emphasizing movements most easily seen, we find an anticipation of Lovaas' initial emphasis on training words with readily discernible visual components.

> I felt I should try a last resource, which was to lead him to the use of speech through the sense of sight. . . . Here the problem was to practise his eye in observing the mechanism of the articulation of sounds, and to practise his voice in the reproduction of the sounds by the use of a happy combination of attention and imitation. For more than a year all my work and all our exercises were directed towards this end. In order to follow the previous methods of insensible gradation, I preceded the study of the visible articulation of sounds by the slightly easier imitation of movements of the face muscles, beginning with those which were most easily seen. Thus we have instructor and pupil facing each other and grimacing their hardest; that is to say, putting the muscles of the eyes, forehead, mouth and jaw into all varieties of motion, little by little concentrating upon the muscles of the lips. Then after persisting for a long time with the movements of the fleshy part of the organ of speech, namely the tongue, we submitted it also to the same exercises, but varied them much more and continued them for a longer time. (Itard, 1932, pp. 85-86)

Since his efforts yielded nothing more than unformed monosyllables, he resigned himself to failure in teaching speech. This negative verdict, rendered with such finality by Itard himself and uncritically accepted historically, obscures some important facts. First, at a much earlier stage of training Itard had, in fact, elicited some highly satisfactory imitations of speech sounds. Victor's vocalizations included three consonants, the French *l, d,* and liquid *l,* and all of the vowels except *u.* Following training, he emitted the word *lait* when receiving milk, although not as a request. These productions were vastly superior to the unformed monosyllables obtained in the final training effort. Second, it should be noted that Victor obtained a relatively high level of abstraction in terms of reading comprehension; for example, his ability to demonstrate correct interpretations of sentences containing verb forms.

The present writer believes that, in comparison with the remarkable achievement of teaching Victor to comprehend reading, the attainment of at least a limited amount of meaningful vocal speech might have been relatively simple. With fading added to Itard's technique, it quite possibly could have been achieved incidentally to reading instruction.

Itard established requesting by showing or giving Victor the object when Victor looked at the printed word representing the thing desired, or alternatively, he indicated the word when Victor was given the object. Eventually, when Victor wanted something, he requested it by silently indicating the word. At this point, the following procedure might have been employed: The experimenter would have trained Victor to request several objects by indicating the corresponding printed words. Then, since *lait* had once been quite clearly enunciated and had, in fact, been previously emitted after seeing milk (though not as a request), the experimenter would have chosen this word next. He would have trained Victor to select and point out the correct word from a list of words. On each successive presentation a new list would have been given with the words in a different order. As the next step, when Victor indicated the word, the experimenter would have held the list near his own mouth, pointed to the printed word and simultaneously enunciated *lait*. He would then have had Victor point to and simultaneously imitate the word, following which the milk would have been presented as reinforcement. On successive occasions the experimenter would have faded out his own enunciation so that Victor would enunciate and point to the word without prompting prior to receiving the drink. When Victor had learned to request milk *before* seeing the liquid, the experimenter would have gradually faded the printed word on successive lists until it eventually became invisible. All that would have remained of it would have been a blank space on the list. Finally, even the space would be faded so that he would simply be presented with a list of words from which *lait* was omitted. If necessary, the list itself would be withdrawn. By this time, the act of verbally requesting milk should have been established.

In summary, it can be seen that Itard and Seguin approached imitation training from exactly the same point of departure as do the Skinnerians. They recognized that a vast amount of learning occurs with remarkable efficiency through the process of imitation. Such training frees the teacher from painstakingly developing each new response to be taught. The problem, then, was to establish imitation as a generalized process. Clearly, Seguin's concept of mimical generalization is equivalent to Gewirtz' & Stingle's (1968) definition of generalized imitation. Counterparts for even the specific details of what is identified as Skinnerian training methodology can be found in Itard and Seguin. Thus, the method of insensible gradation is what Isaacs, Thomas & Goldiamond, (1960) labeled *successive approximations*. And in Seguin's gradual withdrawal of his hands as physical prompts for speech imitation, we can see a clear example of fading. Although some procedural details vary, others are amazingly similar. For example, Seguin, like Baer et al., tackled speech imitation after having established the imitation process through non-verbal, motor acts. He already knew what Lovaas later had to discover for himself: that syllables should be taught "from the lips backwards, from the seen to the unseen."

Unlike the Skinnerians, Itard and Seguin did not use probes to test for the development of generalized imitation during the course of training. Yet, despite the fact that it was administered after the completion of an extensive course of training, Itard's circle problem can be considered a test of imitative generalization. In point of fact, Victor's successful performance appears to be a more impressive demonstration of generalized imitation than can be found in any of the contemporary studies reviewed in this chapter.

Typically, the course of historical research leads to the discovery of some ancient antecedents to a modern scientific development. After duly acknowledging that the ancients had in a very general way anticipated the development, their work can be quickly dismissed. Ordinarily such work lacks any specific connection with the present scene. The nineteenth-century work of Itard and Seguin on imitation training is a rare exception to this typical state of affairs. They anticipated not only the procedural aspects; but also foresaw the technical meaning of generalized imitation, and devised some procedural innovations as yet not rediscovered.

NOTES

[1] This material will be published separately in the *American Journal of Mental Deficiency*.

[2] Initially, an individual may need a highly obvious, even exaggerated, cue for his behavior. With learning, the cue may gradually be diminished. For example, in training a profoundly retarded individual to sit down on command, one may initially have to combine the words "Sit down" with an exaggerated hand gesture and a light touch to the shoulder. Gradually, the touch and then the gesture can be reduced and eventually eliminated, with the vocal instruction being sufficient to elicit the behavior. The gradual elimination of gesture and touch is an example of fading. It can be said that control of the learned behavior is eventually transferred to the verbal command.

[3] For an application of this approach to linguistically deficient, culturally and economically deprived, but nonretarded, ghetto children, see Risley (1968).

[4] For a brief but stimulating film account of this work, see "Reinforcement Therapy, available free on loan from the Smith, Kline & French Laboratories.

[5] Hewett's (1965) speech training of an autistic child illustrates how Lovaas' program eventually promotes the development of meaningful language, e.g., spontaneous requests for desired items in the absence of the objects themselves.

[6] After reading this manuscript, Dr. Robert Liberman informed me that Dr. Todd Risley has linked Seguin's work with generalized imitation training and

specifically with the work of Baer, Peterson & Sherman. For details, see T. R. Risley, Behavior Modification: An Experimental-Therapeutic Endeavor, in L. A. Hamerlynck, P. O. Davidson & L. E. Acker (eds.), *Behavior Modification and Ideal Mental Health Services,* the First Banff International Conference on Behavior Modification (Calgary, Alberta, Canada: University of Calgary, 1969).

[7] Although the procedure involved the reinstatement rather than the initial training of speech, a case study of a catatonic schizophrenic (Isaacs, Thomas, & Goldiamond, 1960) involved an approach almost identical to Itard's. Thus the experimenter successively reinforced and thereby "shaped" a series of behaviors eventuating in speech, i.e., ". . . eye movement, which brought into play occasional facial movements, including those of the mouth, lip movements, vocalizations, word utterance, and finally, verbal behavior" (p. 9).

Courtesy of William G. Stephens and Hester M. Hughes

part 3

Kephart — A Contemporary Approach

chapter 5

Kephart's Theory

Newell Kephart is acknowledged as a leading authority in the field of sensory education. His work will provide a theory and correlated educational program representing the present-day scene. Because it is anchored in contemporary theory, Kephart's system provides a highly suitable point of departure for examining the theoretical and applied aspects of modern sensory education programs.

Kephart's work represents a cognitive approach to the interpretation and remediation of learning difficulties. In his stage theory of mental development he describes a series of increasingly efficient strategies for processing information from the environment. These stages must be learned sequentially. If learning at an earlier level is incomplete, learning at higher levels must inevitably suffer. This aspect of his theory resembles Piaget's work (1952) and Kephart acknowledges a direct influence. From Hebb's theory (1949) Kephart has drawn a neuropsychological model through which he accounts for the disruption that occurs in the learning process of disabled learners. Kephart has been influenced by the theory of Gestalt psychology, not only in the modified version expressed by Hebb, but also and more directly from the work of both Werner (1961) and Strauss (Strauss & Lehtinen, 1947; Strauss & Kephart, 1955). While his theoretical rationale for treatment strategies comes largely from Hebb, many of his practical remediation procedures reflect the influence of Maria Montessori (1964), who in turn was strongly influenced by Seguin. For example, Kephart's emphasis on learning writing before reading corresponds to positions taken both by Seguin and by Montessori. Kephart has also been influenced by developments in the field of optometry and once worked in collaboration with Getman (1962) whose theory closely parallels Kephart's on several points. It is also clear that Kephart has influenced the field of physical education and has, in turn, been influenced by it (see Ismail & Gruber, 1967). While his emphases and treatment goals differ from those traditionally involved with the field of physical medicine and rehabilitation, within recent years he has been developing techniques that are increasingly of interest to practitioners in that field; for example, his work on kinesthetic figure-ground.

For Kephart, understanding the child comes from understanding his cognitive structures, i.e., how he experiences the world. It is difficult to see the world through the eyes of the handicapped child, to understand his disrupted processes from the normal adult's frame of reference. Through his stage theory of cognitive development, Kephart aids the adult's understanding by identifying distinctive levels of qualitative functioning. Once identified, there are corresponding remedial procedures for effecting a resolution of the child's arrested cognitive development. A further complication arises from the fact that many children learn to compensate for their cognitive handicaps; thereby these may go undetected. Kephart insists that it is only through a careful study of moment-to-moment performance that such areas of disruption can be detected. For example, one could correctly assemble a jigsaw puzzle by focusing entirely on matching individual pieces without ever conceptualizing the final product (design or picture). Another example — the final product of copying the Gesell divided rectangle ⊠ may be an accurate facsimile of the original. Yet, the child may have drawn eight lines radiating from the center rather than four bisecting lines. Though undetected in the final product, this fragmentary approach in a school-age child would suggest a qualitatively lower-level perceptual process which would predispose the child to academic failure.

Kephart draws heavily upon hypothetical constructs, i.e., inferences about actual events that go on inside the organism between stimulus and response. He feels that we can best fill the gaps in our knowledge concerning stimulus-response relationships through such provisional explanations. In the Hebbian component of his theory, he refers to actual neurological structures, such as synapses, and functional events, such as reverberating neural circuits. He apparently believes that his application of Hebbian theory or a closely related approach will one day be validated in the laboratory. Other hypothetical constructs, especially those of later-ality and directionality, while not based on Hebb's theory, are nonetheless internal events postulated to account for observed behaviors. For example, without laterality, an internal sense of sidedness, the child lacks the groundwork for perceiving directional sidedness in the reading situation and will thereby confuse *b* and *d*. The use of hypothetical constructs clearly differentiates Kephart from the functional analysis of behavior in which the Skinnerians endeavor to confine their explanations solely to the level of observable events.

Another factor that differentiates him from the Skinnerians and places him in Piaget's camp is his emphasis on the motor component of intellectual development. According to Kephart, at the earliest stages the child's information-processing strategy is largely motor in nature. If his motor patterns are inadequately developed, he is literally unable meaningfully to contact and apprehend the world around him. In later stages the motor component becomes subservient to the child's evolving perceptual and conceptual capacities. Initially, however, intellectual deficiency is tanta-mount to a disrupted and undeveloped motor system.

KEPHART'S DEVELOPMENTAL SEQUENCES

Kephart's developmental stages represent a series of qualitatively dis-tinct, increasingly effective and efficient strategies for processing informa-tion from the environment. For Kephart, learning proceeds from inside to outside. The child's development could be characterized in terms of transi-tional stages beginning at the level of proprioceptive or internal bodily awareness and culminating in the development of abstractions beyond im-mediate environmental data.

The infant's first developmental task is to become aware of his own body. The significant stimuli are inside the skin and are of proprioceptive origin. The most important stimuli are transmitted from the vestibular organs of the inner ear and from kinesthetic receptors in muscles and tendons.

How the child learns from such internal data might be clarified by an analogy from space flight, which, though incomplete, will hopefully provide an appropriate phenomenological frame of reference for Kep-hart's theory.

Imagine yourself going to sleep at home. Waking, you find you are sealed in some type of enclosure. (It is, in fact, a space vehicle orbiting the earth, but you are not aware of this.) Inside, it is pitch-black; you cannot see outside and your condition is one of weightlessness. The only moveable object within the cockpit-enclosure is a control stick which, unknown to you, activates elevators and ailerons — control surfaces that cause the vehicle to tilt, or to rise and fall, when moving through the atmosphere. You are, however, not *in* the atmosphere so control surfaces have no effect. Further, due to your weightlessness, you are unaware that the craft is spinning slowly on its axis. You manipulate the control stick, uselessly, but there is no correlation between this voluntary movement and other bodily sensations. In general, you do not know the nature or the function of your enclosure. The problem is to determine what is happening to you and whether or not you have any control over the situation.

While these circumstances depict a claustrophobic nightmare, they also suggest the problems involved at the earliest stages of learning. Clearly, the first piece of required information is that of a *correlation* between voluntary activity and resultant feedback. Such learning, however, cannot occur in orbit. For the necessary correlations to occur we must add the all-important factor, *gravity*. This could be accomplished by slowing the speed of the vehicle until it went out of orbit and entered the earth's atmosphere. Assume that you, as the unknowing "pilot," were again unaware of such a change. For lack of anything else to do, you continue moving the single control, but this time a movement is correlated with a unique set of bodily sensations. Thus, you move the stick to the right and you experience vestibular stimulation and increased tactual feedback from the right side of the body. Further, there is a felt discrepancy between your right and left sides. You move the stick to the left, then forward and back. Each movement, in turn, is associated with a distinctive pattern of bodily sensation. As you learn this series of correlations between kinesthetic patterns incidental to voluntary movement of the control stick and passively experienced bodily sensations caused by resulting changes in position, you develop a frame of reference within the darkened cockpit. At this point you are still helpless and unable meaningfully to guide the craft. Yet the time is not wasted because you are establishing a *system of coordinates* into which you can potentially plug other data as they become available. As your gliding craft gradually loses altitude, the opaque covering over the cockpit disappears and you find yourself peering through a translucent, but not transparent, window. You can discern only the horizon line — that demarcation between the darkened earth and the sky above. At this point, you do not know that it is actually the horizon or that you are viewing anything "out there." It is just an ill-defined boundary, lacking details. Now, however, you have a source of visual input which can be fed into your previously established kinesthetic-tactual-vestibular coordinate system. You push the control stick forward and the horizon line floats upward, you push it to the left and it tilts; you repeat these actions, always with the same result. You are now *matching* visual data against prior kinesthetic, tactual and vestibular data. Your experiential frame of reference has expanded. Thus, visual input is correlated with previously integrated kinesthetic, tactual and vestibular input — the movement of the line acquires meaning in terms of a bodily frame of reference; it tilts when you tilt.

At this point, the translucent windshield is replaced by a semi-transparent one. You become aware that there *is* an "out there." In addition to the horizon gradient or line of demarcation, new gradients of lightness and darkness appear corresponding to land and water masses. However, you have not identified them as such. Nor, for that matter, are you even aware that you are circling the earth. Nonetheless, as you continue to orbit you detect a certain regularity in the *succession* of gradients, and as you lose altitude the gradients become more *distinct*. You conclude that you are, in fact, orbiting a planet with irregular surfaces. If the gradients represent differences in elevation, the craft would have to be carefully maneuvered to effect a safe landing, but you lack sufficient detail to distinguish between a mountain and a plain as prospective locations for such a landing.

Finally, the semi-transparent window is replaced by a fully transparent one and you can, for the first time, see details of the terrain below. You must now reappraise your situation based on the *relationships* between such details. Effecting a safe landing is not merely a matter of finding level ground, but rather level ground of adequate length. Further, the accessibility of level ground must be considered in relation to other features of the terrain; for example, a valley nestled within a mountain range may be sufficiently long but inaccessible. At this point your visual frame of reference is expanded to its full extent. Yet, although it has become predominant, it is still operating in correlation with and in ultimate reference to the originally established proprioceptive coordinate system.

From this point on, with the exception of the final descent, you can continue to view the surface below. However, your focus of attention shifts to making calculations related to a strategy for getting the craft safely down; calculations such as estimations of velocity, possibilities for last-minute corrections in gliding path, etc. While based on the outer scene, these abstract manipulations transcend it; that is, they relate to future possibilities, rather than to the immediate realities of sensory input.

With these details in mind, we can now consider the imaginary space flight in relation to Kephart's conception of developmental stages.

MOTOR STAGE

In the motor stage the child is "learning how to experience his environment" (Kephart, 1968, p. 20), how to contact it and to control this contact. He learns to control bodily experiences by repeated actions providing internally generated perceptual information from muscles and joints. Yet as he thrashes about in the crib, there is little consistency in his behavior. He does not appear to be attending to the kinesthetic information. But with increasing skill and control, these data become systematized and coordinated.

Compare the movement of the infant's arm with the initial movements of the control stick in the orbital condition of weightlessness. Like the infant's actions, they had no meaningful effect. When, however, the craft stopped orbiting and entered the earth's atmosphere and gravitational field, it was possible for the motor feedback from manipulations of the control to be correlated with other, consistent patterns of bodily sensation. The differential pattern of sensations from the right or left side of the body related to the motor activity of moving the control stick to the right and left, thereby tilting the craft, can be compared with the earliest learning of *laterality,* an internal sense of sidedness. An internal system of coordinates, or body schema, is beginning to develop. The body schema will provide a frame of reference from which the child will explore the world.

MOTOR-PERCEPTUAL STAGE

During the motor stage, patterns of visual and auditory information are received through the eyes and ears. Yet only gradually do the perceptual patterns stemming from environmental input become associated with the mass of at least partially systematized motor-kinesthetic information. At this point the visual and auditory inputs can begin to take on meaning through the *matching* of perceptual data to motor data. In order for such matching to occur, however, there must be consistency in both motor and perceptual input.

Consistency of perceptual information from the environment is obtained through voluntary control of the eyes — by pointing them toward the source of information which interests us. Since the infant has poor control over his eyes he must depend on guidance from the hand which by now is under voluntary control. The child moves the hand and teaches the eye to follow. Eye-hand control develops. In this way, "the hand leads the eye and provides the control for the perceptual-motor exploration" (Kephart, 1968, p. 24). Gradually, the eye begins to receive the same information as the hand; turning one's eyes to the right becomes equivalent to reaching to the right. Through such a translation process *directionality* begins to emerge. At this stage, motor information is the standard of reference.

During the motor phase and through most of the motor-perceptual stage, the infant continues to receive visual information, but it is essentially meaningless. Kephart speculates that it consists of little more than a vague differentiation of figure and ground. The infant's mother may be perceived as a kind of undetailed, amorphous "blob," crudely differentiated from the background of the room in which she stands.

The most basic of all figure-ground relationships is that of kinesthetic figure-ground, requisite for the later acquisition of visual figure-ground (Kephart, 1969a, p. 20). The infant must learn to distinguish the pattern of kinesthetic feedback stemming from his voluntary movements from the general background of kinesthetic feedback arising from muscles not specifically involved in the action.

PERCEPTUAL-MOTOR STAGE

One can explore an object much more rapidly and efficiently with the eyes than with the hand, and can gather a much greater quantity of information. For this reason, the eye soon takes the lead in environmental exploration. The hand is relegated to confirming or supplementing visual information. Since directionality is now established, perceptual information has attained consistency. Consequently, perception can take the lead in the perceptual-motor match.

In terms of the progression of the space flight, we have analogously proceeded to the definite establishment of a coordinate system developing out of the kinesthetic-tactual-vestibular match (control stick movements v. differential patterns of bodily sensation). The removal of the opaque cover and the view of the ill-defined horizon correspond to awareness of visual input which is, as yet, meaningless. Further manipulations of the control stick reveal correlative changes in the visual input. Visual information gradually takes on significance when fed into the previously established bodily coordinate system. The latter, however, still predominates. The hand moves the controls and the experience of the eye vis-à-vis the movement of the horizon follows. The two channels of information are in agreement. A specific control movement results in a predictable tilt of the line. Yet there is still no awareness of an "out there." For all you know, the visual display could be coming directly from the surface of the window. Directionality is developing, but visual information still lacks practical significance relative to environmental adjustment.

PERCEPTUAL STAGE

Upon attaining the perceptual stage the child can begin to make discriminations and comparisons between objects in the environment, independent of motor involvement. Yet even in the absence of a motor act, meaningful visual perception is still dependent upon a prior established kinesthetic frame of reference. This fact seems contradicted by the child who has failed to achieve integration at the perceptual-motor stage or earlier and still performs many perceptual tasks with seeming adequacy. For example, he can select an accurate match for complicated geometric designs from a series including only slightly different alternatives. Yet appreciation of any design as an organized whole, or gestalt, is first achieved through motor activity. Without such a foundation, visual perception must remain fragmentary. As indicated in the previous example of the jigsaw puzzle, the perceptually deficient individual performs on a piecemeal basis. He uses only a part of the available perceptual information to complete the task. The figure or gestalt, which is a function of an *organization* of the individual elements and is greater than the sum of these elements, is missing. Here is a lower-level perceptual process, normal at an earlier stage, which may now pass for a mature one.

Copying tasks often reveal perceptual difficulties successfully concealed in matching procedure. For example, a child, able to select the duplicate of a particular triangle from a series of variations on the original, may be unable to copy it due to a lack of *sequence*. Sequencing is the *ordering of events in time*. It is a *motor-temporal system* which must be "projected onto outside events" (Kephart, 1964, p. 205). Copying the triangle is spatial, but it is also temporal and sequential. It gradually evolves, line by line. On a higher level, sequencing is involved in the systematic progression of logical reasoning.

Sequencing is, in turn, based on fundamental motor-temporal capacities. The most basic of these is *synchrony*, which is observed "when muscles move in concert," and *rhythm*, which occurs "when muscles move alternately or recurrently" (Kephart, 1964, p. 205).

Beginning with the perceptual stage, *language* assumes an important functional role. For example, the most efficient way to summarize the seemingly endless variations of objects on which to place things is through the single word "table." Through the medium of that single word one summarizes the perceptual characteristics which refer to all such objects.

PERCEPTUAL-CONCEPTUAL STAGE

The great advantage inherent in perceiving the world in terms of wholes or gestalts lies in its efficacy as a means of organizing information. We immediately recognize a square as such and do not have to identify it by a laborious counting of sides and angles; "squareness" is identifiable at a glance. Similarly, a major improvement in information processing occurs when the child attains the perceptual-conceptual stage. At this stage, elements consist of single gestalts, such as tables of various shapes, sizes and colors. The child's concept of "table" is an abstraction arising from the common properties of all tables previously perceived. When the child is asked to define a table, he does not describe a specific one; rather, he is able to define it in terms of the properties common to all tables. This entails the ability to integrate many gestalts.

In terms of perceptual development, the mythical space trip has progressed to a level corresponding to events transpiring during the successive appearances of the semi-transparent and the completely transparent windows. Thus, there was the definite establishment of an external frame of reference in which increasingly distinctive *details* were drawn from a relatively homogeneous background. The repetitive succession of such details indicated the presence of some kind of organized whole (a planet), but the nature of the whole remained undetermined. Finally, with the full attainment of details and their organzation, the whole was recognized for what it was — the earth, which was then conceptualized as one planet in a system of planets.

CONCEPTUAL STAGE

At this stage, the child's concept comes to involve an increasingly broader integration of present and past perceptual information. As the breadth of concepts broadens, so also does the child's efficiency in dealing with conceptual problems.

Since the perceptual stage, the contribution of language has become increasingly important. The word "table" summarizes the characteristics of all tables without the individual's having to recount their common perceptual properties. So also does the still more abstract word "furniture" refer to the integration of a series of such individual abstractions. Thinking has progressed still further from its perceptual and motor referents.

Just as it is possible to simulate a satisfactory perceptual performance in a matching task without first having established an adequate foundation at the perceptual-motor level, so also is it possible to simulate conceptual functioning without an adequate perceptual-conceptual base. Although the child may read well and be able to manipulate symbols with facility, his symbols lack a grounding in earlier motor behavior. The *perceptually* arrested child has difficulty with copying and drawing; the *conceptually* arrested child fails when he tries to apply what he has read in a practical situation.

CONCEPTUAL-PERCEPTUAL STAGE

By now, conceptual development has proceeded to the point that it dominates the act of perception. Children at the detail level of perceptual development deal with only a fragmentary part of the whole and never appreciate it as an organized totality. In normal development the child begins systematically to explore all features of the whole and to integrate them. At the conceptual-perceptual level, the individual may short-cut the perceptual process, and seemingly revert to dealing with no more than a few elements. However, in actuality, he fills in the gaps and perceptually constructs the organized whole with no more than a sampling of its parts. His ability to synthesize has developed to an advanced level. Similarily, he is able to make predictions about events by sampling relevant information prior to the event's actual occurrence.

The two preceding stages correspond to the final stages of the space flight. Thus, when faced with the necessity of landing the craft you had to consider the relationships among detailed features of the terrain. Finally, you considered the significant possibilities that transcended the view below and you began making predictions regarding the final touchdown.

PRINCIPLES OF REMEDIATION

The child with a learning disorder suffers a pervasive "interference with the process of integration" (Kephart, 1968, p. 43). [1] This breakdown of integration is reflected in poorly coordinated motor responses. Fragmentation is also noted in perceptual functioning, as in the tendency to deal with elements rather than organized wholes. Corresponding disruptions of process are detectable in the child's conceptual functioning. According to Kephart: [1]

> Throughout all his behavior, this child gives the impression that his world and his responses to it exist in bits and pieces with little connection between them, rather than in clusters of similar items held together in well-knit wholes. He continues to respond to items rather than to situations and his behaviors are specific skills rather than adaptive responses.
>
> . . . think of this breakdown of integration as a failure in the development of generalizations. (p. 43)

Treatment and remediation at whatever level of developmental arrest involves the establishment of generalization. Although the specifics vary, the general treatment strategy is the same at all levels; it "requires the simultaneous awareness of a large number of related items and the relationships between these items" (Kephart, 1968, p. 44). The items vary according to the developmental level under consideration — they may be anything from motor to conceptual.

With the normal child, generalization occurs automatically, sometimes in spite of the teacher's efforts to the contrary. The normal school-age child cannot help but perceive a square as an organized whole. It is a compelling perceptual impression. In contrast, the disabled learner must be painstakingly taught to perceive in this fashion. He can seldom attain form perception on his own. Still worse, he learns to mask his deficiency by compensatory procedures that he is loathe to abandon, because they are at least partially workable.

The first step in the development of a generalization is the *acquisition of an initial datum* which Kephart describes as follows:

> This initial datum is an isolated fact, if we are dealing with a conceptual generalization; it is a perceptual element, if we are dealing with a perceptual generalization; and it is an isolated motor skill, if we are dealing with a motor generalization.
>
> The acquisition of such an isolated datum appears not to be a complex neurological process. Such data can be acquired by a rote process which appears not to involve large masses of neural tissue at one time. It rather appears to depend upon the establishment of a relatively simple circuit from a specific stimulus to a specific response. (1968, p. 47)

The initial datum is acquired as easily by the child with a learning disorder as by the normal child. It is in the *elaboration of the initial datum,* the second phase of generalization development, where the disabled learner first encounters trouble. The normal child elaborates the initial datum by *spontaneously varying* his performance; children with learning disorders do not. For example, in the course of rail-walking, a normal child will vary his posture, walk sideways and then backward, etc. Such variations prevent boredom and present a continuing challenge. In contrast, the disabled learner is likely to avoid all such variation and to forego experimentation in favor of a single set procedure. Consequently, appropriate variations must be provided for him. These variations have to be carefully graded — on the walking board a minor shift of balance may cause the child to lose his balance completely and fall off the board.

Just as concepts are no better than their perceptual and motor-kinesthetic referents, so also do conceptual generalizations rest on a foundation of motor generalizations. The primary responsibility of the special education teacher is to supply many variations which the child lacks the creativity to supply for himself. This is more easily said than done. The teacher, from the perspective of normality, finds it difficult to conceive of meaningful variations that are small enough to be absorbed by the child. What she may interpret as a minor variation, he may experience as a completely new task.

Kephart accounts for the disruption of the process of elaboration in terms of Hebb's brain model. Within this context, malfunctioning of a single neural unit results in a disruption that fans out in non-linear fashion and influences many units. Because of this, experiences associated almost automatically in an intact individual remain separate and distinctively different for the neurologically damaged. What for the teacher is simply a variation on a single activity requiring only a minor adaptation of performance, he may experience as an entirely new task. Repeated demands for what the child experiences as major adaptations generates resistance manifested either in rigidity or frustration.

In rigidity, the child prefers to perform an activity over and over again in the same old way. Unlike a normal child, he does not become bored. Kephart assumes that rigidity has, in part, a neurological basis. Another contributing factor is the fear of failure. In any event, the teacher must carefully but firmly press for a performance. Once the rigidity is broken the child responds as if freed from an invisible restraint.

While the rigid child's resistance is specifically focused on the task, the frustrated child's resistance is diffuse, often encompassing the entire situation, including the teacher. With frustration it is necessary to reduce, rather than increase, the demands of the situation as pressure results in further disorganization. The task should be simplified rather than merely altered.

The third phase in the development of generalization is concerned with the *integration of elaborations*.

> Just as the elaboration of the initial datum was facilitated by variation in the information presented to the child, so integration is furthered by the presentation of the same information in different ways. This latter process has been called *redundancy*. Such redundancy involves the simultaneous presentation of identical information in different ways. In such a process, the information is held constant and its presentation is varied. This constancy of the information serves to emphasize the similarity of experience and hence the relationship or integration of experiences. (Kephart, 1968, p. 66)

Redundancy is achieved by presenting information through different sense avenues (visual, auditory, and tactual-kinesthetic). Although various educational techniques have incorporated multi-sensory approaches, they are often incorrectly applied. For redundancy to work one must present the *same* information *simultaneously* through different sense modalities. Unfortunately, the child may be taught reading visually and writing kinesthetically but neither subject through a visual-kinesthetic approach. Too often, in actual practice, he may receive multi-channel information simultaneously — but not the same information; or he may be exposed to the same information — but at different points in time, e.g., the child traces a form with his finger while looking out the window. It may also happen that while redundancy is achieved, it is applied too early; that is, before the child has acquired the necessary elaborations of the initial data.

The type of element involved in the teaching of generalization varies with the developmental stage. Since much has already been written on the subject of conceptual generalization, Kephart focuses more on the lower levels. If the child has not achieved generalization at the perceptual level, form and figure-ground perception will be weak. For this child, learning to read presents special difficulties. Since he discriminates on the basis of perceptual elements — lines and angles — rather than of organized wholes, he is ill-equipped to deal with the complicated perceptual task of learning how to read. At the "look and say" level of reading instruction he may get by with his inadequate process (Kephart, 1960, p. 85). He identifies words by characteristic elements; for example, the word $\boxed{\text{toot}}$ sticks up at both its beginning and its ending. However, when he is later required to analyze words he lacks the necessary integrative process. He is left with a jumble of pieces or elements. In effect, he cannot see the forest for the trees.

Walking is to locomotion at the motor level, as lines and angles are to form perception at the perceptual level. Walking is a specific skill; locomotion is a motor generalization. When the child has acquired locomotion he can adapt a variety of movement techniques — walking, running, crawling — to the requirements of the situation. He attends to the purpose of the movement without having to be concerned with executing it. He is free to engage in "systematic motor exploration" of the environment with "a motor activity which is sufficiently flexible that it can be controlled with only a monitoring function" (Kephart, 1960, p. 75). He is free to respond and, through such exploration, he perceptually organizes the environment. In the course of motor training the development of specific skills should be avoided. The child may become proficient at a circumscribed performance, (e.g., writing his name) but when the same letters are contained in other words, he cannot execute them. Such a "splinter skill" remains at the level of an element rather than a generalization.

NOTES

[1] N. C. Kephart, *Learning Disability: An Educational Adventure* (West Lafayette, Indiana: Kappa Delta Pi Press, 1968). All quotations from this book are used by permission of the publisher and Kappa Delta Pi, an Honor Society in Education.

chapter 6

Kephart's Program—An Evaluation of Theory and Practical Application

An exhaustive evaluation of Kephart's system will not be undertaken in this chapter. Rather, the focus is on gaining a perspective of his work through a detailed examination of several theoretical and research issues. For example, to clarify where Kephart's cognitive approach stands vis-á-vis behavior therapy, his work is compared with studies by Macpherson and Patterson. In the Kephart-Macpherson comparison, it is clear that both (taking Jacobson's progressive relaxation program as a point of departure) independently developed almost identical treatment methodologies. It is in the subtleties of Kephart's program, expressed in the pervasive influence of the central theme of balance, that we detect the distinctive influence of his theory. In the Kephart-Patterson comparison there is at least a limited overlap in treatment goals; that is, bringing hyperactivity under control. But, in both their methodologies and their underlying treament philosophies, Kephart's and Patterson's approaches are fundamentally different. With a new technique, Kephart directly attacks the hyperactivity problem; Patterson focuses upon and selectively reinforces instances of quiescent behaviors with the aim of increasing their frequency and duration. Although it is only Patterson who can offer hard experimental data, both men apparently succeed in controlling hyperactivity. But, as an illustration of a point made by Helson (1969) about theoretical differences, there is a marked discrepancy in terms of *where* they end up. Patterson's subject is seated quietly in the classroom with eyes directed at the printed page. Kephart's subject is outside the classroom, and reading may not even be under consideration.

Attention is given to the values and potential pitfalls involved in the use of hypothetical constructs, such as body image. This discussion includes the all-important problem of obtaining the appropriate measurements to evaluate such a construct. While the sampling of studies is limited and selective, it should serve to explain key methodological issues. And although the phi-phenomenon may be given more attention than it deserves, the discussion will, hopefully, bring to light some of the complexities and subtleties involved in the field of perceptual measurement. It should also clarify some intriguing aspects of Kephart's theory, such as that, under some conditions, brain-injured, presumably perceptually deficient individuals should have *keener* than normal discrimination abilities.

There will be notable omissions. For example, the work of House & Zeaman will be given only a passing reference. Here the writer makes what is frankly a value judgment — that the Russian work on the orienting-exploratory reaction holds much greater promise for a productive application in the training of atypical children than does the somewhat related work of House & Zeaman.

The writer will include material ordinarily omitted. Basic to the divisiveness, and even animosity, existing between cognitive theorists, such as Kephart, and the behavior therapy group, including the Skinnerians, is a series of emotionally charged, existential issues such as the question of purpose. An attempt will be made to reconcile these points of view and show that the positions are less contradictory than they may first appear.

Finally, it should be made clear that, while Kephart's approach will be reinterpreted in terms of both operant conditioning and the current Russian position, it is not the writer's intent to exclude Kephart's own theoretical system. For example, in the previous chapter on escape-avoidance conditioning it was *not* implied that Kephart's program is reducible to the escape-avoidance model. The point is that the model enabled us to make a connection, to find a common meeting ground for seemingly mutually exclusive points of view. If it is possible to reveal a thread of continuity where none seems to exist, the effort is worthwhile. Whatever may be the scientific pitfalls of hypothetico-deductive systems, Kephart's theory, as he has applied it, has been a creative instrument. For Russian or Skinnerian alike, or, for that matter, for anyone interested in the training of controlled movements, Kephart's work on kinesthetic figure-ground should be required reading. Far from placing Kephart in a procrustean bed of operant theory, an important objective is to reveal his uniqueness. In the final analysis, regarding theories, the writer subscribes to the position taken by Claude Bernard:

The theories which embody our scientific ideas as a whole are, of course, indispensable as representation of science. They should also serve as a basis for new ideas. But as these theories and ideas are by no means immutable truth, one must always be ready to abandon them, to alter them or to exchange them as soon as they cease to represent the truth. In a word, we must alter theory to adapt it to nature, but not nature to adapt it to theory. (1957, p. 39)

It is hoped that the following discussion will promote that sense of scientific spirit eloquently described by Bernard more than a century ago.

The truly scientific spirit, then, should make us modest and kindly. We really know very little, and we are all fallible when facing the immense difficulties presented by investigation of natural phenomena. The best thing, then, for us to do is to unite our efforts, instead of dividing them and nullifying them by personal disputes. In a word, the man of science wishing to find truth must keep his mind free. . . . (*ibid.*)

SOME ASPECTS OF THEORY

THE MOTOR BASIS OF PERCEPTUAL DEVELOPMENT AND THERAPEUTIC PROGRAMMING

Kephart's theory rests on the assumption that perception and cognition, including the capacity for abstraction, ultimately develop from a motor base. Although the necessary differentiated motor development may vary from person to person, especially among the brain-injured, without the necessary motor elaborations and generalizations, intellectual growth will be impeded and distorted. Kephart would agree with Piaget (1952) that the earliest manifestations of intelligent behavior are motor in nature and that they predate the appearance of language.

Kephart is primarily concerned with strategies of information processing. He claims that at the earlier levels of development there is a significant motor component in these strategies. As the child grows older, information is acquired mainly through the exteroceptors (eyes and ears). But remedial treatment for the older, slow learning child requires the appropriate therapeutic reintroduction of the motor component. Even for the normal child, concepts are ultimately anchored in motor experience. What, then, is the evidence for the primacy of a motor component in strategies of information acquisition at the earlier developmental levels?

The question can readily be recast in terms of the relative significance of S^Ds obtained through motor activity. For example, in the tradition of Seguin, Kephart uses templates at the earliest stages of his training program for the appreciation of form (Kephart, 1960). The child runs his finger around the edge of the template following the movement with his eyes. Meanwhile, he counts angles and attaches an appropriate verbal label when the tracing is completed. The training is of an abstract nature; it involves the identification of forms, such as squares, triangles, and diamonds, rather than such practical objects in the environment as toy cars and houses. Yet it can be described as a method for a coordinated acquisition of visual and kinesthetic S^Ds for what will eventually become a purely visual discrimination.

Some of the strongest support for Kephart's position comes from the Russians. At times, the Russian theoretical position so closely resembles Kephart's that, with but a few changes in terminology, certain quotations might readily be attributed to Kephart himself.[1] Note, for example, the developmental sequence outlined by Zaporozhets in his description of an experiment by Ruzskaya.

> In the first stages, the function of examining and modeling could only be performed with a palping hand while the eyes played an auxiliary role, that of tracing the movements of the hand. But later the eye became able to solve independently such problems of perception by tracing the outline of the figure as had been done by the palping hand. Very interesting transitional forms could also be observed when the child could differentiate figures visually but his eye movements were accompanied by some movements of the hand modeling the form of the object at a distance, thus organizing and correcting the processes of the visual examination of the object.
>
> Later the children passed to purely visual orientation. In the first stages the movements of the eye were very extended (Zinchenko) and the child visually traced the whole outline of the figure perceived, modeling its peculiarities in detail. In the last stages of the formation of perceptive processes (after the child was trained for a long time in recognizing and discriminating figures of a certain kind), exploratory movements of the eye became reduced consistently, concentrating on the separate, most informative features of the object. It was at this stage that the highest form of internalization of perceptive process was achieved. On the basis of earlier external models that were created with the help of movements of the hand or eye, for example, and were repeatedly compared with the object and corrected according to its features, there was formed at last an internal model — a constant and orthoscopic perceptive image. . . .

> Now, without any extended exploratory operations, one short glance at the object, the distinguishing of some characteristic feature, can signal into action the whole internal model and thus lead to the immediate grasping of the properties of the perceived object. (Zaporozhets, 1965, pp. 99-100) *

The above account corresponds perfectly with Kephart's model of the functional interdependence of tactual-kinesthetic and visual perceptual development; the training program parallels his use of templates in training form perception (see Kephart, 1960, pp. 185-90). The reference to training the child to trace the outline of the figure with his hand can be correlated with observations made by Gellerman (1933) in his classic comparative study on form discrimination learning. Especially significant was the following:

> This "tracing" behavior of the chimpanzees appeared entirely spontaneously. It occurred without possibility of human suggestion and imitation of human action. This type of response has never been observed before in infra-human primates. In the opinion of the writer the "tracing" behavior had definite symbolic significance and was of fundamental importance. (Gellerman, 1933, p. 33)

Investigatory tracing behavior can be related to Russian research on the development of perception in the preschool child[2] which centers around the study of *orienting-exploratory movements.*[3] For example, Zaporozhets (1965) reported a study by Zinchenko and Ruzskaya on the development of pre-schoolers' "acquaintance actions" which revealed transitional stages varying from the three-year-old's catching movements, to the six-year-old's tracing the whole outline of the figure with fingertips. The more mature forms of acquaintance actions were correlated with the increasing accuracy of visual identification of objects explored tactually. Children with immature acquaintance actions, when taught the more mature approach, showed a corresponding improvement in visual identification. In another study (Zaporozhets, 1965), the same experimenters had pre-schoolers familiarize themselves, in the following ways, with flat wooden figures of irregular forms: (a) by looking at them only; (b) by touching them only; (c) both by looking at them and by touching them; and (d) by inserting them into the corresponding recesses in a board

---

*A. V. Zaporozhets, The Development of Perception in the Preschool Child, in P. H. Mussen (ed.), *European Research in Cognitive Development,* Monographs of the Society for Research in Child Development, 1965, 30(2), no. 100, 82-101. All quotations from this work are used with permission of the publisher.

(practical manipulation). When later asked to identify the figures from a group of unknown figures, three- to four-year-olds who performed practical manipulations made the fewest identification errors. The advantage of practical manipulation over "looking only" noted at the three- to four-year-old level (15.4% versus 50% errors) disappeared by ages five to six (both 0 errors).

What ties the Russian program still closer to that of Kephart's is their developmental research on the role of eye movements in perceptual functioning. Zaporozhets (1965, p. 86) described how Zinchenko and Ruzskaya filmed the eye movements of children while they examined objects they were later to identify from a group of objects. The development of their visual perceiving actions was analogous to the previously described manual acquaintance actions. The three- and four-year-olds' eye movements were completely within the figure. The eye movements of the four- and five-year-olds were also confined mainly to the figure, but the movements increased in frequency. While they still did not trace the outline, there were movements seemingly oriented to the size and length of the figure. Also there were "groups of fixing points . . . related to the most specific features of the object" (*ibid.,* p. 87). By the age of five or six, children began ocularly tracing the figure's outline but they usually looked at only one specific part, ignoring the rest. The eye movements of six- to seven-year-old children, however, ". . . followed . . . the outline of the figure, as if reproducing or modeling its form" (*ibid.,* p. 88). While three- and four-year-olds identified only 50% of the figures they originally examined, the six- and seven-year-olds with the *active* method of examination, correctly identified all of them. Further, experiments by Boguslavskaya show that they could also "solve more difficult sensory problems connected with adequate reproduction of perceived figures in the process of drawing, constructing, modeling, etc." (*ibid.*).

The interaction between visual and motor acquaintance actions was studied by Sokhina who used "concrete modeling . . . in teaching children to analyze visually a complex form while constructing it according to a given model" (Zaporozhets, 1965, p. 92). Simple geometric models were cut out of solid black cardboard, e.g., two contiguous houses of different heights. Parts necessary to reproduce the model (triangles and squares) were mixed with such various inappropriate parts as quarter circles, and placed below it. The whole display was placed under glass and children, four to seven years of age, were instructed to select the elements necessary to construct a replica of the model. Each child was then given the elements he had selected and asked to construct the replica. After several successive failures, the child was given white paper duplicates of the correct elements which he then placed over the model. In the process of correctly superimposing these elements on the model the child learned to make a correct visual analysis of the task. Subsequently, most children could correctly designate the necessary constituent elements without this preliminary exercise in "concrete modeling." According to Zaporozhets, sensory training such as this provides "a basis in sense perception for some of the simplest, most basic conceptual operations" (1969, p. 118).

The Russian studies reflect the transition from *executive* movements, whereby the child "fixes" the object for the purpose of observation, to *modeling* movements, whereby he explores the object and thereby forms a corresponding perception. Seguin's work on the development of prehension takes us through a similar developmental sequence. Yet Seguin also provides a step *prior* to the development of executive movements — to the training of the "idiot hand" of a child who resists all attempts at developing purposeful manipulation. Seguin, with his tremendous practical understanding of what is required to get the most primitively functioning child actively to contact the environment, tells what to do with children who do not naturally develop even executive movements (see page 90).

But where does Kephart fit into all of this? The answer is that he provides the basis for manual and ocular orienting-exploratory movements through prior training on the gross motor level. In much the same fashion as did Pryor (1969) in her work with porpoises, Kephart has focused on the development of spontaneity by means of programs specifically introducing the factor of motor variability. But motor variability in the form of manual and ocular exploration of objects constitutes the necessary basis for the development of a more purely visual perception. To the extent that Kephart's gross motor variability training transfers to the sphere of such processes, we see a continuity and therapeutic complimentarity between gross motor training and orienting-exploratory behavior.[4] Though this assertion must remain tentative pending experimental verification, the expectation of transfer of training seems quite reasonable.

For this writer, Russian theory regarding the transition between manual exploration and visual perception is more immediately understandable than is Kephart's. This is because the Russians proceed more directly, in an empirical sense, from one stage to the next. Thus, the relationship between tactual-kinesthetic and purely visual investigatory actions seems much more direct than that between laterality and form perception. And, note that both the tactual-kinesthetic and visual manifestations are recorded in terms of observable events, while the laterality and body schema events must be inferred.

Whatever the difficulties with Kephart's theory, there is no denying the outstanding nature of his contributions regarding therapeutic methodology. For example, in comparing Ruzskaya's and Kephart's procedures for teaching perception of simple forms, it will be noted that the latter's procedure was far more elaborate and that it provided for a carefully engineered fading of both tactual-kinesthetic and visual cues. Kephart has an elaborate program for training form perception that entails practical manipulation in the construction of match stick forms, pegboard designs, and such (Kephart, 1960, pp. 259-75). Similarly, his program for teaching counting involves transfer of stimulus control from tactile-auditory experiences to totally visual or auditory perception (Ebersole, Kephart & Ebersole, 1968). Kephart sees this transfer as a transitional step toward abstract thinking apparently in much the same way as does Zaporozhets.

Conceptually, the works of Seguin, Kephart and the Russians all converge in the clincal example of Itard's attempts to teach Victor to distinguish between knife and razor. Up to that point, Itard had pursued a program of sensory education confined completely to what the Russians would describe as artificial, "abstract" forms. It was only with the introduction of practical manipulation that Victor truly comprehended what he read. A man with lesser clinical sensitivity than Itard's might have failed completely to recognize the nature of Victor's conceptual limitations. The subtle nature of this problem is explained by Strauss & Kephart*:

> It is very difficult to test the adequacy of the concepts which a child understands by a given word. His impression derived from the word is his alone; we can never know exactly what the nature of this impression is. The only clues which we can get are through the use of other words which are themselves open to the same difficulties as the word which we are examining. We never know how much of the meaning of a word used by another is the exact meaning which the other had in mind and how much is meaning read into his word by us. If he can use the word in a fashion which permits us to read meaning into it, we assume that he himself had in mind the same meaning. His meaning, however, might be much more restricted than ours and we would not be aware of this fact. Therefore, the proper use of language in itself may not indicate the adequate use of concepts even though language is necessary to the formation of concepts.
>
> It is probable that the high language performance of many brain-injured children may be explained in somewhat that fashion. Illustrations abound of instances where their language ability breaks down in situations where they are required to manipulate concepts prior to use in language. An eleven year old brain-injured boy who had a

*A. A. Strauss and N. C. Kephart, *Psychopathology and Education of the Brain-Injured Child. Vol. II: Progress in Theory and Clinic.* New York: Grune and Stratton, 1955. All quotations from this book are used by permission of the publisher.

Wechsler verbal I.Q. of 140 was told the story of the bird who saw a bee drowning in a stream. He flew down and picked the bee out of the water and set him free. Later the bee saw a hunter taking aim at the bird. He flew to the hunter and stung him on the hand. When the boy was asked what was the meaning of this story he replied, "The hunter ran out of the woods." Here was a child who performed very well in the language area, as his score on the verbal test indicated, but who, when he was required to manipulate concepts and appreciate the relationships which we usually think of language as dealing with, fell down completely. Numerous other illustrations lead us to feel that in many cases the language development displayed by these children does not adequately reflect their ability to deal with the concept which the language symbolizes.

In the second place, we have pointed out that the development of language in the child permits him to gain perceptual experience vicariously. He can augment his poor perception by accepting in its stead the perceptions of other people conveyed to him through the medium of language. It would, therefore, be possible to conceive of an individual who built himself a perceptual world which was only in part his own and in part given him by others. He might, therefore, be able to develop necessary concepts by using in effect other people's perceptions where his own are inadequate.

In the third place, we can display a rather remarkable language facility by using language which we hear or read and repeating it in a rather parrot-like fashion. Many a college student has a facility for listening to a passage and returning it on an examination in a rote memory fashion without having the slightest idea of what the passage means. It is possible that much of the language of the brain-injured child can fall in this category. If he has difficulty in performance activities, he has little left but language. It might be expected that he would attempt to impress those around him through the use of language. The rote memory use of what he has heard other people saying would be an easy way to achieve this end.[5] (pp. 209-10)

Following the Skinnerian model of programmed instruction, O. K. Moore (1963) developed an elaborately programmed electric typewriter. With this device he has taught three-year-olds to read. Yet, what if it had been applied to the above-mentioned brain-injured boy? It seems possible that he might have learned to read, but without an adequate conceptual basis.

An intriguing recapitulation of Kephart's description of the normal developmental process occurs in human adults adapting themselves to the long-term wearing of distorting prisms or lenses. One aspect of this work, conducted by Ivo Kohler at Innsbruck, is summarized by Werner as follows:

First, they learn to master space on a sensorimotor level; that is, they are able to move about without error. But, though they may be able to ride a bicycle quite skillfully, the visual world as such may, at this stage, still be extremely confused, upside down, or crooked. The further development toward visual adaption shows some remarkable features: the objects seem to fall into two classes, things-of-action and purely visual things. The observer conquers first the things-of-action and only later purely visual things. For instance, observers wearing prisms which invert left and right can see an object already in correct position if it is part of their own actions, but incorrectly — that is, reversed — when purely visually grasped. In a fencing situation, a subject sees his own sword correctly pointing toward the opponent, but at a moment of rest it becomes visually inverted, pointing toward himself. By the same token, a little later in development any object-of-action, such as a chair or a screwdriver, whether it is actually handled or not, is correctly transformed, whereas purely visual objects, such as pictures or printed words, remain reversed. Only at a last stage the differences disappear, and complete transformation of the visual world is achieved. (1957, pp. 129-30)

PERCEPTION AND CONCEPTION

Kephart deals extensively with the sensory aspect of visual perception. He feels that the infant's earliest perceptions are vague and ill-defined. This notion is contradicted by the work of Fantz (1961) who has provided evidence that even newborns have pattern-vision capacities. Kephart[6] argues that Fantz's claim may stem from a misinterpretation of the significance of the visual fixations on which his technique is based. It is certain, however, that Fantz has challenged the validity of Kephart's claim that the newborn sees only ill-defined blobs.

The experimental evaluation of Kephart's assumptions regarding perceptual development entails some challenging measurement problems; for example, the inability to copy a form does not necessarily demonstrate impaired sensory perception. An interesting example of an attempt to assess the intactness of the sensory aspect of form perception independently from its praxic aspects can be found in the work of Bortner & Birch (1960) with brain-damaged adults. These authors criticized Wechsler's claim that his block design test involves the ability to perceive and to analyze forms. They noted, ". . . it is possible that difficulties in block design reproduction may be more sensitive indicators of apraxia than of explicit perceptual disorganization. . . . It would follow that failures in block design reproduction often be unaccompanied by difficulties in the appropriate perception of the presented model" (Bortner & Birch, 1960, p. 49). They tested this hypothesis by administering the Wechsler block design test in standard fashion requiring the subject to reproduce designs with as many as twelve varicolored blocks. An alternative procedure required the subject to select from actual block models, previously assembled, the one which correctly matched that model depicted on the design card. The results indicated that, in 81% of the cases of failure to construct the design, the patients were nonetheless able to designate a correct reproduction. This finding lent support to the notion of "functionally autonomous" perceptual and perceptual-motor (or action) systems.

Kephart's theory implies that brain damage would precipitate regression to a lower level of perceptual functioning. The Bortner & Birch study thus strikes a blow at Strauss and Kephart's (1955) assumption that form perception is disrupted in brain-injured individuals. Yet Kephart has an ingenious way of interpreting such data that could preserve the notion of Bortner & Birch's brain-damaged subjects' having operated with a lower-level perceptual process. Thus, Kephart described how a child might correctly place a triangular block into its appropriate formboard recess by referring solely to a single element, the apex angle, without seeing or attending to the rest of the figure (Kephart, 1960). Theoretically, Bortner's and Birch's patients could have discriminated variations on the correct block design by responding to a single rotated block or element while ignoring the form of the total design. Therefore, Bortner and Birch failed to rule out the alternative interpretation that, while their brain-damaged subjects correctly performed form discrimination (matching) tasks, they did not necessarily discriminate *by means of* form.

A Kephart-type interpretation of the above block design study, with its phenomenological framework, presents an unusually challenging problem in research methodology. As Bortner & Birch demonstrated, the motor factor should be eliminated from tests designed to measure the sensory aspect of visual perception. This automatically rules out most of the available instruments, including the time-honored Bender-Gestalt. As already indicated, purely visual matching tasks are also open to criticism on the grounds that a seemingly adequate performance could be effected by means of a low-level perceptual process. Other complicating factors intrude such as those of motivation and attention. While the latter can be largely controlled through techniques developed in the context of operant conditioning, operant techniques have the disadvantage of requiring the subject to learn the discrimination procedure as the basis for later discrimination testing, with a consequent contamination of results. With these limitations in mind, Trabasso & Bower (1968, p. 175) discussed the need for a "non-learning" testing procedure. Still another problem —

with forms as simple as circles and triangles, the available measurement techniques for subjects above mental age two are little more than tests of reaction time. Yet, according to Kephart's theory, older children and even some adults with above-average verbal intelligence may be deficient on such a level. This problem might be handled by presenting the forms at extremely short exposure intervals, under conditions of reduced illumination, depicted against distracting backgrounds, and so forth. But by obscuring the perceptual task, one diverges from the goal of directly measuring form perception. With infants, Fantz's fixation technique measures the infant's ability to discriminate between forms. But in much the same fashion as Kephart might have criticized Belmont's and Birch's work, Hershenson points out the limitation of fixation techniques as follows: "Newborns may respond to a portion of a form, for example, a border or an angle, rather than to the entire stimulus" (1967, p. 331). Ball approached this measurement problem through an application of the *phi-phenomenon.*[7]

The phi-phenomenon, or *apparent movement,* is at once a compelling and a universal phenomenon. It is so compelling, in fact, that most laymen are surprised when its true nature is revealed. Phi, of course, is the "motion" seen in motion pictures and television. What the viewer actually receives is a series of still pictures separated by intervals of darkness. Common experience tells us that we do not statically retain the image of a picture from one frame to the next — the result would be a blur. Rather, the interval is filled with a continuous movement as we are successively exposed to slightly but distinctly changing views of an event in progress. We cannot resist the perceptual experience of movement during the course of observing a motion picture. In fact, there is good evidence that it is mediated through lower brain centers.

An example of phi corresponding more closely to the present application can be found in the familiar neon sign depicting an arrow rhythmically moving back and forth. The arrow on the right is turned on and off. There is an interval of darkness followed by the illumination and extinction of the arrow on the left. As this cycle is repeated the arrow seemingly jumps the spatial gap, continuously oscillating back and forth. If, however, we sufficiently increased the rate of oscillation, the constantly moving arrow would stop moving and we would observe two arrows flickering on and off rapidly, while staying in place. If we then gradually reduced the rate of alternation, the point would be reached at which the two stationary arrows again formed a single moving arrow — this would be the subject's threshold for phi.

What if one of the arrows were turned around so that they pointed at each other? One result would be a delay in the development of oscillatory movement. The rate of alternation would have to be significantly lower for movement to occur than it would be for arrows pointing in the same direction. The difference in the two thresholds, measured in milliseconds of darkness interval between successive flashes, could then be used as a quantitative index of the discrimination of difference in *spatial orientation* of the arrows. The discontinuity introduced by a change in spatial orientation results in a significant change in threshold — it makes it harder to see phi. In fact, *any* change in one of the figures — brightness, form, color or size — produces the same effect. Thus, phi is a sensitive indicator of anything that disrupts perceptual continuity. It is this characteristic that makes it applicable to the present measurement problem.

With phi, measurement can be achieved without the examiner's referring to the forms of the two figures. This is done by beginning at a high alternation rate with two identical circles, flickering while in place, and awaiting the subject's own spontaneous report of fusion and movement as the examiner slowly reduces the alternation rate. Following this demonstration, the subject is instructed to continue reporting whenever the two lights come together and move back and forth. With this established, other forms can be substituted for the circle (e.g., paired square and triangle) without even referring to form. The subject continues reporting when the two lights come together.

While taking this test requires some pre-training there are important differences distinguishing it from the operant conditioning approach to discrimination measurement. One is that the procedure is mediated by an innate process that the individual spontaneously reports without prompting. The second is that when the subject reports fusion, the question of the motivational aspects of attending to the figures is automatically handled. In other words, if he can report movement, he is, of necessity, attending to the figures.

Consider these figures: □ ⌇ . According to Kephart, for the subject at the detail level of perceptual development, they are actually more distinctively *different* than they appear to a person with intact form perception. This is because, for the person with mature form perception, we have altered an element (side), but not the identity of the form as a square. But if you perceive only elements, the change from a straight-sided to a wavy-sided square must produce a major disruption of *continuity*. The defective perceiver would thus be expected to show a significantly *greater* discrepancy in thresholds for paired straight-sided squares, in contrast to paired straight-sided and wavy-sided squares, than would a normal perceiver. This, then, is a *quantitative* measure of what Kephart posits as a *qualitatively* different perceptual process; a process that, under some conditions, may lead to *keener* than normal discrimination.

The actual results were negative: both reading disability cases and matched normal achievers discriminated the two pairs to the same extent (Ball, 1968). On the basis of this finding and a series of related perceptual studies, Ball concluded that Kephart's assumptions regarding a pervasive lower-level perceptual process involving detail rather than form discrimination is incorrect. On the sensory level, at least, form perception was not disturbed in the clinical subjects.

In contradiction to Kephart, this writer believes that the organism may perceive a form in the gestalt sense of an organized whole that is greater than the sum of its parts and *still* employ only an isolated element during instrumental learning. Many years ago, Lashley (1938) found that rats, in learning a discrimination that enabled them to avoid a fall into a net, responded to isolated details while ignoring the totality of the form. This was an instrumental learning situation — actions based on correct discriminations yielded a rewarding consequence. In terms of the original discrimination, utilization of the detail cue paid off as well as would utilization of the entire form. In contrast to instrumental learning tasks, a unique feature of phi as a measurement technique is that the subject need not "use" the cues from the stimulus patterns. [8] Since he experiences them passively and spontaneously through the modality of an innate response, they automatically exert their influence in the most primitive and compelling sense. There results a relatively pure measure of perception, but this measure does not tell us how the subject would use aspects of such perceptual information during instrumental learning.

According to Trabasso & Bower, studies of cue utilization in normal adults indicate that reliance on partial information is not limited to animals. They noted the following:

> These findings indicate that a subject may notice, name, experience a cue in close temporal contiguity many times with the correct response, and still not learn the cue-response correlation. Noticing and using a cue for the auxiliary purpose of naming or identifying it is quite different from noticing, learning, and using a cue for classifying the stimulus patterns. The sampling theory is concerned with the probability that a cue will be used in the second sense, that it becomes effective in the focus used for classification. In the first sense or "noticing," most of our subjects probably notice and identify most of the available cues on many trials throughout the acquisition series; they reveal this by being able to recall at the end of training the values of the attributes. In the second sense of "noticing," however, our results suggest that the subject is learning and using for classification only a small number of attributes at any one time. (1968, pp. 85-86)

Kephart's theory of perceptual development may apply quite well to instrumental learning which includes learning to read. Perhaps the child who discriminates the word *toot* on the basis of detail cues does, in fact, perceive the stimuli as organized on the sensory level. The point is that he still misreads the word and is in as much difficulty as if he could only perceive part of it. More important, Kephart's remedial procedures appear effective in forcing the child out of a restricted pattern of inadequate, single cue utilization.

If Kephart's perceptual learning approach is recast into an instrumental learning framework, support can be found for his claims regarding the maladaptive consequences of detail-oriented, rather than generalization-oriented, perceptual training. A study by Ball & Campbell (1970) indicated that a detail-oriented Montessori procedure may indeed impair conceptual learning, i.e., acquisition of Piagetian conservation of volume.[9] Support for Kephart's assumptions regarding the progression from the detail to the constructive form level of perception is found in the previously mentioned Russian developmental studies. The developmental progression from an immature utilization of partial cues to a systematic exploration of contour was noted both in the tactual-kinesthetic and the visual spheres.

CONCEPTUAL-PERCEPTUAL STAGE

At the conceptual-perceptual stage, Kephart asserts, conceptual development has proceeded to the point that it dominates perception. Once again, he refers to perception from the standpoint of sensory organization, and, unlike his claims regarding the earlier stages of perceptual development, the phi technique provided evidence supporting the validity of this notion on the sensory level.

The experiment (Ball, 1964) stemmed from the work of Scheerer (1949), a Gestalt psychologist. He claimed that conceptual performance in a sorting task could affect the way in which forms were perceived on the sensory level. The task was based on the fact that a flat, wooden, diamond-shaped form could be sorted as readily with a triangle as with a square. Thus, a triangle, though a three-sided figure, resembles the upper half of a diamond. An unrotated square, though lacking the apex pointedness of a triangle, is nonetheless quadrilateral — like the diamond. Most borderline retarded (and also most normal) adults spontaneously sort the diamond with the triangle but quite readily respond to hints that it might be sorted with the square. After the shift is made, most subjects can readily provide the correct rationale, i.e., both are quadrilateral. Scheerer believed that subjects who correctly shifted with the aid of hints not only reconceptualized the problem, they actually *saw* the diamond as less triangular and more square-like. This is precisely what Kephart's theory would suggest. However, testing the validity of the claim is a tricky affair.

Once again, measurement involves the difficult problem of utilizing simple forms with adult subjects without obscuring or complicating the perceptual act. Not only that, but the same test must be administered both prior to and after conceptual sorting. This requires a subtle, indirect measurement of form perception so that the subject's performance is not biased by the intervening experience. Also, there must be no practice effect from the first to the second administration.

Specifically, the subject was tested for movement thresholds for paired diamond and square and paired diamond and triangle immediately before and immediately after the sorting task. Pre-test phi thresholds correlated with sorting behavior; the diamond and triangle combination was perceived in motion more readily than the paired diamond and square. Yet for those who, with hints, shifted to sorting diamond with square, the post-test threshold relationships were reversed. This is consistent with the notion that, at least temporarily, the diamond did appear more square-like. That the threshold change was not an artifact of some disruptive effect from the sorting task is indicated by the retained reliability of the phi technique at post-testing.

The existence of a conceptual-perceptual stage receives additional confirmation from the previously described Russian research on the development of ocular-motor scanning movements. Thus, at an early stage the child discriminated on the basis of isolated details; he then progressed to scanning the entire contour; finally, at the highest developmental level, he reverted to a sampling of details. It appears that, at this stage, he can conceptually fill in the gaps and short-cut the perceptual process. Perception has assumed a role secondary to conception.

SOME ASPECTS OF PRACTICAL APPLICATION

Evaluating Kephart's contribution to the understanding and treatment of atypical children has, to be sure, its tough-minded and strictly objective aspects. Yet in the final analysis there is a subjective, even gourmet-like, aspect that enters the picture. It is something like appraising a pleasant-tasting homemade soup which, despite a thin broth, is generously supplied with chunks of meat and vegetables. If our gourmet interest sets us on the track of subtle ingredients, once detected, they can be evaluated objectively. A new and very significant ingredient is that of kinesthetic figure-ground.

KINESTHETIC FIGURE-GROUND

Through the motor and motor-perceptual stages the infant is reputedly acquiring kinesthetic figure-ground. Kephart believes that kinesthetic figure-ground is basic to the acquisition of all other figure-ground relationships, including the visual. Therefore, from the point of view of learning disabilities, the ultimate pay-off for training in kinesthetic figure-ground occurs in the classroom. Normal children are believed to acquire this learning in the course of unprogrammed family experience. For the hypokinetic or hyperkinetic child specific training may be required (Kephart, 1969a, p. 20).

When kinesthetic figure-ground is established, voluntary movements are differentiated. The muscles involved in the specific movement receive more energy and show greater tonus than other muscles of the body. The hyperkinetic child, however, is tight in his behavior. His movements are explosive. Tonicity is not selective — his entire musculature enters into any of his movements including those involved in maintaining balance. The child is hyperactive and disruptive in the classroom. Due to the generalized muscular tonicity, voluntary movement cannot emerge as "figure" against such a "ground." This child has difficulty learning to write because such action requires differentiated movements and correspondingly differentiated patterns of tonicity. When he attempts to write, every muscle is innervated. This generalized tonicity is revealed in a muscular overflow manifested in extraneous movements (e.g., movement of the tongue) correlated with his attempts to write.

Kephart's treatment of the hyperkinetic child takes Jacobson's (1938) principle of progressive relaxation as its point of departure. This principle involves teaching the individual to relax one body part at a time beginning with the peripheral and moving into the central parts. Kephart has adapted this system primarily through substituting non-language training procedures for Jacobson's system of verbal instruction.

Kephart's treatment program for the hyperkinetic child begins as follows:

> The child is placed in a semi-supine position. The therapist sits on the floor behind the child. The child's upper torso is held firmly against the chest of the therapist. This semi-supine position is the

easiest in which to begin. Relaxation is easiest when muscles are slightly, but not completely flexed. The semi-supine position allows the legs, arms, and waist to be slightly bent, thus providing slight flexion for the muscle groups involved.

Hyperkinetic children tend to maintain balance through a wide-spread over-stimulated response of the entire musculature. When relaxation removes one or more muscle groups from this widespread response, the maintenance of balance becomes precarious. Therefore, when they are asked to relax, aid must frequently be provided to support balance.

The child leans against the therapist who supports the upper part of the body with his arm. The head is maintained in an upright position and in line with the body by the therapist. If balance is lost or the child, sensing a balance problem, tightens up in response to the balancing reflexes, the therapist tightens his grip on the child thus supporting balance and at the same time cluing the child that relaxation has been lost. With practice the therapist can become very sensitive to such responses of the child and can clue him in anticipation of a balancing response thus preventing the overt loss of relaxation. When the child has become accustomed to the semi-supine position, he is encouraged to relax his foot and toes. Descriptive language meaningful to the child is used, such as: "Make your foot loose and limp," "just let your foot go," "Let it lie all by itself," etc. At the same time manipulate the ankle and toes. This procedure will probably require two people. (Kephart, 1969b, unnumbered) [10]

In similar fashion the child is progressively taught to relax all body parts. He learns the feel of normal movements by passively experiencing manipulations; for example, appropriate manipulation of the foot allows him to feel the normal spring of walking. Visual cues are added as when the child is taught to recognize how his feet look when relaxed. Care is taken to avoid a buildup of overflow tension in non-participating muscle groups (e.g., in the left leg while the right leg is worked). When relaxation is achieved, the child is verbally instructed to relax the part and then to move it. The therapist watches closely to see that tension does not develop during the movement, and the child himself is encouraged to watch for such signs of tension.

At a later stage in the training of kinesthetic figure-ground, Kephart focuses more specifically on the development of effective voluntary movements. In the following quote he demonstrates his approach to the differential development of writing skills.

When the child has learned to move out of relaxation, he must learn to make voluntary or constructive responses without the development of tension in those parts of the body not directly involved in the task. Frequently, in an effort to control a constructive response, the child tenses all the musculature of the body. Instead of aiding control, this excessive effort, breaks up and destroys what control he has. He thus throws himself into a vicious circle in which he develops excessive tension in an effort to exert control over his movements. This very tension, however, destroys the control. In an effort to restore control, he responds with even more tension, the result of which is to further break down control. The harder he tries, the greater his failure.

The solution to this problem lies in reversing the cycle. The child must be taught that, when he begins to lose control, he should relax in the interest of gaining control, rather than tense for this purpose. Now that the child knows what relaxation is, how to recognize it and how it can augment movement responses, he can be taught to use this information in the solution of his problems. He will need to be taught how to make constructive movements out of relaxation and how this procedure augments the control of these responses. . . .

Give the child a crayon and a sheet of news print. Ask him to scribble aimlessly on the paper while paying attention to what he is doing. The attempt here is to elicit movement out of the relaxed position with a minimum requirement for attention to the nature of the movement or its results. Hence the use of scribbling rather than copying at this stage. Observe carefully to see that no excess tension develops in the muscle groups considered previously. Pay particular attention to the feet. Frequently children display the tension developed by such constructive tasks in the responses of the feet. The feet may be hooked around the legs of the chair, the legs and feet may show excessive tension or there may be excessive shuffling or movement of the feet.

Watch the neck and shoulders to see that excessive tension does not develop. Watch that the child does not assume an atypical posture in an attempt to relieve the tension which has developed.

If tension develops, manipulate the involved muscle groups until relaxation is restored. Then continue the task. If an atypical posture develops, stop and restore the desired posture, then continue. Encourage the child to recognize when relaxation has been lost and the effect of this loss on his performance.

The child is asked to move with a minimum of perceptual control. The demand for perceptual control should now be increased.

Ask the child to trace a simple motif drawn on the newsprint with a marking pencil which produces a broad, heavy line. This line requires perceptual monitoring during the tracing, but because it is so broad and heavy, does not require precision of monitoring. (Kephart, 1969b)

This writer has gone into what may seem excessive detail regarding figure-ground training because it illustrates implications and interrelationships which transcend Kephart's own work and provide an enriched context. It illustrates not only the stimulating possibilities but also the complications involved in dealing with even so specific a contribution.

What is the supporting evidence for Kephart's assumption that the above training eventually has anything to do with the way the child *sees* the world? As yet, there is none. In this respect, kinesthetic figure-ground stands only as an unproven hypothesis in a developmental theory. Yet there is one immensely practical implication — the possible efficacy of the technique for training individuals suffering a disruption of controlled voluntary movements due to brain damage.

Although, once again, research validation is lacking, the technique has many important implications. One intriguing relationship linking Kephart with a seemingly contradictory point of view was recently reported by Macpherson, a behavior therapist. Those who identify themselves as behavior therapists differ among themselves in theoretical orientation; some are strictly Skinnerian and totally reject hypothetical constructs while others employ such constructs to some extent. In the main, however, the behavior therapist's orientation could be considered in opposition to Kephart's brand of cognitive theory.

Macpherson (1967) clearly identifies himself as a practitioner of behavior therapy. As did Kephart, Macpherson used Jacobson's program of progressive relaxation as his point of departure. However, since his patient, a 60-year-old victim of Huntington's chorea, had normal intelligence, he could utilize Jacobson's standard system of verbal instruction. The problem was, at least in part, the converse of that described by Kephart: unlike the hyperkinetic child, the patient previously had had smoothly functioning voluntary movements. But like the child, she had trouble carrying out these movements. Her pre-training attempts to oppose involuntary movements with voluntary ones only increased them. Kephart's hyperkinetic child experienced a diffuse muscular activation from which he had to learn to distinguish those feelings of muscular tension specifically identified with voluntary movements. In both instances, then, the patient must learn to identify those kinesthetic S^Ds related to a selective pattern of muscular activation.[11] It is a problem in discrimination learning. One set of stimuli, those arising from extraneous muscle groups, must be ignored, while those leading to coordinated functioning must be responded to. In either case, the problem is one of helping the patient to identify the appropriate S^Ds from a confusing array of stimuli.

Macpherson began with conventional relaxation training. With the attainment of a satisfactory degree of relaxation, his patient was trained in carrying out voluntary movements. The second phase entailed training her to attend to sensations associated with the onset of involuntary movement. By means of an electromyographic recording technique, muscle potentials were recorded from a limb being trained and were fed through an audiometer and headphones. An incipient involuntary movement produced noise prior to the appearance of overt activity, and in this way, she learned to identify the inappropriate stimuli. In the final stage she was asked to respond to the appearance of these stimuli with total relaxation. At the end of a year of treatment, involuntary movements were almost entirely absent.

In Kephart's procedure, the electromyograph is replaced by the therapist. Supporting the child in a semi-supine position, he strengthens his grip on the child as soon as he detects an inappropriate tightening up. This cue operates to clue the child precisely as did the noise for Macpherson's patient. The child then learns progressively to relax other body members and to make voluntary movements out of a condition of relaxation.

Though the treatment objectives significantly differ in certain respects, it can be seen that the treatment strategies, while arising from diverse theoretical frames of reference, are essentially the same. Macpherson expressed concern over the fact that the instructions given in training may be excessively difficult for the patient with organic brain damage. Kephart, however, anticipated this problem. He has shown the way in which Jacobson's procedures might be appropriately adapted to the needs of such individuals.

Kephart's initial training procedure reflects a basic theoretical emphasis. Thus, as is characteristic of Kephart, he relates his first training steps to the problem of balance, which he considers the point of origin for all learning. This concept, when related to avoidance conditioning, makes a great deal of sense. Note that Kephart infers that while the hyperkinetic child is standing, relaxation of one or more muscle groups imperils total balance. This is because the child does not know which muscles can be safely relaxed and which cannot. Therefore, activation of the entire musculature is, in fact, a successful avoidance response and is reinforced. Since loss of balance represents the potentially most dangerous consequence of muscular incoordination, inappropriate contraction is most powerfully learned in this context. And, since inappropriate tension tends to overflow to other muscle groups less centrally involved in balance, it certainly seems logical to begin with this problem. For example, if relaxed finger movements were learned first, then relaxation would be negated when uncertain balance activated generalized muscular tension.

While inefficient muscular activation is powerfully reinforced as avoidance behavior relative to balance, it might also be true that the attainment of coordinated balance is the most significant experience of mastery for the uncoordinated child. And since "the human organism is reinforced simply by being effective" (Skinner, 1968, p. 62) this could constitute an unusually powerful reinforcement for the child and his parents — another reason for starting with balance.

In Kephart's description of initial relaxation training from the semi-supine position it is apparent that he exercises total physical control over the child's posture and movement. In the example, the child was cooperative. Kephart would, however, exercise physical control if the child were resistive. Zaslow (1967), in his paper on the treatment of autistic children through "rage reduction," emphasized the necessity for complete physical control including the need to overcome motor resistance. Unaware of the prior work of Seguin (see page 71), he claimed for himself the distinction of being the first to incorporate total motor control in a treatment program.

Common to Kephart's and Macpherson's procedures is the fact that muscular relaxation becomes intrinsically reinforcing. With this in mind, these techniques can be compared and contrasted with one described by Ferster & Simons[12] as follows:

> Frequently Miss Simons will deprive a child of his freedom or an article of clothing and make their return contingent on a particular performance. One day when William, a verbal autistic child, screamed, kicked and in general thrashed about, Miss Simons first took his shoes off. Then she held him by a sheet around his waist, his arms free, so that she could hold him at arm's length without being kicked or bitten. As he calmed down, she loosened her hold and as he behaved primitively she tightened it until finally the conditions for going over to the sofa where he could get his shoes were that he walk calmly, holding her hand lightly . . . .
>
> Initially, William's tantrum was an aversive stimulus which strongly controlled the behavior of all of those around him. Adults around William either stepped out of his way as he attacked or they tried to stop the tantrum. When they stepped out of his way, William was controlling them by presenting an aversive stimulus which was terminated by their escape. When they remained and interacted with William's tantrum he was also controlling since the tantrum provided many aversive stimuli which they would have to terminate or escape from if they remained in the vicinity. Miss Simons first reversed William's control of her by taking his shoes off and restraining him. The restraint gave her a reinforcer which she could apply to some behavior of her choice. So long as the boy behaved primitively she held him tightly. When he relaxed, she released him. This experience provided a series of contingencies in which tantrum

behavior was not reinforced (the sheet remained tight). Walking toward the sofa "voluntarily" was reinforced by escape from the restraint . . . . (1966, p. 69)

As with the Kephart and Macpherson procedures, the end result of controlling the individual was a state of relaxation. Yet, in his interactions with Miss Simons, William did not progress to the point at which relaxation became intrinsically reinforcing. In fact, she used escape from physical control to reinforce a behavior incompatible with a tantrum (voluntarily walking toward the sofa). The point of this comparison is that subtle but significant differences may exist in techniques for physically controlling children in a treatment situation.

Turning to Kephart's exercises for the development of controlled writing movements, we encounter another striking parallel from the field of behavior therapy — Wolpe's (1958) technique of systematic desensitization or counter-conditioning. Wolpe's technique, which is also based on Jacobson's program, assumes that irrational fear, as in the case of phobia, is incompatible with a state of relaxation. If, for example, a person had a snake phobia, he would be gradually put through a hierarchy of situations related to snakes which might begin with imagining the presence of a snake safely locked up in a zoo and ending with the actual handling of snakes. At each step the subject learns to relax in the presence of the imagined or the real stimulus. In this way the snake becomes a cue, or S^D, for relaxation rather than tension and anxiety.

If "tension" could be reinterpreted as "emotional tension" and if Kephart's writing program were relabeled, "a treatment procedure for a handwriting phobia," it could almost pass as an example of counter-conditioning. Although Kephart intervenes with direct physical manipulations, like Wolpe, he promotes relaxation in the context of a typically tension-producing activity. A hierarchy is involved in the gradation of motor activities. Again like Wolpe, he takes the subject through a series of increasingly tension-producing experiences: he starts with a playful, minimally threatening "scribbling" and progresses to a formal tracing task demanding perceptual control. Since the subject continues to relax, even in the presence of a more demanding task, voluntary movements can occur without the disruptive effects of muscular tension and subsequent loss of control. Kephart's program should also be effective for the treatment of writer's cramp in individuals without neurological injury.

Kephart's technique for training the hyperactive child contrasts with the treatment strategy developed by Patterson in a Skinnerian framework. Unlike Kephart, Patterson was not concerned with the development of coordinated movements. Yet both pursued the general objective of reducing hyperactive behavior and establishing studying behavior. Patterson's study entails only a small segment of what Kephart strives to achieve in his work with hyperactive children. However, it does represent at least a limited amount of overlap and serves as a point of departure for comparing the two approaches.

Patterson (1965) worked with an extremely hyperactive, minimally brain-injured child in a classroom setting. This child was engaged in disorganized, hyperactive behavior most of the time. The problem was defined as one of developing attending behaviors. Since these behaviors were emitted so infrequently and were of extremely short duration, special care was taken to reinforce them with minimal latency. In making reinforcement contingent upon attention — in this case, looking at a book while seated — it was hoped that the stimuli of the classroom setting would be established as S^Ds for studying rather than disorganized and disruptive behaviors. The procedure involved reinforcing the boy at the end of ten-second intervals in which only attending behaviors occurred. As an added feature, he earned reinforcements (candy and pennies) not only for himself but also for the rest of the class. This technique effectively produced the desired changes.

The first question, as yet unanswerable, is which technique is more effective in reducing hyperactive behaviors in the classroom. However, there are additional points of comparison that raise interesting questions regarding the broader implications of each of these approaches. Thus, Patterson's approach to hyperactivity corresponds to the strategy enunciated by Isaacs, Thomas & Goldiamond (1960) regarding the approach to abnormal behaviors in general; Patterson bypasses the hyperactivity, focusing instead on increasing the probability of the occurrence of adaptive behaviors which did occur, however infrequently, from the outset. Effectiveness of treatment is then measured in terms of the increasing proportion of adaptive behaviors and the relative decrease in hyperactivity.

A Skinnerian-type criticism of Kephart's approach would be that he sets out to treat hyperactivity directly. Further, he deals, not with observable environmental events, as does Patterson, but with kinesthetic figure-ground and other inferred hypothetical constructs inaccessible to examination.[13] Kephart would aver that he deals directly with the "cause" of hyperactivity. Patterson implies that he neither knows nor cares about an inferred cause — the only data of significance are subsumed by observable events. Now consider where each of these positions has led its proponent operationally. One critical difference is in terms of where Kephart first behaviorally engaged the hyperactive child; in this case, in terms of his balance problem rather than his classroom studying behaviors.

Ultimately, it may prove that, in terms of the specific objectives Patterson set for his hyperactive subject, he may get the job done, perhaps more efficiently and in less time than does Kephart. Yet, we cannot afford to ignore the philosophies and perspectives inherent in each approach. As with the comparison between Kephart and Macpherson, differences in the orientations of Kephart and Patterson had important consequences in terms of *where* they engaged the problem. The writer agrees with Helson who said, "Theories do make a difference . . . even small differences in theory may have important consequences on where one finally comes out in scientific work" (1969, p. 1006). Philosophy and perspective are also involved in the long-term implications of specific treatment efforts. This point has been incisively expressed by Scott, Burton & Yarrow. They note the following:

> Those concerned . . . with applying reinforcement principles in educational programs face additional questions to those which may arise in experimental settings. Some aspects of the general issues raised . . . may only be clarified in long-range experimental approaches to real-life situations . . . . They force one to extend one's perspective beyond that of describing the functional properties of a stimulus-reinforcer in terms of expected and immediate change in the frequency of a single aspect of overt behavior. (1967, p. 63)

The Russian, Luria, has developed a theoretical position and correlated training recommendations almost identical to those expressed by Kephart in the context of kinesthetic figure-ground.

> Any voluntary movement involves a complex group of muscle innervations, in which may be distinguished the innervations of the *leading muscle groups* composing the basic motor structure, and the innervations of the muscle groups forming the *motor background*. For example, when a person holds a pencil and begins to write, the role of the dominant group is played by the finger muscles of the right hand and the role of the motor background by the muscles of the forearm, shoulder, neck, and trunk, which themselves do not play an active part in the movements of writing but provide the motor background which gives optimal dynamic conditions for the performance of the complex movement. If for some reason this dynamic background is absent and the correct distribution of muscle tone in the various segments does not take place, the complex movement cannot be performed satisfactorily. (Luria, 1966, p. 147)[14]

LATERALITY AND BODY IMAGE AS HYPOTHETICAL CONSTRUCTS

The development of kinesthetic figure-ground is part of what Kephart describes as *laterality,* an internal sense of sidedness. As in the former, the latter involves a sorting out of internal, proprioceptive feedback from body movements. Laterality is the foundation for *directionality* which, in turn, is the basis for perceiving direction in space.

Laterality is a concept with common-sense appeal. Watching an infant's movements in a crib it seems obvious that the infant is learning how his motor equipment works and that this knowledge must, of necessity, involve proprioceptive feedback. Also, such learning must include an internal awareness of body sidedness. Observing the infant's ocular pursuit movements, one is readily convinced of the validity of Kephart's description of a "midline translation problem" when he notes one eye stop at the midline while the other independently continues its sweep. And in reading Head's (1925) clinical accounts of brain-injured, aphasic World War I veterans, one is impressed by their selective failure in imitating movements that involve crossing the midline (e.g., touching left ear with right hand), while the ability to imitate ipsilateral movements (e.g., right hand to right ear) is intact. Such phenomena can readily be demonstrated. The question is this — are they actually manifestations of a developmental process prerequisite to all later learning? An attempt to answer this broad question might begin with the following empirical questions: (1) is laterality deficiency, in fact, related to learning handicaps? and (2) does laterality training result in enhanced capability in the handicapped learner?

Roach & Kephart (1966) present evidence of a significant relationship between laterality measures and academic performance. The limitation inherent in this kind of evidence arises from the fact that the demonstration of a significant correlation between two events does not prove that they are *causally* related. This fact was clearly brought out in a study of brain-injured adults conducted by Semmes et al. (1963), who demonstrated a relationship between a measure of personal orientation and a test of extrapersonal orientation. The relationship in question was very much the same as that between laterality and directionality in Kephart's system. Did the correlation reveal the presence of a pervasive perceptual defect basic to both functions? Or were both disturbed because of the anatomic overlap of brain structures responsible for each, an overlap that insured simultaneous damage? With such damage both body awareness and spatial orientation could be impaired and yet be functionally and developmentally independent. Semmes et al. did not resolve this question, and neither has Kephart.

Does laterality training produce enhanced learning ability? Since laterality is but one part of a developmental process and, of itself, is an inadequate basis for academic learning, it would be meaningless to try to relate laterality training directly with academic performance. Higher level perceptual and cognitive skills cannot be considered apart from Kephart's overall training program. With these limitations in mind, Ball & Edgar (1967) designed a hypothetico-deductive type of study incorporating a developmentally appropriate criterion of training results. We sought to determine whether sensory-motor training generalizes to non-practiced performances relevant to body image or, on the contrary, yields only specific and circumscribed skills.

One of the criterion measures was Head's hand, eye, ear test, previously mentioned. Like Head's aphasics, the normal kindergarten child typically imitates the examiner's cross-lateral gesture, (touching left ear with right hand) with an ipsilateral response (touching right ear with right hand). This midline-crossing difficulty is what Kephart would describe as an outward manifestation of laterality deficiency. Since Head's test was a criterion measure, care was taken to avoid training activities related to crossing the midline of the body or identifying facial features. Additional criterion measures were Benton's right-left discrimination battery which, unlike Head's non-verbal test, involves spoken commands, and his finger localization test. The latter measures the subject's ability to designate on a schematic diagram the fingers touched by the examiner both in full view of the subject and again with subject's hand behind a screen.

Daily sensory-motor training sessions of fifteen- to twenty-minutes duration were conducted in small groups for a period of 3½ months. Post-testing revealed that the trained subjects increased significantly in their ability to cross the midline, while control subjects persisted with ipsilateral responses on Head's test. Neither of the Benton tests produced significant differences between experimental and control groups.

The results were in the predicted direction and supported the validity of the laterality construct. However, the experiment was criticized, and with some justification, on the grounds that improvement on Head's test could have been a function of imitation training occurring incidental to the sensory-motor program. If this were true, the changes noted need not have involved an internal sense of sidedness. The children could have become more proficient at any kind of imitation, regardless of its nature. In this context, crossing the midline was significant only to the extent that it was a more complicated task than was an ipsilateral item. This criticism was at least partially overcome by an improved and extended version of the above design which involved teen-age, moderately retarded, institutionalized males (Maloney, Ball & Edgar, 1970). The factor of imitation on Head's test was minimized by employing a version requiring the subject to imitate various pictorial representations of the sixteen items, instead of directly imitating the examiner's touching his own eye or ear. Additional criterion measures consisted of Benton's finger localization test and a test requiring the subject to touch parts of his own body corresponding to points indicated on schematic diagrams of a man's body. The Purdue Perceptual-Motor Survey was administered to insure that the experimental subjects attained significant progress in sensory-motor skills. A new feature of the training program was the addition of specific finger training. This was provided to the experimental group and to a control group upon completion of the sensory-motor training phase. In addition to a "no treatment" control group, a second control group was added, the members of which received individualized attention while engaging in an active program which did not include gross motor activity. The latter group was introduced to control for interpersonal attention and motivational factors. The results were in agreement with the previous study: the sensory-motor group made relatively greater gains on Head's test and the Personal Orientation Test. As before, both experimental and control subjects improved on finger localization, but to essentially the same extent.

While this study lent further support to the laterality construct, it also suggested a serious limitation in its applicability. The problem arises from the very reasonable expectation that the attainment of a differentiated awareness of body sidedness (laterality) should generalize to an awareness of finger location. The finger training intervening between sensory-motor training and the post-test should have provided every opportunity for such a transfer to take place. Since it did not occur, a question must be raised regarding the generality of body schema itself. If there are specific and autonomous sidedness and finger schemata, this renders highly questionable the notion of a general body image. Further, it attenuates the expectation that laterality generalization will carry over to the schema of ocular movements. But it is on the basis of such generalization that directionality is assumed to develop.

While laterality can be operationally defined in terms of midline crossing difficulties, the general notion of body image is another matter. As a vehicle of explanation, its applications reveal the pitfalls and dangers of hypothetical constructs in general. Thus, the notion of an internal model of the body has an immediate appeal. It can be applied to many and varied situations. It is a tremendously flexible and adaptable concept. And therein lies the fallacy — in explaining everything, it explains nothing. Since it is presumably "well known" that body image is related to cognitive learning, there is presumably ample justification for applying diverse, unvalidated movement techniques as part of remedial programs for slow learners, reading disability cases, and so forth. Indeed, since so many wonderful transformations are supposedly occurring "inside the skin" it might even appear boorish to ask for proofs of validity in terms of demonstrable, environmentally defined variables. Here is a comfortable idea with common-sense appeal. But we must ask the embarrassing question — what has been the payoff from this idea in terms of solid, scientific knowledge? The scientific status of the concept was summarized by Benton as follows:

> In general, the construct of the body schema remains vague and ill-defined. The role of the various sensory components and of the language functions, its mode of operation and its modifiability remains unspecified. Moreover, if the test of the value of an explanatory hypothesis be its predictive power, it must be said that for the most part the value of the construct for this purpose has still to be elucidated. (1959, p. 138)

The notion of body image has been extended to explain a variety of body disturbances, among them, hypochondriacal preoccupation, depersonalization, and somatic delusion (Benton, 1959, p. 137). When the so-called facts so easily fall into place through the use of constructs such as this, complacency develops and scientific progress may be seriously impeded.

As noted above, an attempt has been made to objectify the laterality component of the body image concept by means of the operationally definable hand, eye, ear test. But even that test has problems that cannot completely be resolved. Use of the orienting response as a measure of tactual perception can potentially circumvent the limitations of evaluation techniques such as the hand, eye, ear test including the problem of the incidental training in imitation, motivation to take the test, attention, and comprehension of directions. With the OR approach these factors are simply not involved. A recent chapter by Ball, Gabriel & Ackerland (1971) suggests that an OR technique may be an effective means of measuring finger schema (finger localization) while the subject, blindfolded, does nothing. The subject cooperates only to the extent of relaxing and remaining still. Otherwise, there are no directions to follow and nothing to do. In this sense, it is potentially a relatively pure and direct technique of body image measurement.

In summary, it appears that while Kephart's laterality construct has received some support experimentally, the general notion of body image presents numerous difficulties.

MOTOR-TEMPORAL SYSTEM

What is the significance of writing as a skill and what is the best technique for teaching writing to an educable, mentally retarded child? Bijou and his associates (Birnbrauer, Bijou, Wolf & Kidder, 1965), in the Skinnerian tradition, approached the problem directly, employing the model of programmed instruction. They focused on writing itself, and efficiently proceeded to shape this skill with a sequential program. The equipment used and the training stages incorporated in the program were described by the authors as follows:

> An illuminated tracing box was used to ensure that the model being traced was clear and to provide a means of controlling the amount of time that the pupil could see and trace the model. At first, the light was on almost continuously, thus providing continuous information about the lines to be traced. Then, the proportion of light-on time was decreased to "wean" the child from tracing and to transfer control to lines on the paper and other cues used in free handwriting.
>
> The program began with tracing simple strokes which permitted a wide margin of error . . . . Then, the margin of error was gradually decreased and the complexity of the models was increased to include letters and letter groups . . . . When the pupil traced these models competently, with reduced light-on time, the second stage began.
>
> During the Tracing and Copying stage, two types of items were presented, one providing both a model to trace and one to copy; the other, only a model to copy. The latter served as tests of the acquisition of copying. . . .
>
> [In] The third stage, Copying, . . . the models are still further removed and more complex. . . . Script models that the pupil translated into cursive were also introduced. After this stage, for the most part, writing practice was incorporated into other exercises. (1965, p. 362)

The authors acknowledged that the technique cannot stand alone, especially when pupils "are not motivated to learn and have not acquired the prerequisite attentional and study skills" (*ibid.,* p. 363). This suggests that the student's failure points up the need for a more powerful reinforcer and that he should be shaped to sit at the teaching machine and work appropriately.

Consider the application of the above program to a brain-injured adult described by Luria (1966). This man, with only a slight hesitation, read simple material with little or no difficulty. However, in writing from dictation he made many peculiar errors in spelling. Since Bijou's program necessarily involved spelling, it might reasonably have been used for retraining. Providing the speed requirement were not excessive, the ex-soldier might have proceeded well with the copying of script models but unexpectedly failed when required to write cursively. Following Bijou's approach to trouble-shooting, the factors of motivation plus attentional and study skills would be examined. In an appropriately engineered environment and with correctly arranged contingencies he should learn to write. Therein lies the problem, or does it?

Luria, starting with a theoretical orientation similar to Kephart's, placed the patient's writing difficulties in a broader context. For Luria, writing is but one expression of a *kinetic melody*. Spelling problems were only one manifestation of a pervasive underlying disturbance of this generic function. Instead of concentrating solely on cognitive skills such as writing, Luria carefully analyzed the man's motor processes. Apart from slight slowness and clumsiness, the patient was normally coordinated and "was able to move about and look after himself perfectly well" (Luria, 1966, p. 228). It was not until he was required to carry out *sequential* motor patterns that he showed obvious impairment:

> The patient was asked to tap on the table simultaneously with both hands — the right made into a fist, and the left with the open palm, altering the corresponding positions of the hand each successive time (a test of reciprocal coordination). Instead of interchanging the movements smoothly and performing both components simultaneously, the patient made a series of individual movements, each requiring its own impulse. (*ibid*, pp. 228-29)

Luria describes his patient's performance in more complex activities as follows:

> The patient was asked to draw three symbols in succession: O □ +, which were shown to him once. He easily drew these symbols in the proper order. When he was asked to draw the shape ⌐Ⅳ⅂Ⅳ⅂Ⅳ by a rapid and *continuous movement*, he could only do this very slowly, by fixing each link separately and verifying his drawing with the specimen.
>
> The formation of a skilled movement in the form of a smooth "kinetic melody" met with insuperable difficulties: When the patient was asked to close his eyes or to draw a figure more quickly, the structure disintegrated and the patient either began to repeat the same link over and over again, or he abandoned the task, declaring that his hand could not feel what it had to do. Characteristically, prolonged practicing of this task caused very little change, and only with the introduction of visual control — with analysis of every link of the movement to be performed — could the patient overcome his difficulties. (*ibid*, p. 231)

His seemingly adequate performance in copying a circle, square and cross *separately* is consistent with the expectation, expressed above, that he could have copied individual script letters adequately. The spelling problem is consistent with his difficulty in drawing the continuous, irregular, saw-tooth pattern. Luria looked at something Bijou did not consider, namely, the patient's ability to write with eyes closed, and learned that he was totally dependent on visual control. The soldier's disruption of kinetic melody is what Kephart would relate to sequence, synchrony, and rhythm, all aspects of the "motor-temporal system."

What Luria discovered, as would have Kephart, is a deficit that Bijou's approach would not reveal. Limited to Bijou's orientation, the teacher might be deceived by the soldier's adequate initial performance. That is, shaping by successive approximations is a *continuous* process, and, if it breaks down, one returns to an earlier point in the program and perhaps looks for a better reinforcer. Following Sidman & Stoddard (1966), it may be determined that the subject's problem could be remedied by the insertion of several additional steps to compensate for what may have been an excessively large increment in the program. For Luria's patient, however, this approach is incorrect because the underlying *process* of writing is disturbed. Initially, while copying script he *overtly* could have performed satisfactorily. Yet the assumptions that have made programmed instruction a twentieth-century technological breakthrough in education do not apply to him. This is not a theoretical issue; it is based on Luria's observations regarding the breakdown of performance with eyes closed and with continuous movement. The discontinuity in performance was a qualitative one.

Using Kephart's terminology, the soldier's abnormality is reflected in the perceptual-motor match. The motor component of the match — in terms of motor generalization rather than of motor skill — had been severely disorganized due to brain injury. Because of a selective retention of the capacity for visual guidance, he could, in some circumstances, compensate for and even conceal the impairment. The impairment of basic motor generalization is further reflected in a difficulty in sequence, synchrony and rhythm, clearly revealed in the test of reciprocal coordination of hand movements. A Kephart-type evaluation would lead to further questions, e.g., regarding the patient's reading performance. Because of the disruption of motor generalizations attained during early childhood, it could be assumed that the conceptual base for the subject's reading of even simple material might be seriously impaired. However, such a consideration involves theoretical assumptions that go beyond the purely empirical facts of the spelling difficulty, which was basically a problem of subtle impairment of motor-kinesthetic organization.

This case is intended to make a point: while it seems most likely that Bijou, a skilled clinician, would uncover the true nature of the problem within a short time, Kephart's cognitive approach more readily would lead one to discover the empirical facts underlying the soldier's disrupted spelling ability. Aside from the validity of Kephart's theoretical assumptions, his approach would predispose one to look for certain kinds of cues and to ask certain kinds of questions. It would also seem that serious questions can be raised regarding many current applications of programmed teaching as applied to individuals with impaired functioning.

The soldier maintained a semblance of visual-motor adequacy by matching the motor to the visual. If, however, the visual aspect is deficient relative to the motor, the individual may reduce or eliminate visual input during a performance. Kephart (1968) described a child who looked out of a window while tracing a square with his hand. That this inattention was not necessarily an idiosyncratic behavior problem is suggested by the fact that such phenomena are not uncommon among young children. For example, Bruner (1969) cited a seven-month-old who literally shut her eyes in the midst of reaching for a cup. He observed, "If a reach involves some conflict between the line of vision and the course the hand must follow (detour-reaching), the child is especially likely to look away or close his eyes as he reaches" (p. 66). In terms of reaching, the child lacked what Kephart describes as a motor pattern. It was still a specific skill, not a motor generalization. She was preoccupied with the problem of reaching on a moment-to-moment basis. Under these circumstances it is difficult to keep the purpose of the movement continuously in mind. It is a major accomplishment merely to keep the hand going in the right direction.

How should we interpret the infant's performance?[16] Does she have an "attention" problem? Could we accelerate her development through shaping her by successive approximations to fixate continuously on the cup? On the other hand, would continuous fixation during reaching turn out to be what Kephart describes as a "splinter skill?" Perhaps flexibility in reaching strategies develops through generalizations that occur later on when the child learns to walk — when she progresses from motor skills to motor patterns. Perhaps learning to get around detours flexibly is best reached on the gross motor level. If such is the case, generalization might best proceed from gross motor learning to reaching. Definitive answers to these questions appear to be lacking. Yet it is significant that Kephart's theory stimulates their formulation.

Previously established motor generalizations were disrupted in Luria's patient. But what happens if, instead of being disrupted, they have never been developmentally established? In such instances, the individual, when faced with the demands of writing instruction, lacks the necessary motor-perceptual basis for such learning. His motor-temporal processes consist of ungeneralized, fragmentary splinter skills. Such was the plight of a mildly retarded ten-year-old boy being taught to write numbers by tracing dotted lines.

After correctly tracing a series of dotted 6s, he was required to execute an additional 6 completely on his own. Moving his pencil downward, he drew a vertical line, hesitated, and then executed a clockwise circle producing a pendulum-like representation of the number. Since he had been practicing counter-clockwise circles on the dotted 6s, there was a total discontinuity between practice and performance. Was this a chance occurrence? Was it an expression of negativism? That it was neither is suggested by manifestations of the same phenomenon in other contexts. Thus, when simply asked to draw a circle, unlike most right-handed children, he executed it in a clockwise direction. A "lazy-eight" — the number 8 drawn on its side (see Kephart, 1960) — was drawn on the blackboard and the writer traced over it several times with chalk. The direction of movement was such that the loop on the left side was executed clockwise. When the chalk reached the point of intersection in the middle of the figure, the direction changed so that the loop on the right side was traversed counter-clockwise. When the child was invited to trace the pattern he imitated the writer's execution of the left-hand loop correctly, tracing it clockwise. But when he came to the point of intersection, instead of reversing direction, he changed course tracing the right-hand loop clockwise. On a second occasion, upon reaching the intersection, his chalk completely left the "track" and he failed to regain it — his performance "fell apart."

The boy was locked in to a clockwise execution of circular patterns. Performance of the 6 was completely discontinuous with practice. One need not invoke theoretical concepts such as laterality or directionality in interpreting this boy's learning problem. Here was *negative transfer of training* involving motor-temporal performances predating school experience. He may also have lacked a spatial-numerical concept of 6. But the issue at hand was one of learning to execute the written symbol of that quantity.

The boy's problem in executing the 6 was based on a rigid motor-perceptual pattern incompatible with an acceptable production. If one approached the boy's difficulty in terms of Bijou's model, remediation would probably be attempted through a gradual fading of the dotted lines or by backing up and repeating the training sequence through successive approximations. If the underlying problem were that of a weakly or indefinitely established motor-perceptual pattern specific to the number 6, the Skinnerian strategy would probably pay off. Yet in this instance, a restricted, locked in pattern must be disrupted and in its place the child must attain a generalization. Primarily through the modality of chalkboard training, he would need to acquire ease in executing circles in either direction, with either hand, from varied positions, with varied speeds, etc. (see Kephart, 1960). In view of this, no further attempts at teaching the number 6 should be made pending the development of such a generalized concept of the circle.

VERIDICALITY AND PURPOSE[15]

For Kephart, and many other cognitive theorists, operant conditioning might appear to be a mechanistic psychology employed by its practitioners to usurp control from the individual and lead him toward a blind, unreasoning acceptance of externally imposed, predetermined goals. Kephart's program represents the antithesis of such an orientation. This is especially evident in his emphasis on training spontaneity and in his concept of *veridicality*. But are these notions necessarily irreconcilable with the operant conditioning framework?

Pryor's (1969) work in training porpoises clearly demonstrates a capability for training spontaneity with a specifically Skinnerian approach. And from an operant conditioning point of view, her procedures are essentially the same as Kephart has used with children both on land and in the water. What differentiates Kephart from the Skinnerians is his long-standing concern with the problem of developing spontaneity, and the extent to which it remains a guiding concept pervading his system.

Implied in Kephart's concept of veridicality is the notion of an immutable truth. He differentiates it from validity by agreement. The latter, as in the practice of driving on the right-hand side of the street, is a matter of accepted usage. Not so for veridicality, which is based on parameters of the universe (e.g., gravity) existing independently of man's intentions or interpretations. To the extent to which the child's early learning is based on veridical phenomena, it is grounded in truth and the child is on his way to developing a realistic view of the world and himself in it. Learning based on veridicality avoids the implication of manipulation by others. Kephart claims that, as the child gains control in the course of relating to the problems of veridical learning, such learning becomes self-rewarding.

Compare Kephart's notion of veridicality with the following statement by Skinner (Evans, 1968, p. 62): "The human organism is reinforced simply by being effective." Bijou and Baer extend Skinner's concept to the early adaptive learning of infants.

> Behaviors which succeed are considered skillful; those which fail are viewed as clumsy. If the skillfulness itself produces a pattern of proprioceptive stimuli, then that pattern could be a discriminative

stimulus associated with positive reinforcers and avoiding negative ones. Similarly, if the clumsiness itself produces a pattern of such stimuli, that pattern could be discriminative stimulus for the loss of positive reinforcers, the continued presence of negative reinforcers, or the presentation of new negative reinforcers. Then skillfulness and clumsiness would acquire reinforcing functions. Skillfulness would acquire a positive reinforcing function, and clumsiness a negative reinforcing function.

In these situations, behaviors which are skillful would be self-reinforcing; behaviors which are clumsy would be self-punishing. In other words, skillful behaviors would grow steadily in strength, and clumsy ones would become weak, by virtue of their own inherent characteristics, and independently of any other reinforcers they may produce or avoid. Such self-reinforcement has the great advantage of operating within chains, and then *just* at the moment when they can do the most good. The baby then would display skillful behaviors on many occasions when these behaviors accomplish nothing other than their own action — he should "play" with his environment. By playing with it, he displays skill: he displays control of his environment, making it work, move, be held, be still, make noises, make sounds — in effect, be his to make function. (Bijou & Baer, 1965, pp. 102-03)

These quotes from Skinner and Bijou describe a process that seems completely consistent with Kephart's account of veridical learning. And to the extent that they support the use of natural environmental consequences instead of other reinforcement procedures, the Skinnerians are actually promoting the notion of veridicality (see Ferster & Simons, 1966). Once again, the difference seems primarily a matter of emphasis.

It is significant that over a period of time procedural differences between Kephart and the Skinnerian camp have tended to fade. In a previous discussion it was noted that Baer, a prominent Skinnerian, did not take the time to shape movements according to the traditional laboratory version of the operant conditioning procedure (see page 58). To do so would have been a waste of time. Instead, he initially trained the non-imitating child to move in much the same way as Kephart would have taught "Angels in the Snow" (Kephart, 1960). The one notable difference is in the type of reinforcer used. [17]

Skinner and Bijou suggest that sheer control of nature and of oneself as a part of nature is reinforcing. Although they would avoid attaching the label "purpose" to the preceding statement, it would seem to be quite reconcilable with the concept of purpose as Kephart might use it. Here is something universal and pan-cultural, inherent in human experience within the bounds of earthly parameters. It is not a process shaped by someone pursuing the child with a bag of M & Ms — it is veridical.

There are still other areas of agreement. Training through operant conditioning may appear to be a series of increasingly complex, but nonetheless mechanistic, applications of reinforcement strategies. The individual may seem in danger of becoming an increasingly sophisticated robot. This would indeed be true if humans operated like computers and we were sequentially providing increasingly complicated programs. Yet while the computer analogy might be useful in some circumstances, the teacher-student relationship is severely distorted if we overdo the analogy. Despite arguments to the contrary, Seguin's aphorism, "Man sows and nature fecundates," applies to the operant approach. Based on some insights gained from Cecil Colwell,[18] Ball (1968) reflected on this question relative to the relationship between extrinsic and intrinsic reinforcement. The discussion focused on the problem of teaching a profoundly retarded child to ride a tricycle. Unlike normal children, many profoundly retarded have to be specifically taught to sit down on the vehicle, to remain seated, and even to press down on the pedals. These behaviors can be shaped using food as a reinforcer. The procedure appears mechanistic and indeed it is. The child conforms to the trainer's preconceived goals — not his own. But once the child activates the pedals he experiences movement through space in a new-found way — he realizes the intrinsic reinforcement of tricycle riding. The mechanistic shaping led the child to the threshold of discovery. Once the door was opened, the shaper could bow out. The child's joyful fulfillment was beyond his art or craft. It was an activation of a human potentiality. The purpose of tricycle riding is expressed in this potentiality.

Kephart himself is not exempt from the allegation of behavioral manipulation. This issue can be evaluated relative to his handling of the problem of rigidity.[19] In breaking through rigidity, Kephart unequivocally imposes his will on the child. The child's choice in the matter is not considered. At least temporarily, Kephart imposes his goals, albeit for the long-range good of the child. Qualitatively, the issue of manipulation applies as readily to Kephart as it does to the Skinnerian who initially shapes the child to ride the tricycle without his spontaneous or willing participation. But there is a further point: it seems quite possible that the child's resistance to the training procedure might be gradually overcome by successive approximations, and the emotional reaction and struggle that almost inevitably result in a direct and frontal approach to behavioral change might thereby be avoided. Consequently, the child's active and willing participation might be obtained sooner through behavior shaping.

There is, of course, the danger that one could distort operant-type training by failing to appreciate the transitional possibilities for moving from extrinsic to intrinsic reinforcement. This once occurred to the writer in the course of teaching an orthopedically and visually handicapped youngster to ambulate in a walker. Stepping was evoked by posturally "setting up" the child so that a step would be likely. When this occurred it was quickly reinforced with milk and enthusiastic praise. The steps gradually became more frequent and he began to move under his own power. He became more animated and smiled at the writer. While the writer continued to reinforce each step with milk, this act was not merely redundant; it actually *disrupted* what had become a spontaneously joyful physical and social experience for the child. This anecdote illustrates the point that, even in the process of repeating essentially the same overt behavior, the reinforcing nature of the situation may undergo marked changes. Although on the speech rather than the motoric level, the writer saw his experience duplicated in the Lovaas film, "Reinforcement Therapy." In one scene, Ricky, an autistic child who had already received considerable training in naming objects in the environment, suddenly "cut loose" and, with a rising pitch of excitement, gleefully named everything in sight. The trainer expressed her enthusiastic approval but food reinforcement and even appropriate timing of social reinforcement were totally unnecessary. Exactly the same phenomenon can be found in the record of Anne Sullivan's training of Helen Keller.

The pivotal experience of Helen Keller, immortalized in both stage and film accounts of her life, was described by Anne Sullivan as follows:

April 5, 1887

. . . something very important has happened. Helen has taken the second great step in her education. She has learned that *everything has a name, and that the manual alphabet is the key to everything she wants to know.*

In a previous letter I think I wrote you that "mug" and "milk" had given Helen more trouble than all the rest. She confused the nouns with the verb "drink." She didn't know the word for "drink," but went through the pantomime of drinking whenever she spelled "mug" or "milk." This morning, while she was washing, she wanted to know the name for "water." When she wants to know the name of anything, she points to it and pats my hand. I spelled "w-a-t-e-r" and thought no more about it until after breakfast. Then it occurred to me that with the help of this new word I might succeed in straightening out the "mug-milk" difficulty. We went out to the pumphouse, and I made Helen hold her mug under the spout while I pumped. As the cold water gushed forth, filling the mug, I spelled "w-a-t-e-r" in Helen's free hand. The word coming so close upon the sensation of cold water rushing over her hand seemed to startle her. She dropped the mug and stood as one transfixed. A new light came into her face. She spelled "water" several times. Then she dropped on the ground and asked for its name and pointed to the pump and the trellis, and suddenly turning round she asked for my name. I spelled "Teacher." Just then the nurse brought Helen's little sister into the pump house, and Helen spelled "baby" and pointed to the nurse. All the way back to the house she was highly excited, and learned the name of every object she touched, so that in a few hours she had added thirty new words to her vocabulary. Here are some of them: *Door, open, shut, give, go, come,* and a great many more.

P.S. . . . Helen got up this morning like a radiant fairy. She has flitted from object to object, asking the name of everything and kissing me for very gladness. Last night when I got in bed, she stole into my arms of her own accord and kissed me for the first time, and I thought my heart would burst, so full was it of joy. (Keller, 1965, p. 187-88.)

There is a parallel between the above incident and Victor's acquisition of the meaning of knife and razor (see page 39). As with Victor, this was not Helen's initial exposure to the word because, as Anne Sullivan had recorded previously, *water* was one of the eighteen nouns Helen knew as early as March 31. With Helen, as with Victor, the breakthrough in the acquisition of understanding occurred in a concrete, action context. In a psychological, if not in a grammatical, sense, water emerged as a verb. It was no longer simply an S^D for the satisfaction of a recurrent personal need. Rather, she had contacted those S^Ds that stir the soul of the poet — water in action, shockingly cold and swiftly moving. These discriminative stimuli produced newly experienced ORs, and were, in turn, intrinsically reinforcing. Helen was an energetic, active girl — but due to her sensory limitations she had little else with which to orient except her own body and her own physical appetites. Like Seguin's child (see page 50), she destroyed objects and for the same reason, i.e., this was the most satisfying, most novelty-producing, use of objects. [20] Anne Sullivan brought her to the threshold of experiencing a new set of S^Ds: stimulating, interest-arousing characteristics of the environment. Since words provided the most efficient vehicle for organizing and acquiring more knowledge about these S^Ds, they acquired the reinforcing value they initially lacked. Once these exciting stimuli were accessible to Helen, they took hold like a chain reaction and led her through an ever-expanding horizon of discovery. [21] As with the scientist engaged in pure research, purpose was expressed in discovery for the sake of discovery, not in terms of practical results. The most profound discoveries are often a byproduct of the joyful use of the mind. Could there be a more vivid or meaningful demonstration of human purpose?

Anne Sullivan approached the teaching of Helen Keller just as Seguin would have: she began with the problem of control. In Helen's tyrannical control of her family she was not unlike many so-called autistic children. There were other similarities. Thus, with the exception of her mother, she did not allow others to touch or fondle her, she was hyperactive and manipulated others by aversive behavior. Helen controlled sources of satisfaction in a primitive fashion. Her needs were met with minimal delay. Since she did not need to discover many of the S^Ds of objects as a means of satisfying her needs, many potentially stimulating S^Ds remained undiscovered. Like Seguin's goblet-breaking child, she derived pleasure from immediately breaking objects rather than using them appropriately. It was only after Seguin's child learned out of necessity to use and preserve the object as a means of satisfying his thirst that it could become the subject of sustained visual regard. During such sustained viewing the child could discover its intrinsic value as a beautifully colored object. Similarly, as Anne Sullivan made Helen completely dependent upon her for the satisfaction of the most basic needs, Helen was forced to deal with the environment in an active and sustained instrumental manner. It was only after she became oriented to environmental S^Ds for their survival value in instrumental learning that she could discover those intrinsically rewarding stimuli associated with cold running water.

Helen can be likened to a physically intact but somewhat lethargic profoundly retarded child who has to be shaped to ride a tricycle. He has to be brought to the threshold of those intrinsically reinforcing experiences of which he is entirely unaware and which are as yet inaccessible. But as he eventually moves through space he springs to life — he now has a purpose for movement. For Helen, such a newly acquired discovery of intrinsically reinforcing S^Ds led to a similar motivational breakthrough.

What is sensory education in its largest meaning? *It is the realization that eyes and ears do not a sensing person make*. It is in this greater meaning, if not in the details of her pedagogy, that Montessori demonstrated the most profound understanding. Consider her program of training in silence.

> The children, after they had made the effort necessary to maintain silence, enjoyed the sensation, took pleasure in the *silence* itself. They were like ships safe in a tranquil harbour, happy in having experienced something new . . . . They *forgot* the promise of sweets,

and no longer cared to take the toys, which I had supposed would attract them. I therefore abandoned that useless means, and saw, with surprise, that the game became constantly more perfect, until even children of three years of age remained immovable in the silence throughout the time required to call the entire forty children out of the room!

It was then that I learned that the soul of the child has its own reward . . . . (Montessori, 1964, pp. 211-12)

She adds the following:

In life about us, there exist inexhaustible fonts of aesthetic enjoyment, before which men pass as insensible . . . . (*ibid.,* p. 222)

It would thus appear that Helen Keller's initial state can be taken as a metaphor representing much of mankind. It is quite possible for an adult to have grown up in an American city never to have known silence as Montessori understood it. Even with normal hearing he may be sensorily deprived, even ignorant in the most profound sense. How could such an individual make a judgment about a pressing environmental issue such as noise abatement? The point is that appreciation of an important social and environmental *value* is beyond his grasp. It is thus the higher role of the teacher to instruct others in the art of listening to those vibrant melodies heard only in silence. But to lead others to awareness he must himself be an aware, spontaneous and open person — else he will be teaching with extrinsic reinforcement at that very moment when discovery can take hold and give wings to the imagination.

NOTES

[1] The development of Russian sensory education is best understood by seeing how it has diverged from the traditional schools. In the following quote, Zaporozhets differentiates the Russian approach from those of Montessori and Decroly. Though Zeaman and House are not mentioned, their work can be classified with training approaches emphasizing artificial "abstract" forms.

We can now define more precisely what the principal points of difference are between our system and the formal didactic systems (of Montessori and others) and between the "substantive" or "pragmatic" systems, as they are otherwise termed — those proposed by Decroly and others. In the former type the focus was mainly on training children how to distinguish and recognize artificial "abstract" forms which had been selected for teaching purposes. Under these systems, however, children were not taught how to use such forms as standards they might apply when trying to isolate and reproduce qualities they perceived in reality.

By way of reaction to this formal didactic method, the adherents of the "substantive" systems of sensory training tried to acquaint children with the diversity of forms, colors, and sounds to be found in the world. But on the whole they failed to equip the child with a means of becoming oriented to his surroundings. Consequently, both these systems were completely unsatisfactory, for they did not provide tasks that would consistently develop methods by which a child could orient himself to the world of perceptible phenomena.

As we pointed out, the Soviet program of sensory training provides ways in which the child will successively master a system of conventional standards of sense data. He is taught how to use these effectively to analyze and synthesize the qualities he perceives in surrounding objects. This use of standards requires that, in addition to a knowledge of sensory patterns (graphic ideas about the basic colors, elementary forms, etc.) a child be able to compare these with qualities in real objects; that he also be able to detect other relationships between the parts of objects.

For example, Boguslavskaya's experiments (1963) indicate that what a child learns about a triangle (as a figure having three angles) from teaching materials that use equilateral triangles, will prove valuable in orienting him to his surroundings only if he is specifically taught how to compare other variants of this figure with the pattern he has learned. Thus, even 4-to-5-year-old children can be taught how to make a visual comparison of triangles in terms of their general proportions, the type of angle at the apex, and the like. When new figures were shown to children in these experiments, they said that these were also triangles, only that one was "tall and kind of pointed" while another was "tiny and wide."

More complex skills, however, are needed to analyze combined forms which have compound structures — the typical composition of most objects in the world around us. After all, objects that form regular squares or circles are to be found more rarely than Montessori assumed. In the majority of cases the forms of objects a child sees about him in his life at home, in the animal and plant figures he perceives, represent an intricate combination of a number of simple geometrical elements. The child has yet to learn to break such combined forms down into their elements and, on the basis of his analysis, try to recreate the forms (through drawing, modeling, design work, etc.)

An experiment designed to develop skills of this type in preschool-age children (that is, the ability to analyze the spatial characteristics of compound objects) is to be found in research by Sakulina (1963).

She taught children to recognize the general form which characterizes an object as a whole. What she did was to teach them how to distinguish the basic form of an object (of the major part, the largest area of the figure) and the form of its details. It is only by acquiring skills such as these that a child can effectively use his store of sensory patterns to analyze and synthesize the reality he perceives. A program of sensory training ought certainly to provide ways in which these skills can be developed. (Zaporozhets, 1969, pp. 92-93)

An exceedingly interesting perceptual interaction between "abstract" geometrical elements and environmental objects is seen in the classic work of Goldstein & Scheerer (1941). One brain-injured patient, when given a set of sticks, was unable to reproduce the position of a single stick, whatever its orientation. However, when faced with the seemingly much more difficult task of reproducing a house consisting of 10 to 12 sticks, he succeeded. According to Goldstein & Scheerer, he succeeded in the latter task because of its "concrete" meaning. They observed, ". . . to build the house presupposes a mental set on the part of the patient which is easier to assume than the abstract attitude required for the grasping of "mere spatial position." (p. 19)

This case is significant from a perceptual learning standpoint. Thus, there is the implication that retraining in the constructive use of perceptual elements could be accomplished through the relatively intricate but conceptually concrete objects from the patient's everyday environment. For example, the patient was unable to reproduce an upward-pointing angle consisting of two sticks. Yet, while copying the house he apparently succeeded in reproducing the angle as the concrete representation of a roof. With this as a point of departure a teaching program could be evolved. Through generalization of the specific concrete representation, the patient's appreciation or orientation in the abstract might gradually be restored. Luria (1963) calls this process "conceptual reconstruction." A patient unable to reproduce the figure ⌐Ʌ Ⱶ may succeed if it is suggested that it represents the Russian world ПАПА. He noted, ". . . as a result of this reconstruction, the patient very soon masters this motor pattern almost without error. Subsequently he often automatizes the process, and the defect is compensated" (p. 112). An example follows:

Patient Zheg (Wound of the left pre-motor area)

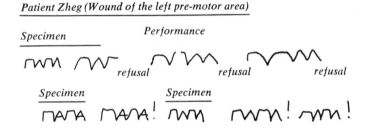

Note: Luria used a tremendously overlearned performance (writing a familiar word) to restore the motor-perceptual process basic to drawing the irregular sawtooth pattern. With developmentally arrested children, however, residuals of higher-level learning are absent. Therefore, training must proceed from the lowest level at which the child failed to achieve integration.

Returning to the Goldstein & Scheerer case, one possible program might involve the patient's reproducing houses with roofs of varying pointedness. Only the two "roof" sticks would be involved, the remainder, representing other details of the house, would remain unchanged. As the patient succeeded in reproducing roofs ranging from nearly flat representations to extremely apex ones, the sticks representing the balance of the house would be removed and replaced with solid black lines. An outline of the lower part of the house would be used by both trainer and subject, each of whom would be reduced to working with only 2 "roof" sticks. Then, as the activity proceeded, the lines representing the house would be gradually faded until the patient was left with the model of two sticks depicting an "abstract" relationship. Assuming that such generalization occurs, the patient then could apply his newly reacquired ability to deal with perceptual elements by directing it to the analysis and synthesis of environmental objects on an abstract level. An ability to deal with perceptual elements acquired through concrete experience with common sense environmental objects might thus be redirected toward a more abstract interaction with the same object.

Perceptual learning would have occurred through the modality of concrete meaning. Compare this with the Zeaman & House (1963) perceptual learning approach. In their learning set procedure, learning to respond selectively to certain perceptual cues is a matter of probabilistic learning — meaning is not involved. That the child will respond to the relevant cue on the first trial is strictly a matter of chance. But if a concrete meaning is initially available and could serve as the springboard for learning an abstract appreciation of perceptual cues, why not start out with meaning in the first place? It would take some clinical effort to unearth such concrete meanings which may vary from case to case, an admitted limitation. But if they exist, why not exploit them?

For this writer, the limitation of the Zeaman & House model, with its emphasis on what the Russians describe as artificial and abstract forms, is that it depends upon an unnecessarily artificial learning situation derived from animal research. Humans, including brain-injured ones of originally normal intelligence and many of the mentally retarded, bring numerous meanings to the learning situation. Why not exploit them? As Ackerland (personal communication, 1969) has suggested it would also seem that such learning would avoid the accidental attachment to irrelevant cues noted by Trabasso (1968). The trainer would know the concrete referent from the outset and could systematically fade it out.

Compared with the Russian work on the orienting-exploratory reflex, the work of Zeaman & House both begins and ends in a relative vacuum. Zeaman & House (1963) have suggested that their work is relevant to Montessori's. To that extent it suffers the same limitations the Russians have appropriately attributed to the latter. This writer's appraisal of the relevance of Zeaman & House is made despite the fact that a recent study revealed transfer from sensory-motor training to learning set acquisition (Maloney & Charrette, 1970). Though transfer occurred, it is difficult to account for it in terms of the relationship between Kephart's theory and Zeaman's & House's. In my opinion, a much more direct, meaningful, and potentially productive tie-in can be made between Kephart's sensory-motor training and the Russian orienting-exploratory reflex. The latter account may eventually provide an interpretive frame of reference that encompasses the above-mentioned experimental results. It may also provide a much broader front for research efforts than would be possible with the limited theoretical perspective of Zeaman & House. Finally, what is perhaps the greatest objection to Zeaman and House is this — learning to discriminate *within* a single dimension may occur exactly as it did with Lashley's rats (see page 136), i.e., on the basis of fragmentary cues, the utilization of which may ultimately lead to negative transfer of training (see Ball & Campbell, page 137, and Trabasso, page 136).

[2] For a highly readable brief account of the Russian system of sensory education at the nursery school level, see Cole & Cole (1968).

[3] According to El'konin (1969, p. 194), Dunaevskii (1956) has shown that the child reacts to stimuli, at least to some of them, not only by directing the analyzer to the source of the situation, but also by hand actions. The orienting reflex which Pavlov characterized as a "what's that?" reflex is thus supplemented by the "what is this for?" orienting-exploratory reflex.

In Seguin's system, the orienting reflex corresponds to "touch proper" and the orienting-exploratory reflex to "tact" (see page 70).

[4] I would predict that generalization from sensory-motor training would result in more mature acquaintance actions in the manual exploration of objects (see previously described study by Zinchenko & Ruzskaya).

[5] Compare the above quote with the following from Gagné (1965), a thoroughgoing learning theorist:

> The great value of concepts as means for thinking and communicating is the fact that they have *concrete references*. . . . But since concepts are learned by the human being via language, there is often a danger of losing sight of this concreteness. Learning can become ovververbalized, which means that the concepts learned are highly inadequate in their references to actual situations. The learner, one may note, 'doesn't really know the meaning of the word,' even though he can use it correctly in a sentence. . . .
>
> The danger of verbal superficiality, and the necessity for avoiding it, is recognized in a number of educational doctrines. 'Learning by doing' is one of these. (pp. 138-39)

To this I would add that Kephart, and also the Russians, have developed techniques that maximize "learning by doing" (for example, see page 130), a fact ignored by Mann (1970) in his critique of perceptual training.

[6] Personal communication, January 15, 1970.

[7] By means of exactly the same stimuli and testing procedure, the phi test affords a *direct quantitative* comparison of the abilities of kindergarten children and adults to discriminate between forms as simple as square and circle.

[8] In a phi experiment by Ball & Wilsoncroft (1967), a diamond shape was suggested by arranging separate neon lights to indicate each of the four corners. The four lights in this half of the array went on and off simultaneously. The second half of the array consisted of only a single bulb. It was expected that, during alternation, the single light would eventually fuse with the adjacent light in the diamond array and that its remaining three lights would stand still. To our surprise, the single light seemed to "disappear" and an intact diamond was seen to oscillate back and forth. This suggests that subjects do *not* respond to isolated elements in the phi situation.

[9] Piaget's task involves pouring the liquid contents of one beaker into a second beaker and making a judgment about volume. For example, when water is poured from a short, wide beaker into a tall, narrow one, many five-year-olds report that there is more water in the second beaker. They note the change in the height of the column of water and, ignoring the compensatory reduction in its diameter, make an incorrect, non-conservation judgment. The exclusive use of the single cue of height, called "centration," corresponds to Kephart's detail level of perceptual development.

The Montessori materials consist of four blocks of wood with insets into which knobbed cylinders are placed. If a cylinder is the wrong size it either does not fit into the hole or, when placed, it extends above or below the surface of the block. Because of this, the error is made immediately evident to most children, and they spontaneously correct the placement. Two of the blocks contain cylinders varying both in height and diameter, e.g., in one block the shortest is the narrowest and the tallest the widest. An adult examining these materials might assume that since cylinders varied in two dimensions, the child, in the course of using them, would acquire the concept of volume. However, following Kephart's maxim regarding the need to study the *process* of the child's actual performance, it was found that the child could correctly place a cylinder by referring exclusively to its diameter, ignoring height. Since this is what the children typically did, this practice in utilizing a single dimension could reinforce "centration" or, in Kephart's terms, a detail or "splinter skill" type of perceptual discrimination. The results supported this notion, i.e., the Montessori-trained children were significantly surpassed on a post-test of conservation by a control group receiving experience with picture puzzles.

[10] N. C. Kephart. Glen Haven In-Service Training Program: Syllabus Learning Disabilities. Denver, Colorado: Learning Pathways, Inc. 1969. All quotations from this book are used by permission of the publisher.

[11] Here is an excellent example of how kinesthetic cues can function as S^Ds for new learning:

> In teaching a person how to cast a fly, it is necessary for him to guide his forward delivery by feeling the gentle pressure release that occurs when the line reaches the end of its uncurving on the backcast. If your flycasting pupil is too eager to spot this cue, he will be rather tense, and his own muscular tension will mask the gentle pressure release that he must use as a signal (Bruner, 1957).

[12] C. B. Ferster and J. Simons. Behavior Therapy with Children. The Psychological Record, 1966, 16, 65-71. All quotations from this article are used by permission of the publisher.

[13] The research application of Macpherson's electromyographic technique to Kephart's kinesthetic figure-ground training might change the status of kinesthetic figure-ground from a hypothetical construct to an appropriate subject for the functional analysis of behavior (see note 2, chapter 1).

[14] From pp. 147, 228-29, 231, Human Brain and Psychological Processes by A. R. Luria. Copyright 1966 by Harper & Row, Publishers, Inc. Reprinted by permission of Harper & Row, Publishers, Inc.

[15] Boyd (1914) evaluated Montessori's beliefs regarding individuality and freedom as factors in education. His brilliant and provocative discussion has retained its relevance over the years.

[16] Seguin described precisely the same behavior (see page 71). For examples from clinical neurology, see Lawson (1962, pp. 28 and 31).

[17] Not only are many so-called applications of operant conditioning operationally similar to those of the cognitively oriented Kephart, but at times they

may not even be classifiable as operant conditioning. A case in point is that of The Token Economy which Skinner embraces as an application of operant conditioning (1967). Yet it seems likely that instead of being an outgrowth of operant conditioning it conforms to Skinner's definition of reward training which he excludes from his framework (1967). Yet, however classified, the important thing is that token economies *are* effective (Ayllon & Azrin, 1968; Schaefer & Martin, 1969; Sibbach, 1969).

[18]Personal communication, 1967.

[19]Rigidity restricts the process of acquiring information. It may also inhibit the appearance of problem solving strategies that the individual has in his repertoire but does not use. Such strategies may not appear until the organism experiences some duress or frustration, as in an escape-avoidance situation. Under such circumstances even the profoundly retarded may show unusual adaptive responses (for example, see page 89). Yet a high degree of frustration need not be involved. In fact, Itard's antecdote regarding Victor's ingenious fabrication of a pencil-holder (see page 41) is perhaps the best statement ever written on this subject.

[20]The child in Seguin's example also received much social reinforcement for this behavior; this also could have been the case for Helen.

[21]John Platt, the biophysicist, has eloquently described the process I am attributing to Helen Keller. Thus:

> Chain-processes seem, and are, so much more *alive* than the rest of the universe. A waterfall. A thunderstorm. Newborn puppies. We feel their changes of form, their setbacks and advances . . . as though we were part of them, as though their reaction systems were our very own. And are they not? Chain-reactions represent the side of nature which is least mechanical, where we can empathize and identify with ongoing and universal processes that we, too, represent (Platt, 1966, p. 56).

Synopsis

The behavioristic and cognitive approaches have contributed importantly to the development of therapeutic techniques of sensory education.
Yet the entire field has suffered from a lack of theoretical parsimony. The
purpose of this book is to develop an integrated view of the field of sensory
education. Within this context, the writer has coordinated the work of
the Skinnerians with that of Kephart, a cognitive theorist. In addition, the
concepts of both are related to contemporary Russian work on the orienting reflex (OR) and the orienting-exploratory response and to the historical contributions of Itard and Seguin. The resulting integration seems
to afford a unique perspective. For example, one of the most convincing
arguments for Kephart's approach to training visual perception comes, not
from contemporary sources, but from Itard's 165-year-old account of
training a feral child. Similarly, in the field of attention, one of the most
skillful and ingenious training applications of what Pavlov later labeled the
orienting reflex was devised by Seguin in the mid-nineteenth century. Kephart's program of training flexibility on the gross motor level provides
a basis for the development of spontaneity, a factor greatly underem-
phasized within the Skinnerian framework. For many atypical children,
Kephart's program may provide a foundation prerequisite to successful
utilization of training in orienting-exploratory behavior.

The overall theoretical integration is summarized as follows: In the
early stages of learning, touch predominates over vision as a means of

acquiring discriminative stimuli about objects. However, the young child acquires these tactual S^Ds inefficiently, as by "catching" an object rather than systematically exploring its contours. Like the blind man who felt only the elephant's trunk, he acquires an incomplete and even distorted concept. If he is a normal child he can quite readily be taught a more mature strategy for acquiring S^Ds. The essence of the mature strategy is its flexibility. Instead of mechanically grasping a form, the child should purposively feel around it, and in an adaptive yet systematic fashion explore its informational content. This is the essence of the Russian orienting-exploratory or "What is it for?" response. But what if the child is brain-injured, retarded or autistic? The normal orienting-exploratory behavior so characteristic of primates (Butler, 1954), is often severely curtailed. In such instances it is necessary to look at some of the factors basic to the orienting-exploratory reflex. Among these are the following:

1. *Awareness:* Unless the individual orients to stimuli associated with an object, learning relative to that object will not take place. The orienting reflex, which Pavlov called the "What's that?" reflex, must occur in response to such stimuli or they will never become S^Ds. Such a pervasive lack of awareness was noted in Ball & Porter's profoundly retarded, blind subjects who, on a sensory level, received sounds from their environment. Like a person habituated to a series of identical stimuli, the sounds did not adequately register. As indicated behaviorally and also physiologically (through the GSR), they failed to respond discriminatively to their own names. Until the children oriented to sound, learning based on sound could not take place. The problem, then, was to condition an OR to sound. This was done by shaping them to pull a lever that terminated a continuous buzzing noise, using food reinforcement. Once the OR was conditioned, training based on auditory S^Ds could have taken place.

Itard's Victor, a feral child, differed vastly from Ball & Porter's blind subjects. He demonstrated very powerful orienting responses to S^Ds associated with survival in the wilderness. Nonetheless, he lacked other ORs necessary for certain kinds of learning. For example, he had to acquire sensitivity to moderate temperature variations. This was achieved through a rudimentary course of sensory stimulation which included warm baths.

At the level of awareness, the problem is one of getting the subject to orient to environmental stimuli of potential significance as S^Ds for learning.

2. *Motivation:* "Negative will," as described by Seguin, represents a pervasive and profound motivational obstacle to the development of orienting-exploratory behavior. In negative will, the child displays a monumental resistance to attempts at eliciting active and adaptive responses. The resistance is often interpreted as an inherent manifestation of idiocy rather than a learned and highly rewarding method of controlling the

environment. Yet, as Lovaas has suggested, by doing nothing the child actively controls others. A further complication with many of these children is that through repetitive, self-stimulating behaviors, they provide their own reinforcement.

Seguin skillfully used an escape-avoidance strategy to overcome negative will and elicit active palpatory movements. In the ladder technique the child reflexively grasped the rungs to avoid falling. Then, with a perfectly timed introduction of pleasant stimuli associated with grasping, Seguin reinforced what was initially a "frightened grasp" and converted it to a purposive prehension of desirable environmental objects. At this point, however, flexibility of prehension remained to be established.

3. *Flexible Adaptiveness:* When the individual learns to walk upright he acquires what Kephart terms a motor skill. But unless he learns to shift his center of gravity through wide postural variations, he will be exclusively concerned with retaining an upright posture rather than exploring the environment. If such is the case, he will move through space in a highly restricted fashion. He will be preoccupied with avoiding a fall rather than experimenting with ways of getting about. If, on the gross motor level, the child is restricted in his ability to locomote adaptively, he probably will be similarly restricted in his manual and visual exploration of objects in the acquisition of S^Ds.

Kephart's therapeutic program represents a systematic and effective means of developing flexible adaptiveness and spontaneity at the motor level (motor patterns). Much as Pryor has done recently, Kephart has for years elicited and reinforced motor variability. And as Pryor has found, variability begets further variability — a kind of creativity expressed in movement. Once established, this spontaneity should generalize to the level of orienting-exploratory movements thereby providing the child entry into an expanded world of awareness and discovery.

Bibliography

Ayllon, Teodoro and Azrin, Nathan. *The Token Economy: A Motivational System for Therapy and Rehabilitation.* New York: Appleton-Century-Crofts, 1968.

Ayllon, Teodoro and Michael, Jack. The Psychiatric Nurse as a Behavior Engineer. *Journal of the Experimental Analysis of Behavior,* 1959, **2**, 323-34.

Ayres, A. Jean. Sensory Integrative Processes and Neuropsychological Learning Disabilities. In J. Hellmuth (ed.), *Learning Disorders, Vol. 3.* Seattle: Special Child Publications, 1968, pp. 47-58.

Baer, Donald M., Peterson, Robert F., and Sherman, James A. The Development of Imitation by Reinforcing Behavioral Similarity to a Model. *Journal of the Experimental Analysis of Behavior,* 1967, **10**, 405-16.

Baer, Donald M. and Sherman, James A. Reinforcement Control of Generalized Imitation in Young Children. *Journal of Experimental Child Psychology,* 1964, **1**, 37-49.

Ball, Thomas S. Perceptual Concomitants of Conceptual Reorganization. *Journal of Consulting Psychology,* 1964, **28**, 523-28.

Ball, Thomas S. Behavior Shaping of Self-Help Skills in the Severely Retarded Child. In J. Fisher and R. E. Harris (eds.) Reinforcement Theory in Psychological Treatment — A Symposium. *California Mental Health Research Monograph No. 8,* 1966, pp. 15-24.

Ball, Thomas S. The Reestablishment of Social Behavior. *Hospital and Community Psychiatry,* 1968, **19**(7), 230-32.

Ball, Thomas S. The Establishment and Administration of Operant Conditioning Programs in a State Hospital for the Retarded. *California Mental Health Research Symposium, No. 4,* 1969. (a)

Ball, Thomas S. Treatment by Escape-Avoidance Conditioning: Historic and Contemporary Applications. *California Mental Health Research Digest,* 1969, **7**(4), 165-75. (b)

Ball, Thomas S. and Campbell, Mary L. Effect of Montessori's Cylinder Block Training on the Acquisition of Conservation. *Developmental Psychology,* 1970, **2**, 156.

Ball, Thomas S. and Edgar, Clara Lee. The Effectiveness of Sensory-Motor Training in Promoting Generalized Body Image Development. *The Journal of Special Education,* 1967, **1**, 387-95.

Ball, Thomas S., Gabriel, Michael, and Ackerland, Valerie. The Orienting Response as a Nonverbal Measure of Body Awareness. To be published as a chapter in J. Hellmuth (ed.) *Cognitive Studies, Vol. 2: Deficits in Cognition.* New York: Brunner/Mazel, Inc., 1971, pp. 135-39.

Ball, Thomas S., Midgley, Peter, Ackerland, Valerie, Nies, Richard and Hord, David. The Orienting Response as a Nonverbal Measure of Neurological Extinction. *Perceptual and Motor Skills,* 1969, **28**, 47-53.

Ball, Thomas S. and Porter, William. An Exploration of the Uses of the Orienting Response. Paper presented at the 91st Annual Meeting of the American Association on Mental Deficiency, Denver, Colorado, May 15-20, 1967.

Ball, Thomas S. and Wilsoncroft, William E. Complex Phi Thresholds of Brain-Damaged Children. *Perceptual and Motor Skills,* 1967, **24**, 879-83.

Bandura, Albert and Walters, Richard H. *Social Learning and Personality Development.* New York: Holt, Rinehart & Winston, Inc., 1963.

Bensberg, Gerald J. (ed.). *Teaching the Mentally Retarded: A Handbook for Ward Personnel.* Atlanta: Southern Regional Education Board, 1965.

Benton, Arthur L. *Right-Left Discrimination and Finger Localization.* New York: Harper & Row, Publishers, 1959.

Berlyne, D(aniel) E. *Conflict, Arousal and Curiosity.* New York: McGraw-Hill Book Company, 1960.

Bernard, Claude. *An Introduction to the Study of Experimental Medicine.* Tr. by H. C. Greene. New York: Dover Publications, Inc., 1957. Originally published, 1865.

Bexton, W(illiam) H., Heron, W., and Scott, T. H. Effects of Decreased Variation in the Sensory Environment. *Canadian Journal of Psychology,* 1954, **8**, 70-76.

Bijou, Sidney W. and Baer, Donald M. *Child Development I: A Systematic and Empirical Theory.* New York: Appleton-Century-Crofts, 1961.

Bijou, Sidney W. and Baer, Donald M. *Child Development: Vol. 2, Universal Stage of Infancy.* New York: Appleton-Century-Crofts, 1965.

Birnbrauer, Jay S., Bijou, Sidney W., Wolf, Montrose M., and Kidder, J. D. Programmed Instruction in the Classroom. In L. P. Ullmann and L. Krasner (eds.), *Case Studies in Behavior Modification.* New York: Holt, Rinehart & Winston, Inc., 1965, pp. 358-63.

Boguslavskaya, Z. M. Development of Means of Visual Shape Investigation In Preschool Children. *Abstracts of the Second Conference of the Association of Psychologists.* Moscow: Izd. Akad. Pedag. Nauk RSFSR, 1963, No. 2. Cited in M. Cole and I. Maltzman (eds.) *Contemporary Soviet Psychology.* New York: Basic Books, Inc., Publishers, 1969, p. 93.

Bortner, Morton and Birch, Herbert G. Perceptual and Perceptual-Motor Dissociation in Brain-Damaged Patients. *The Journal of Nervous and Mental Disease,* 1960, **130**, 49-53.

Boyd, William. *From Locke to Montessori.* New York: Henry Holt & Co., 1914.

Bruner, Jerome. Up From Helplessness. *Psychology Today,* 1969, **2**, 30-33, 66, 67.

Bruner, Jerome. On Perceptual Readiness. *Psychological Review,* 1957, **64**, 123-52, 146.

Butler, Robert A. Curiosity in Monkeys. *Scientific American,* 1954, **190**, 70-75.

Cole, Michael and Cole, Sheila. Russian Nursery Schools. *Psychology Today,* 1968, **2**(5), 22-29.

Colwell, Cecil. Teaching in the Cottage Setting. In G. J. Bensberg (ed.), *Teaching the Mentally Retarded: A Handbook for Ward Personnel.* Atlanta: Southern Regional Education Board, 1965, pp. 159-63.

Davenport, Richard K. and Rogers, Charles M. Intellectual Performance of Differentially Reared Chimpanzees: I. Delayed Response. *American Journal of Mental Deficiency,* 1968, **72**, 674-80.

Delacato, Carl H. *The Treatment and Prevention of Reading Problems.* Springfield, Illinois: Charles C. Thomas, Publisher, 1959.

Doll, Eugene E. Trends and Problems in the Education of the Mentally Retarded: 1800-1940. *American Journal of Mental Deficiency,* 1967, **72**(2), 175-83.

Dunaevskii, F. P. An Attempt to Study the Higher Nervous Activity of Children in the First Years of Life. *Izv. Akad. Pedag.* Nauk RSFSR, 1956, No. 75. Cited in M. Cole and I. Maltzman, (eds.) *A Handbook of Contemporary Soviet Psychology.* New York: Basic Books, Inc., Publishers, 1969, p. 194.

Ebersole, Marylou, Kephart, Newell C., and Ebersole, James B. *Steps to Achievement for the Slow Learner.* Columbus, Ohio: Charles E. Merrill Publishing Co., 1968.

Edgar, Clara Lee, Ball, Thomas S., McIntyre, Robert B., and Shotwell, Anna M. Effects of Sensory-Motor Training on Adaptive Behavior. *American Journal of Mental Deficiency,* 1969, **73**, 713-20.

El'Konin, D. B. Some Results of the Study of the Psychological Development of Preschool-Age Children. In M. Cole and I. Maltzman, (eds.) *A Handbook of Contemporary Soviet Psychology.* New York: Basic Books, Inc., Publishers, 1969, pp. 163-208.

Evans, Richard I. *B. F. Skinner: The Man and His Ideas.* New York: E. P. Dutton & Co., Inc., 1968.

Fantz, Robert L. The Origin of Form Perception. *Scientific American,* 1961, **204**(5), 66-72.

Fernald, Grace M. *Remedial Techniques in Basic School Subjects.* New York: McGraw-Hill Book Company, 1943.

Ferster, C(harles) B. and Simons, J(eanne). Behavior Therapy With Children. *The Psychological Record,* 1966, **16**, 65-71.

Fuller, P(aul) R. Operant Conditioning of a Vegetative Human Organism. *American Journal of Psychology,* 1949, **62**, 587-90.

Gagné, Robert M. *The Conditions of Learning.* New York: Holt, Rinehart & Winston, Inc., 1965.

Gellerman, Louis W. Form Discrimination in Chimpanzees and Two-Year-Old Children: II. Form Versus Background. *Journal of Genetic Psychology,* 1933, **42**, 28-50.

Getman, G. N. *How to Develop Your Child's Intelligence.* Luverne, Minnesota: The Research Press, 1962.

Gewirtz, Jacob L. and Stingle, Karen G. Learning of Generalized Imitation as the Basis for Identification. *Psychological Review,* 1968, **75**, 374-97.

Goldstein, Kurt and Scheerer, Martin. Abstract and Concrete Behavior: An Experimental Study With Special Tests. *Psychological Monographs,* 1941, **53**(2), Whole number 239.

Gray, Burl B. and Fygetakis, L. The Development of Language as a Function of Programmed Conditioning. *Behavior Research and Therapy,* 1968, **6**, 455-60.

Haeussermann, Else. *Developmental Potential of Preschool Children.* New York: Grune and Stratton, Inc., 1958.

Harlow, Harry F. The Nature of Love. *American Psychologist,* 1958, **13**(12), 673-85.

Harlow, Harry F. and Harlow, Margaret K. Learning to Think. *Scientific American,* 1949, **181**, 36-39.

Head, Henry. *Aphasia and Kindred Disorders of Speech, Vol. 1.* New York: Cambridge University Press, 1925.

Hebb, Donald O. *The Organization of Behavior: A Neuropsychological Theory.* New York: John Wiley & Sons, Inc., 1949.

Helson, Harry. Why Did Their Precursors Fail and the Gestalt Psychologists Succeed? Reflections on Theories and Theorists. *American Psychologist,* 1969, **24**, 1006-011.

Hershenson, Maurice. Development of the Perception of Form. *Psychological Bulletin,* 1967, **67**, 326-36.

Hewett, Frank M. Teaching Speech to an Autistic Child Through Operant Conditioning. *American Journal of Orthopsychiatry,* 1965, **35**, 927-36.

Hoffer, Eric. *The Passionate State of Mind.* New York: Harper & Row, Publishers (Perennial Library), 1955.

Hunt, J. McV. *Intelligence and Experience.* New York: Ronald Press, 1961.

Isaacs, Wayne, Thomas, James and Goldiamond, Israel. Application of Operant Conditioning To Reinstate Verbal Behavior in Psychotics. *Journal of Speech and Hearing Disorders,* 1960, **25**, 8-12.

Ismail, A. H. and Gruber, Joseph J. *Integrated Development: Motor Aptitude and Intellectual Performance*. Columbus, Ohio: Charles E. Merrill Publishing Co., 1967.

Itard, Jean-Marc-Gaspard. *The Wild Boy of Aveyron*. Tr. by George & Muriel Humphrey. New York: Appleton-Century-Crofts, 1932, 1962.

Jacobson, Edmund. *Progressive Relaxation*. Chicago: University of Chicago Press, 1938.

Keller, Fred S. *Learning: Reinforcement Theory*. New York: Random House, Inc., 1954.

Keller, Helen. *The Story of My Life*. New York: Airmont Publishing Co., 1965.

Kephart, Newell C. *The Slow Learner in the Classroom*. Columbus, Ohio: Charles E. Merrill Publishing Co., 1960.

Kephart, Newell C. Perceptual-Motor Aspects of Learning Disabilities. *Exceptional Children*, 1964, **31**, 201-06.

Kephart, Newell C. *Learning Disability: An Educational Adventure*. West Lafayette, Indiana: Kappa Delta Pi Press, 1968.

Kephart, Newell C. Address given to a special study institute on "Current Trends for Teaching Orthopedic and Other Health Impaired Children." Conducted by The Spastic Children's Foundation, Los Angeles, Calif., March 13-15, 1969. (a)

Kephart, Newell C. Glen Haven In-Service Training Program: Syllabus Learning Disabilities. Denver: Learning Pathways, Inc., 1969. (b)

Krech, David and Crutchfield, Richard S. *Elements of Psychology*. New York: Alfred A. Knopf, Inc., 1958.

Lashley, Karl S. The Mechanism of Vision. XV. Preliminary Studies of the Rat's Capacity for Detail Vision. *Journal of General Psychology*, 1938, **18**, 123-93. Cited in R. S. Woodworth and H. Schlossberg (eds.), *Experimental Psychology*. New York: Henry Holt and Co., 1954.

Lawson, Ian R. Visual-Spatial Neglect in Lesions of the Right Cerebral Hemisphere. *Neurology*, 1962, **12**, 23-33.

Lovaas, O. Ivar. Some Studies on the Treatment of Childhood Schizophrenia. In J. M. Schlien (ed.) *Research in Psychotherapy*. Vol. 3, Washington, D. C.: American Psychological Association, 1968, pp. 103-21.

Lovaas, O. Ivar, Berberich, John P., Perloff, Bernard F., and Schaeffer, Benson. Acquisition of Imitative Speech by Schizophrenic Children. *Science*, 1966, **151**, 705-07.

Lovaas, O. Ivar, Freitag, Gilbert, Gold, Vivian J., and Kassorla, Irene C. Experimental Studies in Childhood Schizophrenia: Analysis of Self-Destructive Behavior. *Journal of Experimental Child Psychology*, 1965, **2**, 67-84. (a)

Lovaas, O. Ivar, Schaeffer, Benson, and Simmons, James Q. Building Social Behavior in Autistic Children by Use of Electric Shock. *Journal of Experimental Research in Personality*, 1965, **1**, 99-109. (b)

Luria, Aleksander R. *Restoration of Function After Brain Injury.* Translated by O. L. Zangwill. New York: Pergamon Press, Inc., 1963.

Luria, Aleksander R. *Human Brain and Psychological Processes.* Translated by Basil Haigh. New York: Harper & Row, Publishers, 1966.

Lynn, Richard, *Attention, Arousal and the Orientation Reaction.* Oxford: Pergamon Press, Inc., 1966.

Macpherson, Evan L. R. Control of Involuntary Movement. *Behavior Research and Therapy,* 1967, **5**, 143-45.

Maloney, Michael P., Ball, Thomas S., and Edgar, Clara L. Analysis of the Generalizability of Sensory-Motor Training. *American Journal of Mental Deficiency,* 1970, **74**, 458-69.

Maloney, Michael P. and Charrette, Harriett. Note on the Effects of a Gross-Motor Approach to Training Attention Control on Discrimination Learning in Mentally Retarded Subjects. *Perceptual and Motor Skills,* 1970, **31**, 41-42.

Maltzman, Irving. On the Training of Originality. *Psychological Review,* 1960, **67**, 229-42.

Maltzmann, Irving and Raskin, David S. Effects of Individual Differences in the Orienting Reflex on Conditioning and Complex Processes. *Journal of Experimental Research in Personality,* 1965, **1**, 1-16.

Mann, Lester. Perceptual Training: Misdirections and Redirections. *American Journal of Orthopsychiatry,* 1970, **40**, 30-38.

Melzack, Ronald and Scott, T. H. The Effects of Early Experience on the Response to Pain. *Journal of Comparative and Physiological Psychology,* 1957, **50**, 155-61.

Miles, Nancy R. *Aquatic Activities for Children With Learning Disabilities.* Unpublished manuscript, Fort Collins, Colorado: Glen Haven Achievement Center, 1969.

Minge, M. Ronald and Ball, Thomas S. Teaching of Self-Help Skills to Profoundly Retarded Patients. *American Journal of Mental Deficiency,* 1967, **71**, 864-68.

Montessori, Maria. *The Montessori Method.* New York: Schocken Books, Inc., 1964.

Moore, Omar K. Autotelic Responsive Environments and Exceptional Children. Monograph published by the Responsive Environments Foundation, Inc., Hamden, Connecticut, 1963.

Nissen, Henry W., et al. Effects of Restrictive Opportunity for Tactual, Kinesthetic, and Manipulated Experience on the Behavior of a Chimpanzee. *American Journal of Psychology,* 1951, **64**, 485-507.

Patterson, Gerald R. An Application of Conditioning Techniques to the Control of a Hyperactive Child. In L. Ullman and L. Krasner (eds.), *Case Studies in Behavior Modification.* New York: Holt, Rinehart & Winston, Inc., 1965, pp. 370-75.

Piaget, Jean. *The Origins of Intelligence in Children*. Translated by M. Cook. New York: W. W. Norton, Co., 1952.

Platt, John R. *The Step to Man*. New York: John Wiley & Sons, Inc., 1966.

Porter, William. The Conditioning of a Discriminative Stimulus Measured as an Orienting Reaction in Profoundly Retarded Blind Children. Unpublished Doctoral Dissertation, University of Southern California, 1968.

Pryor, Karen. Behavior Modification: The Porpoise Caper. *Psychology Today*, 1969, **3**, 46-49, 64.

Pryor, Karen, Haag, Richard and O'Reilly, Joseph. The Creative Porpoise: Training for Novel Behavior. *Journal of the Experimental Analysis of Behavior*, 1969, **12**, 653-61.

Reynolds, George S. *A Primer of Operant Conditioning*. Glenview, Ill.: Scott, Foresman & Co., 1968.

Risley, Todd. Learning and Lollipops. *Psychology Today*, 1968, **1**, 28-31, 62-65.

Roach, Eugene G. and Kephart, Newell C. *The Purdue Perceptual-Motor Survey*. Columbus, Ohio: Charles E. Merrill Publishing Co., 1966.

Rosenthal, Robert. *Experimenter Effects in Behavioral Research*. New York: Appleton-Century-Crofts, 1966.

Sakulina, N. P. The Significance of Drawing in the Sensory Training of the Preschool Child. In *Sensory Training of Preschool Children*. Moscow: Izd. Akad. Pedag. Nauk RSFSR, 1963. Cited M. Cole and I. Maltzman (eds.) *Contemporary Soviet Psychology*, New York: Basic Books, Inc., Publishers, 1969, p. 93.

Sayegh, Yvonne and Dennis, Wayne. The Effect of Supplementary Experiences Upon The Behavioral Development of Infants in Institutions. *Child Development*, 1965, **36**, 81-90.

Schaefer, Halmuth H. and Martin, Patrick L. *Behavioral Therapy*. New York: Blakiston Division of McGraw-Hill Book Company, 1969.

Schaffer, H. R. and Emerson, Peggy E. The Effects of Experimentally Administered Stimulation on Developmental Quotients of Infants. *British Journal of Social and Clinical Psychology*, 1968, **7**, 61-67.

Scheerer, Martin. An Experiment in Abstraction. *Confina Neurologica*, 1949, **9**, 232-54.

Schoenfeld, W. N. "Avoidance" In Behavior Theory. *Journal of the Experimental Analysis of Behavior*, 1969, **12**, 669-74.

Scott, Phyllis M., Burton, R. V., and Yarrow, M. R. Social Reinforcement Under Natural Conditions. *Child Development*, 1967, **38**(1), 53-63.

Seguin, Edward. *Idiocy: And Its Treatment by the Physiological Method*. New York: Teachers College, Columbia University, 1907.

Seligman, Martin E. P. For Helplessness: Can We Immunize the Weak? *Psychology Today*, 1969, **3**, 42-44.

Semmes, Josephine, Weinstein, Sidney, Ghent, Lila, and Teuber, Hans-Lukas. Correlation of Impaired Orientation in Personal and Extrapersonal Space. *Brain*, 1963, **86**, 747-72.

Sibbach, Lois. Description of the Token Economy Program. In T. S. Ball (ed.), The Establishment and Administration of Operant Conditioning Programs in a State Hospital For the Retarded. *California Mental Health Research Symposium, No. 4*, 1969.

Sidman, Murray and Stoddard, Lawrence T. Programming Perception and Learning For Retarded Children. In N. R. Ellis (ed.) *International Review of Research in Mental Retardation*. Vol. 2. New York: Academic Press, 1966. pp. 151-208.

Skinner, B. F. How to Teach Animals. *Scientific American*, 1951, **185**(6), 26-29.

Skinner, B. F. An Interview With "Mr. Behaviorist." Interview by Mary Harrington Hall, *Psychology Today*, 1967, **1**, 20-23, 68-71.

Skinner, B. F. Interview in Evans, Richard I. *B. F. Skinner: The Man and his Ideas*. New York: E. P. Dutton & Co., 1968.

Soloveichik, D. I. *Scientific Papers of the Pavlov Physiological Laboratories*, 1928, **2**, 2. Cited in R. Lynn, *Attention, Arousal and the Orientation Reaction*. Oxford: Pergamon Press, Inc., 1966.

Strauss, Alfred A. and Kephart, Newell C. *Psychopathology and Education of the Brain-Injured Child. Vol. II: Progress in Theory and Clinic*. New York: Grune and Stratton, Inc., 1955.

Strauss, Alfred A. and Lehtinen, Laura E. *Psychopathology and Education of the Brain-Injured Child*. New York: Grune and Stratton, Inc., 1947.

Talbot, Mabel E. *Édouard Seguin: A Study of an Educational Approach to the Treatment of Mentally Defective Children*. New York: Teachers College, Columbia University, 1964.

Trabasso, Tom. Pay Attention. *Psychology Today*, 1968, **2**, 30-36.

Trabasso, Tom and Bower, Gordon H. *Attention in Learning: Theory and Research*. New York: John Wiley & Sons, Inc., 1968.

Vogler, Roger E. and Martin, Patrick L. In Defense of Operant Conditioning Programs in Mental Institutions. *The Psychological Record*, 1969, **19**, 59-64.

Watson, J. B. and Rayner, R. Conditioned Emotional Reactions. *Journal of Experimental Psychology*, 1920, **3**, 1-14.

Werner, Heinz. The Concept of Development From A Comparative and Organismic Point of View. In D. B. Harris (ed.) *The Concept of Development: An Issue in the Study of Human Behavior*. Minneapolis: University of Minnesota Press, 1957, pp. 125-48.

Werner, Heinz. *Comparative Psychology of Mental Development*. New York: Science Editions, Inc., 1961.

Whalen, Carol K. and Henker, Barbara A. Creating Therapeutic Pyramids Using Mentally Retarded Patients. *American Journal of Mental Deficiency,* 1969, **74**(3), 331-337.

Wheeler, Harvey. The Nature of Dialogue in a Democratic Society: A Conversation. In *The Civilization of the Dialogue.* A Center Occasional Paper. Published by the Center for the Study of Democratic Institutions. December, 1968, pp. 26-33.

Wolpe, Joseph. *Psychotherapy by Reciprocal Inhibition.* Stanford, California: Stanford University Press, 1958.

Zaporozhets, A. V. The Development of Perception in the Preschool Child. In P. H. Mussen (ed.), *European Research in Cognitive Development.* Monographs of the Society for Research in Child Development, 1965, **30**(2) No. 100, 82-101.

Zaporozhets, A. V. Some of the Psychological Problems of Sensory Training in Early Childhood and the Preschool Period. In M. Cole and I. Maltzman, (eds.), *A Handbook of Contemporary Soviet Psychology.* New York: Basic Books, Inc., Publishers, 1969, pp. 86-120.

Zaslow, Robert W. A Psychogenic Theory of the Etiology of Infantile Autism and Implications for Treatment. Paper presented at California State Psychological Association Meeting, San Diego, Calif., January, 1967. Permission granted by author.

Zeaman, David and House, Betty J. The Role of Attention in Retardate Discrimination Learning. In N. R. Ellis (ed.), *Handbook of Mental Deficiency.* New York: McGraw-Hill Book Company, 1963, pp. 159-223.

Index